Lipstick Jihad

Lipstick Jihad

A MEMOIR OF GROWING UP

IRANIAN IN AMERICA

AND

AMERICAN IN IRAN

Azadeh Moaveni

BBS

PublicAffairs   NEW YORK

SH

Published in the United States by PublicAffairs™, a member of the Perseus Books Group.
All rights reserved.
Printed in the United States of America.

No part of this book may be reproduced in any manner whatsoever without written permission except in the case of brief quotations embodied in critical articles and reviews. For information, address PublicAffairs, 250 West 57th Street, Suite 1321, New York, NY 10107.
PublicAffairs books are available at special discounts for bulk purchases in the U.S. by corporations, institutions, and other organizations. For more information, please contact the Special Markets Department at the Perseus Books Group, 11 Cambridge Center, Cambridge, MA 02142, call (617) 252-5298, or email special.markets@perseusbooks.com.

BOOK DESIGN AND COMPOSITION BY JENNY DOSSIN. TEXT SET IN ADOBE GARAMOND.

Library of Congress Cataloging-in-Publication data
Moaveni, Azadeh, 1976–
Lipstick jihad : a memoir of growing up Iranian in America and American in Iran / Azadeh Moaveni.— 1st ed.
p. cm.
ISBN 1-58648-193-2
1. Moaveni, Azadeh, 1976– 2. Iranian American women—Biography. 3. Iranian Americans—Biography. 4. Iran—Social Conditions—1979–1997. 5. Iran—Social conditions—1997– I. Title.
E184.I5M63 2005
305.48'89155073'092—dc22
[B]
2004043184

10 9 8 7 6 5 4 3 2

For my parents,

and

in memory of Kaveh Golestan

CONTENTS

INTRODUCTION

I was born in Palo Alto, California, into the lap of an Iranian diaspora community awash in nostalgia and longing for an Iran many thousands of miles away. As a girl, raised on the distorting myths of exile, I imagined myself a Persian princess, estranged from my homeland—a place of light, poetry, and nightingales—by a dark, evil force called the Revolution. I borrowed the plot from *Star Wars,* convinced it told Iran's story. Ayatollah Khomeini was Darth Vader. Tromping about suburban California, I lived out this fantasy. There must be some supernatural explanation, I reasoned, for the space landing of thousands of Tehranis to a world of vegan smoothies and Volvos, chakras, and Tupak.

Growing up, I had no doubt that I was Persian. Persian like a fluffy cat, a silky carpet—a vaguely Oriental notion belonging to history, untraceable on a map. It was the term we insisted on using at the time, embarrassed by any association with Iran, the modern country, the hostage-taking Death Star. Living a myth, a fantasy, made it easier to be Iranian in America.

As life took its course, as I grew up and went to college, discovered myself, and charted a career, my Iranian sense of self remained intact. But when I moved to Tehran in 2000—pleased with my pluckiness, and eager to prove myself as a young journalist—it, along with the fantasies, dissolved. Iran, as it turned out, was not the Death Star, but a country where people voted, picked their noses, and ate French fries. Being a Persian girl in California, it turned out, was like, a totally different thing than being a young Iranian woman in the Islamic Republic of Iran. In hindsight, these two points seem startlingly obvious, but no one ever pointed them out, probably because if you need them pointed out, you clearly have problems. So I learned for myself, as I endured a second, equally fraught coming of age—this time as a Californian in Iran. I never intended my Iranian odyssey as a search for self, but a very different me emerged at its end. I went looking for modern Iran, especially the generation of the revolution, the lost generation as it is sometimes called. The generation I would have belonged to, had I not grown up outside.

For two years, I worked as a journalist for *Time* magazine, reporting on the twists and turns of Iranian society, through high politics and ordinary life. Since 1998, the revolutionary regime's experiments with political reform—a brief flirtation with democracy—had captured the world's attention. The cultural rebellion of Iranian youth against the rigid, traditionalist system fizzed with unknown potential. As a journalist, I arrived during these times with urgent questions. Was Iran really becoming more democratic? What did young people want, exactly? Did demographics (two-thirds of the 70 million population is under thirty) make change inevitable? Would there be another revolution, or did Iranians prefer this regime to secularize? Were Iranians really pro-American, or just anti-clerical? Often there was more than one answer, maddeningly contradictory, equally correct.

I came to see Iranian society as culturally confused, politically deadlocked, and emotionally anguished. While the vast majority of Iranians despised the clerics and dreamed of a secular government, no easy path to that destination presented itself. In the meanwhile, revolutionary ideology was drawing its last, gasping breaths. Its imminent death was everywhere on display. You saw it when *Basiji* kids, the regime's thug-fundamentalist militia, stopped a car for playing banned music, confiscated the tapes, and then popped them into their own car stereo. You saw it when the children of senior clerics showed up at parties and on the ski slopes, dressed in Western clothes and alienated from their parents' radical legacy. It was there outside the courthouse on Vozara Street, where young people laughed and joked as they awaited their trials and lashings, before brushing them off and going on to the next party.

Iran's young generation—the generation born just before the revolution or along with—is transforming Iran from below. From the religious student activists to the ecstasy-trippers, from the bloggers to the bed-hopping college students, they will decide Iran's future. I decided I wanted to live like them, as they did, their "as if" lifestyle. They chose to act "as if" it was permitted to hold hands on the street, blast music at parties, speak your mind, challenge authority, take your drug of choice, grow your hair long, wear too much lipstick. This generation taught me how to unlock the mystery of Iran—how nothing perceptibly alters, but everything changes—not by reading the newspapers but by living an approximation of a young Iranian's life. That is why I cannot write about them without writing about myself. That is why this is both their story, and my own.

Today, in a quiet room in a country not far from Iran in space, I am finally unpacking the boxes from those two years in Tehran. As I sort through the clothes, peeling veil from veil, it is like tracing the rings of a tree trunk to tell its evolution. The outer layers are a wash of color, dashing tones of turquoise and frothy pink, in delicate chiffons and translucent silks. They are colors that are found in life—the color of pomegranates and pistachio, the sky and bright spring leaves—in fabrics that breathe. Underneath, as I dig down, there are dark, matte veils, long, formless robes in funeral tones of slate and black. That is what we wore, back in 1998. Along the way, the laws never changed. Parliament never officially pardoned color, sanctioned the exposure of toes and waistlines. Young women did it themselves, en masse, a slow, deliberate, widespread act of defiance. A jihad, in the classical sense of the word: a struggle.

CHAPTER ONE

The Secret Garden

You ask me about that country, whose details now escape me,
I don't remember its geography, nothing of its history.
And should I visit it in memory,
It would be as I would a past lover,
After years, for a night, no longer restless with passion,
With no fear of regret.
I have reached that age when one visits the heart merely as a courtesy.

—Faiz Ahmed Faiz

It was so cool and quiet up in the *toot* (mulberry) tree that I never wanted to come down. I didn't have to; the orchard was so dense that I could scramble from the limb of one tree to another, plucking the plump, red berries as I went along. The sweet juice made my fingers stick together, but I couldn't stop climbing. The trees stretched out as far as I could see, a glorious forest of mulberries, ripe for my picking. I loved mulberries, but until that summer in Tehran, I had only tasted them dried, from little plastic packets sold in the Iranian grocery story in San Jose. Riveted by the abundance, and the squishy texture of the berry in its fresh form—a whole new delight—I had spent the better part of the afternoon perched in the shady canopy of the orchard. "Azadeh jan, I am going to count to *three,* and you had better come down," came Maman's glaring voice from somewhere far below. I gave in, but only because of the preliminary pangs of the hideous stomachache to come. Sedigheh Khanoum, one of the farmers who took care of the orchards at Farahzad and who had tended Maman's stomach when she was little, made me tea with sugar crystals, to soothe the cramps. And I lay content on my back on the Persian rug outside, as Maman chatted with Sedigheh about our life in America, debating whether tomorrow I should go after the delicate white *toot,* or the dark red.

Only a very small child in the safety of a walled family compound would have felt liberated in Iran one year after the Islamic Revolution, but I was blissfully unaware of such matters. Finally, I was unleashed, and wanted to stay forever in this country where I could romp about freely. In Iran I could play wherever and with whomever I wanted—in the street, in the backyard, with the caretaker's daughter, with my brand-new duck. When my cousins and I played at our grandparents' apartment complex in California, we had to be visible and within hearing distance at all times. We were tethered to our parents' fears: that we might consort with "street children"—which I later realized only meant normal kids who were allowed to play outside— or that some terrible fate might befall us in this as yet foreign country. If we were to blip off the radar for more than a few minutes, a search and rescue squad would fan out in our pursuit. Neither I nor my cousins tolerated this cloying protectiveness well, and occasionally we would dial 911 in revenge, for the pleasure of watching our poor grandmother or aunt explain to a stern policeman who knocked on the door that "Surely, sir, there is mistake; here we are having no emergency."

In Tehran that summer, I wasn't the only one unleashed. My mother could barely stay put, flitting from house to house, from Tehran to the Caspian and back again; even when she was at home, sitting down, she was gulping in space—high ceilings, drawing rooms vast enough that I could race a tricycle down from one end to the other—as though her lungs had only been partially breathing the whole time she'd been away. I finally saw Maman, my beautiful, proud, mad mother, laughing gustily, instead of the tight-lipped smile she wore as she chauffeured me around San Jose, to piano lessons, to ice skating lessons, to gymnastics, back and forth to school, all by herself. It was often just the two of us, on this trip to Iran, and back in California as well. My parents had divorced shortly after they permanently moved to America in 1976, just a few months after I was born.

She took me to the pastry shop on Pahlavi Boulevard, where we bought the bite-sized creampuffs we had labored over in our kitchen in San Jose, and the ice cream that I forever after associated with that summer in Tehran, that fleeting glimpse of the life we might have had. *Akbar-mashti,* it was called, saffron-colored, dotted with bits of cream and bright flecks of pistachio, perfumed with rose water. Pahlavi ran north-south through Tehran, from the foot of the Alborz mountains downtown, and we walked its northern length, licking our ice cream as it dripped between two thin wafers. Later I would learn that Reza Shah, the late Shah of Iran's father, modeled the boulevard after the arteries of Paris, and that it had been renamed by the revolution Vali Asr (after the Mahdi, the occulted, final iman of Shiism), but that everyone still called it Pahlavi. Years later I would flee down its side streets, tripping in flimsy sandals, away from Islamic vigilantes with clubs who would kill and die to make sure the name never changed back. But that summer it was only an elegant slope of sycamores where Maman would take me for *bastani* (ice cream), where I first discovered that a boulevard could be lined on both sides with a flowing stream, a *joob,* covered with little bridges.

To my five-year-old suburban American sensibilities, exposed to nothing more mystical than the Smurfs, Iran was suffused with drama and magic. After Friday lunch at my grandfather's, once the last plates of sliced cantaloupe were cleared away, everyone retired to the bedrooms to nap. Inevitably there was a willing aunt or cousin on hand to scratch my back as I fell asleep. Unused to the siesta ritual, I woke up after half an hour to find the bed I was sharing with my cousin swathed in a tower of creamy gauze that stretched high up to the ceiling. "Wake up," I nudged him, "we're surrounded!" "It's for the mosquitoes, *khareh,* ass, go back to sleep." To me it was like a fairy tale, and I peered through the netting to the living room, to the table heaped with plump dates and the dense, aromatic baklava we would nibble on later with tea. The day before I had helped my grandmother, Razi joon, make *ash-e gooshvareh,* "earring stew"; we made hoops out of the fresh pasta, and dropped them into the vat of simmering herbs and lamb. Here even the ordinary had charm, even the names of stews.

It was high summer, so many nights we slept outdoors, on the roof of my uncle's building in Shemroon, north Tehran. The servants would carry out the mattresses, the piles of pillows and linens, and we would talk until late, sipping sour cherry juice, before falling asleep under the stars. When the weather turned cold, one of the rooms inside was transformed into a *korsi*—a cozy heap of cushions, carpets, and blankets, arranged in a circle around a central fire of coals, a sort of giant, round, heated bed that served as the venue for winter salons. Each morning, I would sit at my spot at the long table in the airy kitchen, and spin the silver jam wheel, deciding whether to heap carrot, quince, or fig jam on my hot, buttered *barbari* bread, before sneaking off to snuggle under the *korsi*.

It was only once we arrived in Iran that the mystery of our life in California began to make sense. I finally saw the world that had been left behind, and the world our existence in California was dedicated to recapturing. Before that summer, my first visit back, I had suspected my family of collective dissimulation. I would ask my grandfather countless times, "Agha Joon, were you *really* a judge in Iran?" I couldn't conceive how, if the stories were true, they could be reconciled with the only reality that I knew.

I was entirely unconscious at that age of the revolution, and how in classic revolutionary fashion, one social class had overthrown another. Before that came to pass, Iranian society was divided into a tiny upper class, a wide middle with its own distinguishable upper and lower parts, and a sizable body of poor or working class. My mother's family fell somewhere in the area between middle and upper-middle, which meant that they were landowners, and able to send four children to the West for university. Most strands of my father's family were wealthy, and belonged to that upper class that the revolutionaries of 1979 were bent on unseating. One of my uncles had been roommates at Berkeley with Mustafa Chamran, who became one of the leaders in the uprising. They had been friendly in those college days, and when at the dawn of the revolution my uncle was taken to prison, he contacted his old roommate Chamran. No reply. "Your type must go," came a message, through a friend.

Leaving Tehran broke my heart. My pet duck died the week we were to go, and Maman tried to console me with promises of a kitten back home. I was too young to understand that what I didn't want to part with was a newfound sense of wholeness—a sense of belonging in a world that embraced us. The memories of those few months colored the rest of our life in America. They flooded back vividly, when my grandmother cooked jam, when Maman took me with her to the bank, to visit the safety-deposit box where she kept all the jewelry she no longer wore, the gold bangles and dainty earrings our relatives had bestowed on me in Tehran. In times of acute alienation, they were a reminder that things could be different; proof that the often awkward fusion of East and West in our American lives didn't necessarily point to our failure, but the inherent tension of the attempt. At those times when I was most furious with Maman, I would recall the lightness of our days in Tehran, her easy smile and fluid movements, and remind myself of the strength it took for her to build a life in a strange country, alone.

✝

My maternal grandparents came to the United States in the mid-1970s, intending to base themselves for good near Stanford Hospital, where my grandmother's ailing heart could be sustained by a pacemaker and tended by skilled cardiologists. My own parents had attended university in California in the late sixties, along with their many siblings, but like most Iranian students of that generation, they chose not to stay. They returned to Iran with American degrees, and lofty dreams of modernizing the homeland, and discouraging the Shah of Iran from behaving like an authoritarian American puppet. In 1976, my parents married and came to the United States, with no fixed idea of staying forever, but a passing wish to be near my grandparents, lonely in their medical exile. The rest of the family, all their brothers and sisters, remained in Iran, intending to lead international lives traveling back and forth between Iran and the West, the twin poles of modernity and home. Until 1979, the year of the great catastrophe that tossed our lives up into the air, scattering us haphazardly like leaves in a storm.

It came to be known as the Islamic Revolution, though even that term is contested by people like my relatives, who insist it was a populist uprising stolen by fundamentalist clerics. Until 1979, Iran was ruled by Shah Mohammed Reza Pahlavi, a detached, out-of-touch leader whose unpopular government was propped up in 1953 by an American-British coup. The Shah, in the classic style of Middle East potentates, reigned with an authoritarian hand and an allegiance to policies favored by his American backers. He spent vast reserves of oil money on the latest American military technology, but neglected to manage the urbanization and rapid growth that was transforming Iranian society. While he staged baroque, extravagant spectacles in honor of the Persian dynastic tradition, his critics were silenced, and great swaths of Iranian society stayed poor. The sliver that thrived did so flamboyantly, with a Western easiness that provoked the majority of Iranians too traditional and too poor to appreciate the advent of bikinis and Christian Dior. By the late 1970s, resentment against the Shah's regime—for its pro-Western tilt, for its stifling of political dissent, and for economic policies that widened the disparity in wealth—gained momentum, and the revolution unfolded. Some of my relatives left shortly before, when the rumblings grew louder. Of my father's two brothers, one went to prison for his ties to the monarchy; another stayed to cheer the great nationalist revolt.

When radical students took the American embassy hostage in 1979, they transformed a classic revolution into a dramatic confrontation with the United States. The hostage taking energized the uprising and added an iconoclastic dimension, a historic triumph of East over West. That is why, to this day, the Islamic Republic cultivates its stale anti-Americanism, once the life force of the revolution. The freshly minted regime immediately went to war with Iraq, and the two great strategic powers of the Middle East sapped each other's strength for nearly a decade.

To be Iranian in the United States during the 1980s meant living perpetually in the shadow of the hostage crisis. Many Iranians dealt with this by becoming the perfect immigrants: successful, assimilated, with flawless, relaxed American English and cheerfully pro-American political sentiments. Not Maman. I should've known the day I was flipping through old black and white photos of her college years in California. There she stood, with an elaborate beehive, wearing a mini-skirt covered with paisleys, hoisting a placard that read "Palestine is ours!" From my aunts, other relatives, and American family friends who had attended college at places like UC Berkeley and USC in the 1960s, I'd heard stories of a thriving expatriate Iranian student scene—they snorted cocaine, skied, drove fast cars, jetsetting between California, Europe, and Tehran. Why hadn't she been hanging out with them?

Maman imposed on our life in California her strict sense of justice, which others seemed to find noble but which to me was simply an effort to destroy my peace of mind. Often I'd come home from school to find a perfect stranger at the kitchen table, the latest Iranian charity case—an abused wife, a teenage runaway—she'd taken up to rescue. Sometimes these strangers would live with us for weeks, while Maman ignored my complaints that she should be concerned with baking cookies and acting like a normal American parent.

But fate, it seemed, had dealt me a mother who night after night shook her fist at the television, decrying America's latest interference in Latin America, or the brutal crimes being perpetrated against Palestinians. At the time, these tirades confused me. I didn't understand how what happened in Palestine related to us, living quietly in our corner of California. I didn't understand why these distant political conflicts were woven into her consciousness, why they resonated so forcefully.

The high volume of Maman's emotional politics made me feel even more estranged from my friends at school, at an age when nothing is more painful. Their houses were oases of calm, full of candy and movies and carefree parents who took them to baseball games. In these sane households, the biographies of visitors were simple; at our house, even casual acquaintances came through with political résumés ("This is Fereshteh, a reformed

Mujahed; Dariush, who was once Fedayeen . . . "). Only after serious deliberation would I bring the most trusted friends over, exposing them to strange smells, wailing music, and Maman yelling political grievances into the phone ("you'll never believe what these bastards did today in _____!"). For many years my overriding objective in meeting new people was to avoid mention of my Iranianness. That my name gave me away, that people would ask in a smiley, kind way where I was from, and that I would have to say it, "Iran," and watch their faces settle into a blank, this was a permanent source of discomfort. I wasn't sure what made me feel more wretched: being embarrassed to be Iranian, or guilt at being embarrassed. Saying I was Persian helped, but no one knew what or where Persia was, exactly, and there would often be follow-up questions. The adults were marinating in politics, and had little sense of how hard it was on us, the kids.

I can still recall with perfect vividness the first day of school each year, when I would squirm miserably in my seat as the teacher called roll. As she approached the K's and L's, I knew the second she slowed down that she had arrived at my name; that she would bludgeon its pronunciation I had already accepted, but I prayed not to be asked in front of everyone else its origins, to have to utter that word, Iran. Maman suggested I take on an English name for use at school, and I toyed with Elizabeth, the most un-Azadeh name I could think of. I practiced signing my diary entries with Liz, in a flourish of violet ink, but it glowed on the page, embarrassing and alien. I resigned myself to a life of Azadeh, which means "one who is free," a name that became popular right before and after the revolution. As a rebellious teenager, constrained by Maman's rules, my relatives teased me mercilessly. You're not free, neither is Iran. Haha.

As though she knew how earnestly I sought to keep my Iranianness under cover, Maman, my nemesis, would sweep into my classroom each year in the spring, and do a special presentation on Persian New Year (Noruz). Each year I would drag myself out of the navy blue Volvo, its somber, boxy lines a fitting vehicle for my dejected spirit, and watch her patiently unpack the colored eggs, and everything else that went on the *haft-seen,* the ritual table setting of the Seven S's, out of the trunk. "Are you sure you want to go through with this?" I'd ask her. "I think everyone still remembers your presentation from last year." It was always futile, and I would prepare myself for the hour when she would undo what I had spent weeks trying to cultivate: ethnic ambiguity. "The eggs—like your Easter eggs, see how nicely Azadeh has colored them—symbolize fertility; the coins success; the sprouted wheat, new life. Two weeks after the new year, we go on picnics, tie scraps of fabric to trees, and toss the wheat in the river." I tried to visualize what must be going through my classmates' minds: masses of mad Persians flinging clumps of grass into the dank reservoir at the local park. I wanted to kill her.

When she wasn't busy canceling subscriptions to news magazines that were too pro-establishment, Maman tried to find us a niche in California. Finally she did—among the hippie, hyper-educated liberals who sent their kids to alternative school with organic lunches. I condoned this set of acquaintances, despite the peacenik coffees, because they talked so knowledgeably of Iran—its poetry, music, and history—and seemed to think being Iranian was wonderful. In the presence of these hippie friends, my resentment of Iranianness receded.

Around the same time Maman took up Hinduism, and on weekends we drove up to the ashram in Oakland to chant together at children's *satsang*, the practice of coming together in the company of Truth. There were workshops on most everything, from living life with spontaneity to reupholstering the divine source within you. Eventually we switched to a local ashram, but occasionally went to Oakland for many years. The hours I spent cross-legged in these candle-lit, incense-infused rooms were among the only moments I felt comfortable in my own skin. Everyone was too dippy and preoccupied with vegan curry and their chakras to care that we were Iranian; in fact, they thought it was sort of neat, and we were embraced with the squishy affection of people fond of the exotic.

⚘

The Iranian community of northern California, in my youth, was an enclave of constantly shifting associations, of social and financial status, political affiliation, and otherwise. There were older families, like my parents, who had been there longer, but as the revolution churned Iran, it cast out thousands of exiles, many of whom gravitated toward California. In weather, the proximity of beach to ski slope, the climate resembled Iran. Over the next decade, these Iranians would re-establish their social networks, assimilate, and rebuild their lives, with a constant eye at how their co-exiles were faring—who was adapting faster? Who managed to transfer their wealth, and who had to start over? Who was making social concessions in their selection of acceptable acquaintances, and who was becoming more exclusive? All these questions were meant to get at the most important one of all: who had managed to maintain their dignity, keep their way of life intact, and who had been forced, either by financial ruin or mental weakness, to dignify the revolution by allowing it to determine all that was to come? Fate had scattered much of upper-class Tehran throughout Europe and America, but it hadn't absolved the age-old compulsion to weigh ancestry and make authoritative judgments separating the common from the elect. Often when Iranians encountered each other in public, they pretended not to recognize each other as fellow Iranians, speaking English to one another in identical accents. This self-conscious public theater was preferable to acknowledging each other in Farsi, a language that is spoken differently depending on whom one is speaking to. Even my father, the Marxist who spurned class barriers and ridiculed my mother's operagoing bourgeois habits, would whisper *hamvatan,* countryman, to me, in a store, then proceed to address the person in English.

Our relatives, whom I will call the Pakravans, had somehow managed the crossing more proficiently—in suburban northern California their houses multiplied, their cars seemed to upgrade themselves, and with each passing year they acquired more desirable zip codes, until finally they had succeeded in re-creating a sort of life that approximated the one they had left behind. They had shed the shameful compromises imposed by our less well-managed crossing, and the contrast always stung. It was never quite discussed as such—confronting this would have meant also confronting how we had somehow failed. The reasons why they had recaptured their status, forcibly reinstated grace and comfort into their lives, became a source of obsession for Maman, her sisters, the entire family. My great-uncle went in person to the bank in San Jose where everyone managed their finances and demanded the manager tell him how much money Mr. Pakravan had transferred from Iran. I can't disclose that sort of information, he was told. My great-uncle drew his shoulders back. Once a colonel in the army of his Royal Majesty, the Light of the Aryans, now being dismissed by a petty clerk. You *must* tell me, at least who brought more? He did, the bank manager finally said in exasperation. Was it a question of *orzeh* (talent) or timing? The debate raged. But the truth, as it tends to be, was actually rather simple. The Pakravans were savvier with their finances, saving and investing with wisdom and forethought. With my mother's side of the family, not only did fiscal prudence not come naturally, but old habits died hard. Thousands of dollars could be cut down to nothing in a few hours at the roulette table. Annual trips to Europe were deemed necessities. Wardrobes required maintenance. Unsurprisingly, it did not all come together very well. Over the years their laments became a mantra of regret: if only my grandmother had brought her money over when the toman was strong against the dollar (for Iranians, when the dollar equaled seven tomans and before the revolution were interchangeable markers of time); if only she too had bought houses when her savings could have easily purchased them and not waited until the devaluing of the toman made even the rent of a modest two-bedroom apartment a hardship.

Those were the first years after the revolution, when it wasn't clear whether Iran would mutate once again, consolidate, or collapse under the weight of a war with Iraq. How do you make decisions, when your fate hangs in the balance of a country in chaos? How do you force yourself to build a new life, when deep in your heart you hold out hope that the nightmare will end, and your country will be returned to you? My youngest aunt, Farzaneh, who I called Khaleh Farzi, held out hope until doing so became foolish. During my childhood in California, she was one of the most important women in my life, and she became central again in 2000, when I moved to Iran. Just like so many thousands Khaleh Farzi had been drawn to the revolutionary street protests in Tehran without a clear sense of their destination, without any inkling that they would explode the world of which she was so fond. Tehran under the Shah, with a nightlife so dazzling she abandoned her studies in England to come home to party—weekends at the Caspian, smoking grass on the beach in bikinis; weeknights in Tehran, making the rounds of private clubs, drinking champagne in dresses from Paris.

The move from her pre-revolution party life in Tehran to the bedroom she shared with her husband in my grandmother's rented apartment in San Jose, was a shattering, incomprehensible blow. She couldn't drive, there had never been a need; that's what drivers had been for. She never thought she'd need to work, and like so many Iranian girls educated abroad for the principles of being modern and well-bred, she had a useless degree—in her case, in sociology. Soon it became clear that if her husband, Hamid, were to transfer his medical license to the U.S., he would need to pass a bevy of tests in English. That meant many expensive classes. So Khaleh Farzi stopped spending her days wistfully floating through the department stores she could no longer afford to shop at, and donned the scratchy, dull blue uniform of a Woolworth's waitress. I wonder what people thought of her, this shy young Iranian woman with her bobbed hair, delicate gamine features, and sad eyes. I wonder what she minded most: that an Iranian she knew might walk in; that she had a college degree and was serving milk shakes; that this might be reality, and not a bad dream—not a cruel interlude intended to make her value the life she gambled away with what she later came to consider reckless idealism.

As though this all wasn't enough to bear, her own sister, Maman, had the nerve to proclaim the revolution a good thing. Maman had left Iran a few years back, and had more memories of the Shah's oppressive politics; in 1979 she was a single mother of a three-year-old, untroubled by the loss of a glittering social life. And it was still early then. No one knew whether to believe the reports of the countless executions; the full truth of the bloodbath would only emerge later. Full of fire and exultation that the U.S.-puppet Shah had fallen, my mother coaxed my aging grandmother into the car and drove to San Francisco to vote at the Iranian consulate in a referendum to support the newly formed revolutionary government. Khaleh Farzi looked on bitterly.

The trauma of dislocation varied, of course, by generation and gender. Young husbands felt the pain of not being able to provide, with great wounds to their male dignity and self-respect. Older people like my grandparents missed the comforts of retirement in a familiar milieu, with old friends and trusted servants; they felt vulnerable in a strange country, with a language they couldn't speak. But the loss everyone felt together, among the most acute, was the loss of gardens. Trees, flowers, the garden courtyard occupy a hallowed space in Iranian culture. Just look through the photo albums of an old Iranian family. You'll find faded images of parents seated outside on a raised divan covered with Persian rugs, with children playing by a fountain, or amidst a grove of trees, in the background. In one of my favorite stories that Maman would tell me as a child, my great-grandmother, in a fit of wounded rage at my great-grandfather, taking a second wife, ordered the leveling of one of the oldest mulberry orchards—tall, proud trees that had grown for decades, destroyed in revenge for his betrayal. She had found no better metaphor for the death of her love than the destruction of trees. In California, the absence of gardens seemed the bitterest part of our reconstructed lives.

They tried to make do, my grandparents. Their apartment in San Jose, which faced the garbage dumpster, had a small, squalid patch of green out front, covered in coarse, dusty ivy. My grandfather, whom we called Agha Joon, patiently cleared it away, and tried to grow *gol-e shamdooni* (geraniums). Each day he would water them, determined to make something bloom, to resist letting himself go. My grandmother, fiercely proud, had from the beginning decided on a strategy of not caring; if she could not have her orchards at Farahzad, she didn't want gardens at all. When the time came to minister to the flowers, she would roll her eyes, "It's Katouzi, what can I say?" as though my grandfather—whom she called by his last name, in that stately, old way—were watering a desert. Their apartment complex was built around a large pond, with grassy patches on its banks, and on summer evenings we would lay out a rug and loll under the suburban sky with thermoses of tea. My grandmother would cook a huge, steaming pot of fava beans, which we'd unpeel, dipping the hot beans in a vinegary sauce, after popping them out of their long, velvety pods. I wondered whether anyone I knew from school might see us—so absurd, we must seem, all sprawled out on a rug by the pond, eating beans from the pod.

My father, too, was obsessed with the re-creation of a garden. He rented a plot of land in a lot in Saratoga, and each weekend after he picked me up from Maman's, we would drive there to water his patch. He transported me to and from the patch in a white Volvo, the first of many white Volvos to come, with the license plate RAKSH, after the name of the hero Rostam's wondrous white steed, in the *Shahnameh,* the Book of Kings, the ancient Persian epic poem. What's your dad's license plate mean? my friends sometimes asked. Oh, it's just this horse in this one story, I said quickly. Eventually the Volvos graduated to SUVs, still white of course, and RAKSH became RAKSH Jr., bearing us round the wide streets of San Jose, as though the suburbs were a battle.

With seeds he had relatives bring from Iran, Daddy planted rows of eggplant, narrow cucumber, mint, basil, and all the herbs necessary for Persian cooking that at the time didn't exist—at least in their proper variety—at the immense supermarket that everyone else's parents seemed to find sufficient for their produce needs. The only aspect of Iranian culture he cherished, and wanted to pass on to me, was this reverence for nature, which he worried he might not be able to instill amidst the cement and strip malls of San Jose. And so, after monitoring the progress of the Persian herbs, we would take long walks through the hills of Los Altos, stopping at each new tree to note the quality of the bark, the shape of the leaves. Eventually I could distinguish a mulberry tree from a walnut, walnut from almond, and both from the tree that would grow pomegranates. At nights, Daddy would take sheets of white paper and trace the outline of what looked like a bloated cat. He then built me an architect's table, on which I too could learn to draw the proper dimensions of the cat, which he informed me was the accurate geographic contour of Iran. Until I became an adolescent, and insisted on living at the mall, this was all my father and I did together: cultivate herbs, draw the cat-Iran to scale, pass leafy examinations.

Agha Joon, my grandfather, was a gentle, lyrical man, who spent his days in America—almost three decades of them—reading Persian poetry, going for walks, and not learning English. He never complained about the hardship or the crudeness of his transplanted life, and somehow managed to keep that same remote, blissful look in his eyes until the very end. His great joy was also his patch, which he eventually did transform into a wild garden. When I would run back to the apartment after swimming, waiting for my bathing suit to dry, he would point proudly to the blooming flowers, his voice lilting softly with a Turkish accent, from his childhood in the ethnically Turkish region of Iran: Look, daughter, look at what God has created. As a first-grader, it puzzled me that he considered this an offering from God. Besides the fact that everyone knew he shunned religion, the sad, valiant garden seemed more a cause for sorrow than thanks. But seeing the world gently was how Agha Joon coped, and what protected his spirit from a change that had crushed stronger men. This is how he kept the shame of these new circumstances from eating away at him, as it did my grandmother. He ambled around the neighborhood, praised America for its vast malls, the quality of its television channels, the orderliness of its traffic. Eventually he abandoned prose altogether, and began communicating exclusively in verse, remaining connected to us only by the vast stores of poetry in his memory. In each conversation he would dip into his reserves, and find a suitable line or couplet to voice his thoughts. When Maman and I bitterly fought over some new restriction, he refused to take sides. With eyes twinkling through his thick glasses, he would elusively repeat the verse reserved for our arguments—"with the way illuminated, why do you take the darker path? Go then, for you deserve the consequences!"—leaving it intentionally unclear to which of us it was directed.

Only at rare moments did I suspect that Agha Joon was not entirely preoccupied with his flowers, but felt the sting of loss—on those days he would ask Maman to play Banaan, the classical Persian singer whose voice ached with melancholy. He would sit on the couch, pouring his tea into a saucer so it would cool more quickly, sipping it through the sugar cubes held between his teeth. He would sit like that for hours, as the tape played over and over. I would try to turn it down—my friends from school were calling to discuss field hockey, and lip gloss, and I didn't want them to hear foreign wailing in the background. But Agha Joon's hearing was starting to go, and he would look up with such desolate surprise that I quickly turned the volume back up.

As detached as my grandfather was—*dar alam-e khodesh,* in his own world—or had managed to make himself, my grandmother was alert. My cousins and I stopped watching television in her presence, frustrated by her constant demand for translation. What are they *saying,* she would ask, even if she was in the kitchen, her hands stained with green juice, wrist-deep in colanders of minced herbs. To her mild irritation, Agha Joon was content to only watch animal world programs, whose stalking lions and hatching eggs rendered words irrelevant.

Mornings, in the sunlight by the window, my grandmother sat me down to teach me a set of unfamiliar sounds—*al-fatiha,* the opening sura of the Koran. But how can God be good, if he invented Khomeini? I asked, trying to evade the lesson. I didn't want to learn these unintelligible words; I already had my tap-dancing routine and piano scales to memorize. Khomeini has never done anything bad to me *personally,* she said. Well, duh, that's because he didn't know you, I replied, rolling my eyes.

She always had a tin of French raspberry pastilles in her bag, and had named all her children with names beginning with F. Like all Iranian grandmothers, she never called out the name of one per se, but a staccato string of all their names (Fariba, Ferial, Farzi, Fariborz) one of which would inevitably be correct. When we would set out together from the apartment, for the short walk to the grocery store, she slipped her hand into mine, and said, *Asay-e dast-e mani,* you are my hand's cane. I felt this as both a privilege and a burden, knowing that I, barely in second grade, would have to defend her honor at the checkout line. Her acuity was a hundred times more painful for me, because I knew with dread that she felt every backward glance, was stung by every rude word from a pimply, ignorant teenager who only saw a strange old woman in a veil in the line at the grocery store, taking too long to fumble the bills out of her clasp purse, counting them out slowly.

My grandmother cooked often, exclusively Persian food, and in that manner typical to immigrants, exerted some control over her transplanted life through purity of the palette. Since she refused to eat in restaurants, the kitchen became her domain, from whence she spun fantastically delicate custards and fluffy cakes. *Katouzi,* she would call out to my grandfather, come eat. And he would assume his usual place at the table, making his way through a heaping pile of my favorite dish, *adas polo,* fluffy rice with cinnamon, lentils, and raisins drizzled with saffron. Then he would remind us— as usual, in verse, with a couplet that says when the appetite dwindles, the end approaches—that at his prime, he could eat four times the amount of whatever he had just consumed, and drift into his bedroom for a nap.

My mother modeled herself after Agha Joon, seeing only what she wanted to see, impervious to everything else. I was like my grandmother, proud, thin-skinned, sensitive to every backward glance. And so it was with us, as it was with them—a constant friction, a dismay with the other's approach to the world. As Agha Joon planted his garden, enraptured by the petals and leaves, my grandmother ignored it icily, disdainful of its modest size, preferring not to have one at all. As my mother dragged me to operas, where we had to stand because seated tickets were too expensive, I fidgeted sullenly, mortified at being relegated to the serf quarters in the feudal system that was opera house seating. I'd rather stay home and rent a movie, I insisted, than endure that sort of humiliation. But she wouldn't hear of it, and so we went, planted on our feet for hours on end, weekends in a row.

The apartment complex was overrun with other Iranian exiles, and the shoved-up-against-each-other intimacy of condo life—to the chagrin of Khaleh Farzi, who lived with them—erased the social distinctions imposed in Tehran by neighborhood and district. There were Iranians we could associate with, *adam hesabi* (good families), and a slew of undesirables who I wasn't sure whether I should say *Salaam* to. The bogey man of the émigrés was a man who I remember as Mr. Savaki. He had been an official in the SAVAK, the Shah's brutal secret service, and he now spent endless hours by the pool, turning his body on the beach chair as though he was on a rotisserie. I didn't know what *savaki* meant at the time—didn't know it was a byword for torture—except that every grown-up's face drew tight and grave when the word was uttered. When my cousins and I spotted his leathery, wrinkled body stretched out on a pool chair, we would stare briefly at the tattoo of the Shah's face on his bicep, and then flee. On the days he would come by for tea, sitting with Agha Joon to enumerate the flaws of Ayatollah Khomeini, Khaleh Farzi would fume. Maman, I don't understand why you let that man into our house, she complained to my grandmother.

Perhaps the only person more offensive than Mr. Savaki was Mrs. Bazaari—a vulgar rug merchant who prowled the complex in search of *adam hesabi* to terrorize into having tea. We secretly thought she was pleased with the revolution, because her husband could stay in Tehran and sell rugs to the newly rich revolutionaries, while she attempted to social climb among the old guard abroad. Despite the fact that she was now working at Woolworth's, Khaleh Farzi stood her ground; our transplanted circumstances might make us vulnerable to every sort of indignity, but nothing could force her to consort with *bazaaris*. Occasionally the cunning Mrs. Bazaari would find pretexts to gain a foothold in the house, kidnapping Agha Joon in the neighborhood, driving him home, and then claiming she had found him lost, wandering miles away. Khaleh Farzi would wordlessly serve her a cup of tea, in silent protest against the transgression.

That we lived near two immense highways, and could go days without seeing anyone we knew at the grocery store, didn't diminish the tribal and village customs native to Tehranis. Namely, being nosy about the personal lives of people we did not deign to know. For weeks Khaleh Farzi had watched a parade of lovely young women enter and exit the house of an unkempt Iranian man, who lived in the building next door. Baffled that someone so *bireekht*, so ugly, could attract such company, Khaleh Farzi investigated, and learned that he dealt cocaine. It was upon making such discoveries that Khaleh Farzi would lapse into a deep funk, and try not to care that the Pakravans were buying their eleventh columned home in Los Altos. Observing all this as a child, I had the impression that if life in Iran was anything similar, society must be one vast sieve, with everyone trying to catch the people they wanted and filter out the rest.

This émigré political salon convened each Sunday at the condo complex's Sunday brunch, over donuts and coffee. The discussions became engaging enough that soon Iranians from around the city began showing up, and until well into the afternoon—after the last rainbow sprinkle had disappeared—they would debate the state of the country. The Sunday coffee was the ideally neutral space for an inclusive discussion; here the social regulations governing laws of interaction ceased to apply. There was no consensus on anything at all, except the fact that the country had been ruined; No one agreed on whom to blame: Jimmy Carter, the Shah, the CIA, the British, the BBC, the mullahs, the Marxists, or the Mujaheddin?

Sometimes the intricacies and exoticness of this inner Iranian world made me feel lucky, as though I'd been granted an extra life. There was Azadeh at school, who managed to look and sound like the other kids, barring the occasional lunchbox oddity; and there was Azadeh at home, who lived in a separate world, with its own special language and rituals. More often, though, living between two cultures just made me long for refuge in one. Maman's attempts to fuse both worlds, instead of compartmentalizing them, complicated everything. She didn't want to sacrifice anything: neither her Iranian values, nor her American independence. She refused to abdicate one side for the other, not even for a time, and it made our life together harrowing and unruly.

Next door to us on Auburn Way, two blocks from my grandparents' place, lived a single mother with two young girls. Unlike Maman, who had seemingly taken a vow of celibacy after her divorce, the single mom next door went out on dates all the time, and when she decided to stay the night with the man of the week she'd leave her daughters home alone. One night the younger one began to cry, emitting keening howls of fear, which Maman listened to for about half an hour, and then could no longer bear it. She went next door, invited them over, and made peanut butter sandwiches. We watched cartoons, while she set up little beds in our living room, and finally drifted off to sleep in front of the TV. Early in the morning a loud knocking woke us—their mother, still dressed in her evening clothes, was pounding on our door, shouting, and waving the note Maman had left her. She was going to call the police, she screamed, how dare we take her children—kidnap them—out of her house? Maman turned pale, and tried to invite her inside for tea. She explained that the girls had been scared, but that they were fine—see, all snuggly in their pajamas. I could already anticipate my father's angry recrimination come Friday, when he'd come to take me for the weekend, and she would recount the savagery of American mothers, abandoning their children and then terrorizing a neighbor who showed them kindness. "Fariba jan," he would say, "you can't do that sort of thing here. This is *not* Iran, you can't just take people's kids out of their house in the middle of the night."

When it served her purposes, Maman embraced America and lovingly recited all the qualities that made it superior to our backward-looking Iranian culture. That Americans were honest, never made promises they didn't intend to keep, were open to therapy, believed a divorced woman was still a whole person worthy of respect and a place in society—all this earned them vast respect in Maman's book. It seemed never to occur to her that values do not exist in a cultural vacuum but are knit into a society's fabric; they earn their place, derived from other related beliefs. Maman thought values were like groceries; you'd cruise through the aisles, toss the ones you fancied into your cart, and leave the unappealing ones on the shelf. When I was a teenager we constantly fought over her pilfering through Iranian and American values at random, assigning a particular behavior or habit she felt like promoting to the culture she could peg it to most convincingly.

Our earliest battle on this territory was over Madonna. Maman called her *jendeh,* a prostitute, which I considered an offensive way to describe the singer of "La Isla Bonita." On what grounds, I argued, was she being condemned? Was it because she flaunted her sexuality, and if so, did that make out-of-wedlock sexuality a bad thing? My defense of Madonna seemed to infuriate Maman; her eyes flashed, and her bearing radiated a grave, ominous disappointment. It was the same disproportionate reaction she'd show when I would forget which elder in a room full of aging relatives I should have served tea to first, or when I'd refuse to interrupt an afternoon with a friend to take vitamins to an elderly Iranian lady who couldn't drive. Certain conversations or requests, unbeknownst to me, would become symbolic tests of my allegiance to that Iranian world, and the wrong response would plunge Maman into dark feelings of failure and regret.

At the prescient age of thirteen, I realized our Madonna arguments signaled far more serious confrontations to come. Maman's contempt for Madonna seemed like sheer hypocrisy to me. Was this the same woman who thought it regressive and awful that Iranian culture valued women through their marital status, and rated their respectability according to the success or failure of their marriage? The woman who denounced a culture that considered divorced women criminals? She believed it was only modern to consider women fully equal to men, independent beings with a sacred right to everything men were entitled. Somehow, it became clear through her designation of Madonna as whore, that she also thought it fully consistent to believe premarital sex (for women) was wrong, and that women who practiced it were morally compromised. The men she forgave, offering an explanation worthy of an Iranian villager: "They can't help themselves." Women, it seemed, were physiologically better equipped for deprivation. Often our fights would end with me collapsing in tears, her bitterly condemning my unquestioning acceptance of "this decadent culture's corrupt ways," and my usual finale: "It's all your fault for raising me here; what did you expect?"

In Maman's view, America was responsible for most that had gone wrong in the world. *Een gavhah,* these cows, was her synonym for Americans. She'd established her criticisms early on, and repeated them so often that to this day they are seared on my brain: "Americans have no social skills. . . . They prefer their pets to people. . . . Shopping and sex, sex and shopping; that's all Americans think about. . . . They've figured out how corrupt they are, and rather than fix themselves, they want to force their sick culture on the rest of the world." Since she mostly wheeled out these attitudes to justify why I couldn't be friends with Adam-the-long-haired-guitarist or why I couldn't go to the movies twice in one week, or why I couldn't wear short skirts, I wondered whether they were sincere, or tactical.

Her restrictions were futile, and only turned me into a highly skilled liar with a suspiciously heavy backpack. Every morning she would drop me off at a friend's house, ostensibly so we could walk to school together. Once inside I traded the Maman-approved outfit for something tighter, smeared some cherry gloss on my lips, and headed off to class. Knowing I could secretly evade her restrictions helped me endure the sermons, but sometimes the injustice of her moralizing would provoke me, and I would fling jingoistic clichés designed to infuriate her: "Love it or leave it. . . . These colors don't run. . . . No one's keeping you here." At hearing these words come out of my mouth she'd hurl a piece of fruit at me, dissolve into angry tears, and suddenly the fact that I was torturing my poor, exiled single mother filled me with terrible grief, and I would apologize profusely, begging forgiveness in the formal, filial Farsi I knew she craved to hear. In the style of a traditional Iranian mother, she would pretend, for five days, that I did not exist; thaw on the sixth; and by the seventh have forgotten the episode entirely, privately convinced that my rude friends, who didn't even say *salaam* to her when they came over, were responsible for ruining my manners.

When we encountered other second-generation Iranians at Persian parties, I was struck by how much less conflicted they seemed over their dueling cultural identities. I decided my own neurotic messiness in this area was the fault of my divorced parents. The only thing they agreed on was the safety record of the Volvo, and how they should both drive one until I finished junior high. But when it came to anything that mattered, for instance how I should be raised, they didn't even bother to carve out an agreement, so vast was the gulf that separated their beliefs. My father was an atheist (Marx said God was dead) who called the Prophet Mohammad a pedophile for marrying a nine-year-old girl. He thought the defining characteristics of Iranian culture—fatalism, political paranoia, social obligations, an enthusiasm for guilt—were responsible for the failures of modern Iran. He wouldn't even condescend to use the term "Iranian culture," preferring to refer, to this day, to "that stinking culture"; he refused to return to Iran, even for his mother's funeral, and wouldn't help me with my Persian homework, a language, he pronounced direly "you will *never* use." When I announced my decision to move to Iran, his greatest fear, I think, was that something sufficiently awful would happen to me that it would require *his* going back. That he had married Maman, a hyper-ideologue, a reactionary as high-strung as they come, was baffling; little wonder they divorced when I was an infant. Daddy was the benevolent father personified; he couldn't have cared less about curfews, dating, a fifth ear piercing, or whether my hair was purple or not.

There were few times during my adolescence that he intervened, but Maman's attempt to make mosque attendees out of her and me was one of them. Iranians, by and large, are subtle about their piety, and identify more closely with Persian tradition than with Islam. Faith is a personal matter, commanding of respect, but it does not infuse our culture in the totalizing way I have witnessed in certain Arab countries, among many Sunni Muslims. Westernized, educated Iranians are fully secular—they eat pork, don't pray, ignore Ramadan—and so it had never occurred to the exile community to start up a mosque. Hiking groups, discos, political soirees, definitely, but a mosque would have been in bad taste; the revolution had made Islam the domain of the fundamentalists. But Maman was one day struck by worry that I'd grow up ignorant of Islam, and decided some formal religious training was in order. Every four years she seemed to choose a new religious avenue to explore, convinced our lives were lacking in spirituality, and since we had already done Buddhism and Hinduism, and briefly toyed with Mormonism, it was Islam's turn.

That was the summer she enrolled us in a Sunni mosque. It was called the San Jose Islamic Association, but it was really an enclave of super-pious, Sunni Pakistanis who had dedicated their experience in America to avoiding their experience in America. A shabby pink Victorian housed both the mosque and the Islamic Association; bearded men led the sermon, and the women in the back, dressed in *salwar kameez,* dashed off at the final *"allah akbar"* to heat up the *naan.* The sermons were boring, and the Pakistanis were cliquey, but the afternoon morality class was the worst.

Brother Rajabali (or somesuch pious name), a dark, spindly man whose unenviable job it was to make the harsh Sunni morality applicable to our lives in California, had dedicated the afternoon's lesson to sex, and how its only purpose was procreation. Maman nodded gravely, the Bosnian girls scribbled notes to one another, and I sat wondering whether all Sunnis were so narrow-minded. Eventually, I convinced a coalition of relatives the mosque was run by fundamentalist, radical Sunnis who were trying to brainwash me. My grandmother interceded, afraid I would be turned away from Islam forever, and we never set foot again into the sad old Victorian with its angry believers. They still send us their monthly newsletter, full of ads for *halal* meat grocers we never frequent.

The civil war in our house—heralded by the Madonna fight and the

weekly doses of Brother Rajabali—erupted unexpectedly on a fall afternoon, during a placid walk around the neighborhood. By that time I was
well into high school, and envious of friends who had co-conspirator
mothers, always ready to help them primp for first dates, delighted to follow the twists and turns of their teenage romances. I deeply hoped that Maman and I were ready to transcend the don't-ask-don't-tell policy we had
been driven to by the ceaseless arguments of my early teenage years. As we
walked, she turned and with the kindest smile said to me, "Azadeh jan, I
want you to know that if you ever decide to become, ahem, close with your
boyfriend, I'm here for you, and want to know about it. Not to lecture you,
but because I want to be your friend and advise you. There are so many important things you might not be thinking about, and I'm in a position to
help." Maman was devoutly into meditation, yoga, and all the other spiritual hobbies in California that teach a person, even a displaced Iranian,
how to sound far more open-minded, sensitive, and tolerant than they actually are.

A wise voice inside my head told me to be skeptical, but I was so enchanted at the prospect of having a modern mother—already envisioning
us stopping at Planned Parenthood together on the way to the mall—that
with breathtaking stupidity I told her the truth. Immediately red splotches
appeared all over her face, and she began crying, in huge, gulping sobs,
emitting a string of incoherent denials and interrogations: *"Khak bar saram*
[may dirt fall on my head!]. . . . *Vay, vay* . . . You're too young, why did we
ever come to this *mamlekat-e-kharabshodeh* [ruined country]. . . . When??
. . . For how long?" I had been duped, and would pay for it dearly. "What
is wrong with you?" I yelled. "You tricked me! How can you do this, after
asking yourself? You promised to *help.*" The sun sank, and we were still walking. The tears came fast and furious as we did lap after lap around streets
that looked the same. That week, Maman re-enrolled in therapy, banned my
boyfriend from the house, and vilified him with a propaganda campaign
worthy of the darkest dictatorship. The episode cemented a conclusion I
had long been approaching: Being Iranian amounted to psychological torture. It meant bringing a friend home from school, to find an old woman
(there was perpetually a great-aunt or third cousin in town) with a flowered
bonnet on her head kneeling in prayer, or sifting through a vast pile of dried
herbs like a prehistoric gatherer. It demanded a rejection of the only

lifestyle I knew and wanted and offered only vague promises of community inclusion in exchange. And so I decided then and there that Iranianness and I must part.

This break came at a convenient time, just as I was old enough to realize with the sensibility of a young adult, rather than the fuzzy intuition of a child, what a burden it was to be Iranian in America. The hostage crisis had forever stained our image in the American psyche, and slowly I saw how this shaped so much of what we did and strove for as immigrants. We could never take for granted that ordinary Americans—people Maman would encounter at PTA meetings, or at work—would know that the very fact of our living in the U.S. differentiated us from the type of Iranians who held U.S. diplomats at gunpoint for 444 days. Each time I told someone I was Iranian, I would search their face for a sign that they understood this.

Iranians coped with this oppressive legacy in various ways. Some, like parts of my family, willed it away by losing any trace of a Persian accent, and becoming so professionally successful that they entered a stratum of American society sophisticated enough to understand and appreciate their presence and contribution. Some, nearly a million in fact, sought strength in numbers and founded a colony in Los Angeles. They seemed unfazed by their growing reputation for vulgarity and obsession with image; better to be associated with a penchant for BMWs than revolutionary Islam, they figured.

The Iranians who fled the revolution, and those who were already in the United States when it happened, included the country's best and brightest. That they succeeded in their adopted home is not such a surprise. But the image of that Islam-intoxicated, wild-eyed hostage taker was still a shadow that dogged all of us. Whether we were monarchists or not, whether we took some responsibility for what happened in Iran or blamed others, the shame of the revolution placed enormous pressure to be successful, but discreet about being Iranian. As though to make up for this image's awfulness we had to be ever more exceptional, achieve more, acquire more degrees, more wealth, make more discoveries—to become indispensable. All this effort was needed to clear up our nationality's good name; being average, obviously, would not cut it. Redemption became our burden.

These were the preoccupations of my parents' generation of exiles, and it left little energy for ministering to the second generation's delicate cultural transition. We were on our own, as our parents struggled with their nostalgia and political anger. As a teenager I felt there was nowhere to turn, and I often felt invisible, alone with my two irreconcilable halves. Sometimes it felt like we didn't even exist, even though I had proof we did (there were Iranian grocery stores, after all, with too much feta cheese and baklava for our own little circle). We weren't reflected anywhere—not on television, not on radio; we didn't even have our own ethnic slur (the ones for Arabs didn't count), let alone a spoof on *The Simpsons*. It was too overwhelming to dwell in a home wracked with inter-cultural turmoil, within a larger community wrapped up in the awkwardness of arrival, to attempt to bridge my two identities.

At the University of California, Santa Cruz, indeed in probably most universities in California in 1998, there was nothing more pressing to do than amplify your ethnic identity. I groaned under the weight of this discovery; how absurd, that all these silly liberal instructors wanted to take me by the hand and lead me back to the world I had turned my back on. All this heightening of consciousness was fascinating to me, but in a detached, impersonal way. To start with, there was no space for Iranians within the multicultural dialogue everyone seemed so bent on having. We were too new, and didn't have a place yet. And then there was the question of race, in the American sense. Was I brown? All the Iranians I knew seemed to consider themselves Europeans with a tan. Was I an immigrant? My family had always insisted we weren't really immigrants as such, but rather a special tribe who had been temporarily displaced. Iranian women like Khaleh Farzi lived in daily fear of being mistaken for a Mexican—a pedestrian immigrant rather than a tragic émigré. All my life I had wanted to grow my hair long, but Khaleh Farzi always protested and bullied me into cutting it short, a bob just above my chin. "Swingy and chic, not straggly and long, like a Mexican," she would say.

Despite California's demographics, my high school was mostly white and Asian—the children of Silicon Valley yuppies—and it wasn't until college that I encountered a broader canvas of peers. I was a writing tutor for affirmative action students, back when affirmative action still existed in California, and spent most of my afternoons on a sunny, wooden deck overlooking the Pacific, teaching Mexican kids from Los Angeles how to write a five-paragraph essay. My most faithful student was named Andy Ramirez, who had called himself Mexican all his life, and couldn't understand why everyone now insisted on calling him Chicano. He was sweet, cynical, and hard-working, and after two years we got him to the point where a ten-page paper no longer gave him panic attacks. Andy passed through my life only briefly, but he helped change its course. I taught him grammar, and he taught me how to put my life into perspective. As out of place as I'd always felt growing up, I had no appreciation for the degree of inclusion I had taken for granted. Eating organic vegetables, going to the opera, socializing with my mother's academic friends, all the aspects of my life that had become second nature, I now realized, were what made this environment familiar. Andy and I would walk through campus, and I could see how the vast majority of social encounters—with other students, with professors, with the hippies who ran the coffeehouse—made him cringe. There was hardly any social situation that could make me uncomfortable—there was hardly any social situation that could *not* make Andy uncomfortable. For the first time ever it occurred to me I'd actually been buffered against the degree of alienation it was possible to feel as a newcomer in America.

As I watched Andy grow into himself, and develop the intellectual confidence to raise his hand in class, I also began to envy him. He was surrounded by brilliant Chicano professors who encouraged and understood him; who plied him with illuminating books that spoke directly to his experience. He saw his anger and confusion mirrored in poetry, and spent hours unraveling it with thoughtful graduate students who had traveled the same path. In time, awareness and pride replaced ambivalence and shame; in the academic lingo of the place, he had unlocked his internalized resentment of his identity. I saw this evolution not only in Andy but in many of the other students of color who educated themselves about their communities and their past, and found strength and support in the process. The notion of finding power in your otherness, once I got over the pretentiousness of using those sorts of terms, was incredibly compelling. So was the explosive possibility that I could be confident about who I was, the idea that being Iranian didn't have to be about silly emotional culture clashes with my mother, but a sense of self anchored in history.

Andy's academic route to self-discovery offered a fruitful example. Maybe there was something to be gained by studying history dispassionately, without the flushed distortions of family memory and cultural tropes. Within two years I was totally immersed in the Middle East, thrilled to find writers who wrote eloquently about the relationship between East and West, fascinated to discover that the Iranian Revolution had historical roots and wasn't a conflagration designed primarily to upset my family's social caste. In the process of all this academic probing, Iran was demystified—it became a subject I could learn about on my own, a civilization that I could approach from whatever direction I chose. It stopped being only the emotional place and set of rigid norms Maman could use to pull at my heartstrings and play on my guilt. As I discovered contemporary Iranian poetry, some of which I could read on my own, I began to feel, for the first time in my life, that Iranianness was not an obstacle to my independence. For the first time I stopped resisting it. It scared Maman a little, I think . . . that her hold over me was no longer exclusively in her hands. That my loyalty and attachment to things Iranian could exist outside the sphere of our house and our conflicted mother-daughter relationship.

Once I discovered the joys of my own private Iranianness, I was reluctant to dilute it with anything reminiscent of the years of adolescent conflict. Growing up Iranian in America had been arduous and awkward. We had little consciousness of assimilation, because we were in denial of our permanence in America. My mother always made this perfectly clear. We are *not* immigrants. Immigrants come on boats. We came on planes. We were émigrés, exiles, mentally still in between. In such an atmosphere, I had never felt American at all, and so I dispensed altogether with the idea of being a hyphenated American. When people asked me where I was from, I smiled tightly and said, "Iran." Full stop. Shoulders pulled back. Defensive. Knowing perfectly well that the answer was misleading, but too exhilarated by the fresh feelings of pride and coherence to care. In my own mind, I was just plain Iranian; even though the second I opened my mouth, my sentences bubbled with those unconscious "likes," and anyone could tell that California figured in the story. An unintended consequence of this was that I actually began believing it. Soon I came to assume, with reckless confidence, that since I was Iranian, I would feel at home in the one place I was meant to belong—Iran.

CHAPTER TWO

Homecoming

He said I want that which cannot be found.

—Rumi

Arabs dance with their hips, Iranians with their arms and shoulders, concluded Huda, sweeping her waterfall of dark hair out of the way as she adjusted the volume on the stereo. For all the sinewy, seductive motions of an Iranian dance—the hooded, luring gaze, the twitching, butterfly-sweep of the hands—there is no overt sensuality in the movement of the hips. We were fascinated by this, and spent our afternoons in her dorm room before the mirror, executing these various styles to Huda's library of Persian pop music.

Do Afghans dance Baba Karam? I asked her, referring to the most seductive and intricate of all Iranian dances. Huda was from Afghanistan; her grandfather had been president before the turmoil of the Taliban years. While the other second-generation girls of the Islamic diaspora—Egyptians and Pakistanis and Somalis, raised in places like London and New York—bonded by praying together and dancing hip-hop in Cairene clubs, Huda and I fused Persian-Afghan cuisine on her flame-stove, traded stories in Farsi, and shared our longing for Kabul and Tehran. Of these two cities, of course, neither of us had much memory, but they were the poles around which our respective universes centered.

It was exactly one month into my year in Egypt—far too early to conclude I wanted to be elsewhere. It was perplexing to realize that I wanted to go to Iran—a physical journey, not some abstract spiritual one, and *now*, not at some indefinite point in the future. But the slow awareness was also a relief, as though I had finally found out where the honing device planted deep inside me was directed. The path to Iran led through Egypt, spiraling through the region with confusing twists and detours. It wasn't until I was nearly right up against Iran that I realized it had been my destination all along.

The knowledge revealed itself to me one night in Cairo, during the spring of 1999. It was a summery spring, hot enough that by nine in the evening the air hung heavy. Cairo displays its charms at night, so we slipped out from the air-conditioned apartment into the heat, and arranged our chairs in a semi-circle overlooking the lights of the suburban district. It was me, and the only two other Iranian women I knew in this city of millions, where I had come to study Arabic. Somewhere in the city, filed away in the gleaming offices of the Fulbright Commission, was a grant application that claimed I wanted to study this language to prepare myself for researching women's rights in the region. I had suspected for a while that this was only partially true, and tonight I knew for certain.

The balcony belonged to an older Iranian woman who had lived in Cairo for decades. In the intervening years, she had located the Iranians who float through the city, and plucked them into the circle of her company. She had also invited Scheherezade—whom I came to call by her nickname, Shazi—an Iranian correspondent for AP, because she knew that I aspired to journalism. We scarcely knew one another but were brought close by our shared need for the familiar, the company of other Iranian women, adrift in a place where there were few of us.

As we chatted quietly, and sipped our tea—perfumed as Persian tea should be—my own questions bewildered me. They were about the wrong place. Does Cairo smell different than Tehran? I asked. Does the street peddler clanking his way down the alleys yell "rubabekiya" as in Cairo, or something else? The baklava in Tehran is more dense with almonds, isn't it, not too syrupy sweet, like the Egyptian variety? My mind could not focus on Cairo, preoccupied instead with its difference from the Iran of my imagination.

What I wanted, though I chose not to admit it to myself, was to figure out my relationship to this other country, to Iran. Originating from a troubled country, but growing up outside it, came with many complications. Worst of all, at least on a personal level, was that you grew up assuming everything about you was related to that place, but you never got to test that out, since the place was unstable and sort of dangerous, and you never actually went there. You spent a lot of time watching movies about the place, crying in dark theaters, and feeling sad for your poor country. Most of that time, you were actually feeling sorry for yourself, but since your country was legitimately in serious trouble, you didn't realize it. And since it was so much easier and romantic to lament a distant place than the day-to-day crappy messes of your own life, it could take a very long time to figure it all out.

That, really, was why I wanted to go to Iran. To see whether the ties that bound me were real, or flimsy threads of inherited nostalgia. The momentum grew inside me, tentative and slow, but I called it by other names, unprepared to begin fiddling with the rubik's cube of my identity. Going to Cairo bought me time. I was in the same region, short hours away by plane, in nearly the same time zone; closer than I would be in London or New York, separated by a cultural hemisphere, a long journey across time and space of all kinds. A rest house along the way, a caravanserai, Cairo allowed me to dither, to work up my courage. The proximity was comforting; the leap appeared less intimidating.

As we chatted quietly in Farsi, I felt my skin tingling with the possibility of getting on a plane, holding a boarding pass that read Tehran. I tuned back in for Shazi's summation of her recent trip there: "It was unbearable," she was saying, jabbing a spoon into the frosty glass of grated cantaloupe, soaked in rosewater. "I've never seen so much ill in people as I did there." Her shoulders sagged, her eyes, her entire posture recoiling at the thought of Iran.

Eventually, the conversation turned to how long it had been since I visited—don't you want to go, they asked—and I slowly pronounced the words, just to feel them on my tongue.

"I'm aching to go back to Iran. I want to live and work there."

"So go," said Shazi, in that tone of hers I would grow to know so well, flip but deadly serious. Just like that, as though she was suggesting we order pizza.

No one had ever said this to me before. For my tribe of Iranians, the Iranian-American diaspora, Iran was a place you wept and argued over, sang about and professed to pine for, but physically avoided.

But Shazi was different. She still lived in the region, and included Iran in the physical constellation of her life. When Shazi spoke of Iran, her voice changed. She lapsed into this intimate, weary tone that seemed to come from the deepest place within her. It seduced me, this tone, with its echoes of the unspeakable. I wanted to experience what she had, to see what it was that required its own timbre.

We shared a taxi home that night, and as we skittishly tried to cross the yawning wide street—still full of traffic at that late hour—she grabbed my hand nervously. We hovered near the curb for a full five minutes, taking tentative steps forward until a black-and-white taxi hurtled too quickly toward us and we jumped back. "They won't stop, you know," she warned.

A couple of months after that evening, I was still treading water in Cairo, spending a sweaty summer reporting mind-numbing business stories about privatization for a local Cairo weekly, and sucking vast amounts of chunky, fresh mango juice through a straw. Iran still dominated my thoughts. Twice a week, I stopped by the *fakahani,* the fruit vendor, who set up his brimming crates on my corner when the sun set. He promised his perfect, crunchy white apples were exported from Iran, and I bought bagfuls—for my roommate, for my landlady, for Huda. Are you *certain* they're Iranian? I asked him one night, after watching him sell a Russian prostitute a single mango for $10. Yes, I swear to God they are, he said, feigning a look of deep hurt. And so the days went by, and I aired my longing for Iran in the evening fruit bazaar of a distant capital, awaiting a cue that would direct my return.

One slow afternoon, as I read the wires in the elegant, decaying villa in Garden City that housed the weekly where I worked, a breaking news headline immediately caught my eye: "Student Demonstrations in Tehran Descend into Mass Riots." The hard-line judiciary had sparked the riots by shutting down an important independent newspaper, the first publication to criticize the Islamic establishment in years. The newspaper was the banner of an emerging, loose movement of intellectuals and student activists trying to nudge the autocratic regime into recognizing some basic political and civil rights. The students had been demonstrating in Tehran against the newspaper's closure.

The night of their protest, security forces raided a dormitory where many of the demonstrators stayed, breaking down locked doors, attacking students asleep in their beds with clubs and batons. Some students jumped in terror from the balconies of their dorm rooms.

In 1999, the Islamic regime tolerated little dissent, and conducted itself with unchecked brutality. Some of the ruling clerics were checked out, out of touch with the frustration of ordinary people; others were aware, but were warped and fundamentalist enough not to care. The dormitory attack outraged students and everyday Iranians alike, and they poured into the streets by the tens of thousands, chanting death to the regime's leaders, looting buildings. It had all come without warning. Frustration with the country's lawlessness, the poor economy, and severe social restrictions dominated Iranian life. But never since the revolution had grievances exploded into such public turmoil.

Sitting in Cairo, watching this unfold through lines of text on a dusty computer screen, I was stricken. The last time mass riots overran Tehran, a revolution followed. Could it be happening all over again? Without *me?* How could there be another revolution when I still hadn't understood the first one? The thought that Iran might change overnight, undergo another defining upheaval that I would miss, was unbearable. I was naive enough to believe I had a duty to witness history, if only as a tourist-spectator.

I ran home, packed a bag, phoned the travel agent, and rushed to see Shazi at work on the way to the airport. Can you give me phone numbers for sources, I asked urgently, pacing back and forth along the terrace overlooking the Nile. She gave me a strange look. Khanoum, what do you mean sources? These are protests. Your sources are people on the street. I was afraid she would say that. I didn't know the streets of Tehran, and my Farsi didn't include the vocabulary of political rage. I was petrified. I didn't understand how foreign correspondents worked, didn't know it was possible to hire fixers and drivers who could pick you up at the airport and drive you straight to your story. I thought I had to do it all myself. Shazi, please. Just give me some numbers.

Arriving at Mehrabad Airport was ominous, but mostly I was impressed that my Iranian passport, which had acquired dust for years, actually had a function. The long wait for customs check seemed endless, not because of any official, repressive policy, but due to the thick issue of *Vogue* stuffed down my pants. Images of unveiled women were banned in Iran, and I knew the fall fashion issue would never make it past the censor. The customs agent rifled through layers of papers and sweaters, and produced a Botticelli mousepad. He studied the painting on the plastic foam with narrowed eyes, and deemed Venus on the half shell pornographic, tossing her into a cardboard box underneath the examination table filled with other confiscated obscenities.

I arrived, and my aunt and uncle swiftly barred me from leaving the house. *If anything happens to you, your mother will kill us. Have you gone mad, coming here for a reason like this?* I paced around the apartment on Shariati Street, ready to climb the walls; I knew they were right, that it would be stupid to go outside at a time like this, when I didn't even know how to count toman, Iranian currency. Once they realized I was on the verge of doing it anyway, they appointed a committee to help me deal with the riots. A family friend chaperoned me down to the university; another, a journalist, briefed me on everything he knew. We drove to Evin, Tehran's notorious prison, where hundreds of mothers held vigil outside, wailing and demanding to know what had become of their children. Scores of students had been arrested, but no one knew exactly how many. Everyone I spoke to crackled with emotion—fear, adrenaline, fury. Police patrolled the streets around the university, keeping an eerie, post-riot calm.

To absorb and make sense of it all was impossible, but the challenge thrilled me—going home, reporting a cataclysmic news story, rediscovering old relatives. At night I couldn't sleep, as though an electric cloud hovered over me, disrupting my thoughts, tweaking my balance. Overwhelmed, I busied myself with the task of counting the number of students who had been injured, arrested, imprisoned, and killed, respectively. The summer before moving to Cairo, I had interned at Human Rights Watch, and my old boss Elahé was flying in from New York. She had called ahead and asked me to begin reporting a tally. We met at her room in the Homa Hotel. Certain the room was bugged, we communicated by scribbling notes back and forth on post-its, our hands shaking.

Over the next few days, as students flooded in to see Elahé with fresh stories of kidnapped organizers and updates on the injured, I sat and listened. Being a politically active student in Iran, I found out, meant compromising your studies, your safety, your family's safety, and your future. They came alone, and in huddled groups, whispering urgently and eyeing the undercover intelligence agents—unmistakable with their two-day growth of beard and aimless gait—who crawled throughout the hotel lobby. I pushed little tea cakes around, and sat mute in fascination. Everything about them shocked me. First, their belief that the regime could be fixed.

They said the reform movement had bold schemes for challenging the entrenched clergy. Over time, it would revive the Revolution's original ideals, and re-chart the system toward Islamic democracy, setting a defining example for the Muslim world. Clenched between their fists, tucked under their arms and in their backpacks, were the independent newspapers of the day, filled with strident critiques of the ruling clergy. They insisted that there would not be, in fact *should* not be, another revolution.

The revolution of 1979 had already frozen the country's development for two decades; another violent upheaval would only devastate yet another generation, they argued. I listened carefully, fiddling with my pen, realizing with deep disappointment that if these students' views were at all representative (they were middle class, from all around the country) the Islamic regime was here to stay.

Deep in the heart of every Iranian expatriate lurks a hope for another revolution, one that would reverse the catastrophe of 1979 overnight, swiftly and bloodlessly topple the mullahs, and return our country to us. There is a consensus—among Iranian television networks in Los Angeles, exiles who host dinners for congressmen in Beverly Hills and Bethesda— that Iranians will eventually overthrow this regime, and that it is simply a matter of time. That conviction underpinned our lives in the diaspora, and in its defense we saw revenge and redemption for everything we had lost.

I had always thought that way myself, in part because I knew very little about post-revolutionary Iran, but more importantly, because I *wanted* it to be true. As the demonstrations breathed life into my conception of Iran, I saw that the expatriate view—Iran as a static, failed state in unchanging decline—had little to do with the country itself, and everything to do with the psychology of exile. It was an emotional trick to ease the pain of absence, the guilt of being the ones who left, or chose to stay outside. It was a delusion that deferred a mournful truth: that we would never regain the Iran of before 1979, that we would never go back. That if we wanted to deal with Iran as patriots, it would have to be the Iran that existed now, wounded and ugly with its pimples and scars.

I lay awake at night, my old ideas about Iran shattered, with no new framework to understand any better what might happen. The society I had stepped into was precarious, that much was clear. One day, perhaps very near or very far, its current reality would collapse. But how would this happen, barring the bang of revolution? The uncertainty was transfixing, and I spent hours talking until I was hoarse, filling pages with notes, trying to understand.

The slogans the students chanted that summer of 1999, together with the gigantic outpouring of public discontent, fell two decades after the Islamic Revolution and marked an important turning point in its history. Two years prior—in 1997—a moderate cleric named Mohammed Khatami was elected president and promised to transform the Islamic regime into a more gentle, democratic system governed by the rule of law. I remember standing at the magazine stand of a chain bookstore in California, watching other Iranian-Americans cast curious, hopeful glances at the covers that screamed things like "The Beginning of the End" and "Iran's Second Revolution?"

An array of progressive intellectuals and activists of varying backgrounds, ranging from the ardently secular to the liberally Islamist, backed Khatami's efforts. The whole process, from the president's reforms to the grassroots activism, came to be known as the reform movement. The premise that held these disparate forces—socialists, secular intellectuals, both liberal and militant Islamists—together was that Iran could be, indeed must be, transformed from within, without another revolution. This absolutely everyone I talked to agreed with—from my elderly great-aunt who kept a photo of the Shah on her nightstand, to teenage punks who listened to rap and raced motorbikes.

Some of the reformers were concerned with internal political and civil rights, and sought to nudge Iran from autocratic theocracy toward tolerant democracy. If they managed to amend the Constitution, their thinking went, they could abolish or dramatically curtail the power of unelected clerical bodies that ran the country and controlled its economy. Many from this reformist camp, however, wanted to retain the revolution's anti-Western ethos and its commitment to religio-political causes such as the liberation of Palestine. It was a don of the reformist camp, for example, who organized the Palestinian Intifadeh conferences that would be held in Tehran, gathering young and old militants, among them notorious most-wanted-types, to munch on pastry and poke a collective finger in the eye of the West.

Another strand in the reform movement held a pragmatic vision for Iran's future. Their main objective was to redefine the system's mandate along conventional lines—economic growth and the welfare of Iranians. Promoting ideological causes, they felt, kept Iran in a state of fixed tension with the West, and retarded the country's potential as a great power in the region.

Had the reformists been able to agree on priority and strategy, their diversity could have been a source of strength rather than weakness. But they were unable to create a real coalition, and instead bickered among themselves over whether or not to engage with America, over the priority of domestic freedoms, over strategy in dealing with their conservative opponents.

Aligned against these forces stood the old-guard clerical establishment, known as the hard-liners. Just as "reformers" was an umbrella term for diverse political groups seeking change, the "hard-liners" were an equally diverse group, brought together by their allegiance to the status quo. Many were simply outright fundamentalists, Taliban-like in their rigid, backward attitudes toward women, society, and the world outside. Their commitment to exporting Khomeini's Islamic Revolution had not wavered, and they sought to extend Iran's regional influence through support for militant causes. Just as many, if not more, were motivated by money and greed, keen to preserve the rich patronage networks, privileges, and unbridled power the system in its current form allotted them.

The hard-liners, for all intents and purposes, controlled the country. They ran the army and the Revolutionary Guard, had foot militias at their service, held monopoly over state media, and supervised the economy through the *bonyads,* massive funds for the oppressed created after the Revolution. They were custodians of government and law as well, because the elected branches of government—the executive and parliament—were legally vulnerable to the decrees and vetting procedures of the clerical bodies, accountable to the country's supreme religious leader. This position, more powerful than president, was the brainchild of Ayatollah Khomeini, who passed it down to his successor, Ayatollah Khamenei. The photos of both men, with their twin black turbans and dour glares, wallpapered the country.

The history lessons I absorbed during this first visit back helped me understand the struggles revolutionary Iran was facing. But understanding the full splay of the history also complicated my work as a journalist, to document these events for the American media. In my files, generalizations like "reformist, liberal, progressive, moderate" appeared over and over again. My conscience bristled at this language, especially since news stories rarely had room for the historical context required to explain the nuances of these misleading labels.

Writing about Iran as an American journalist, in language that did not get one banned from the country, meant effacing history from the story. It was, to read most written accounts of the political schism, as though real liberals—secular intellectuals, technocrats, and activists with no ties to the clergy—either did not exist or were too irrelevant to be counted as political realities. A conservative politician whom I frequently visited in Tehran had the same complaint, though from a slightly different standpoint. "You journalists, you're painting this story as a fight between good and evil," he said. "You're absolutely right," I told him, though I finished the sentence silently this way: "It's actually a fight between evil and slightly less evil."

President Khatami, perhaps aware that recasting the state's foreign policy would be a task for Sisphyus, set about transforming the style and culture of daily life. By restructuring the upper management of key ministries, he discreetly engineered a more relaxed official approach to Iranians' private lives. The morality police, charged with enforcing the strict social code, began to behave with less regular brutality, and the Culture Ministry issued permits for independent newspapers. In his speeches, he retired the inherited rhetoric of the revolution—martyrdom and death, struggle and enemies—and spoke instead of civil society, dialogue, and openness.

In the early years of Khatami's first term, from 1997 to 1999, Iranians experienced only modest change. I stayed on for a few weeks, during that chaotic, life-transforming first visit, and found the atmosphere decidedly Soviet. My female relatives and I wore dark veils and sandals with socks, wiped off our lipstick when we saw policemen in the distance. My aunt still came along for the ride, if a male cousin was dropping me off late at night, in case we were stopped at a checkpoint. In taxis, my relatives hissed me silent, when I jabbered away critically, suggesting Tehran seemed like a giant cemetery, with nearly every street and tiny alley named for a martyr.

From a purely moral and political vantage point, not to mention an emotional one (what Iranian didn't despise the revolutionary clerics, really, for all they had done?), we considered the reformists suspect, a choice of the less bad among the awful. But did they help transform the way we lived, our habits and sensibilities? They did.

By the end of 1999 and into 2000, the pressures lightened noticeably, and people felt more comfortable behaving in ways that had before seemed reckless. While the legal basis for the regime's oppressive ways stayed intact, the open spirit of Khatami's presidency, and his relentless rhetoric about the rule of law, changed the culture of Iran. For years, public space had been the domain of Islamic vigilantes and the morality police, who arbitrarily terrorized people. Khatami reined them in, and under him Tehran became almost a normal city, with young couples strolling in the park arm in arm, licking ice cream cones.

The demonstrations both fed off and propelled this energy. The hundreds of thousands of people who poured into the streets of Tehran and shouted "Death to the Supreme Leader!" collapsed the regime's façade of invulnerability. More powerful than a mass referendum, as loud as the opening cries for change in 1979, the protests signaled that Iran's nearly 70 million people wanted a different set of rules, a different kind of country. How the clerics in charge would respond, whether they were prepared to change, hung in the balance.

The demonstrations of 1999 also played a central role in my own life. Captivated by the political drama, I knew I had to return and watch the rest unfold. Compared to the stagnant politics of Egypt, the electric, bold debates in Iran, and the open battle for the country's future, were dream stories for a young journalist. A few months later, the regional bureau chief of *Time* suggested I go work in Tehran as the magazine's stringer.

At that time—before the second Palestinian Intifadeh, and well before September 11—Iran was the hottest news story in the region, and the regime didn't allow U.S. publications to base American journalists in Iran. Because I was also Iranian, the regime politely ignored my American birth and passport, and allowed me to come and work. I would be the only American journalist permitted to base myself in Tehran, during what seemed at the time one of the most significant political transformations in the modern history of the region. I packed my bags, and prepared to leave Cairo behind.

My preparations proceeded smoothly, until I announced the decision to my family in California, who were immediately horrified, convinced that torture and certain death awaited me. Relatives from all over the world, of all ages, were recruited to aid the effort of dissuading me. Scandalized Maman, with twenty-year-old visions of political repression of journalists, tried to prevent my going with alternating tactics of fiscal blackmail, admonition, and horror. ("You realize that the physical scars of the torture will

heal, but the nightmares of prison rape will haunt you forever. Your personality will never be the same. Be advised your father will cut you off entirely.
No more ski vacations, nothing. You can fund your own foolishness.")

I tried to avoid the hysteria building around me, though at times I rem-
inisced over the grimmer moments in our family lore—the uncle imprisoned by the revolutionary regime; the great-uncle who hurled himself from
a third-story window to evade the Shah's secret police—and wondered
whether my identity could not be explored in, say, the Iran archives of a really good university library. During these moments of doubt I would leaf
through Goldman Sachs recruitment literature, and contemplate whether
I could endure life with, for example, a giant scar on my cheek slashed by
a vindictive Islamic thug. The terror campaign shook me a little, because
ultimately I didn't really want to die in the course of covering a story, and
didn't know Iran well enough to know this was unlikely. But I reminded
myself these were the same relatives who thought they would be murdered
riding the subway through Manhattan, and went ahead and bought my
ticket.

᛭

During my first weeks back in Iran, in the spring of 2000, the family devoted much time and energy to ensuring I dressed properly. Among the
most concerned was my Khaleh Farzi, who was in her mid-forties, petite,
and marooned in Iran from her two favorite pastimes, jogging and drinking coffee at Starbucks. She and her husband had moved back to Iran in
1998, after long years in New Jersey. During the first year that my uncle
had floated the idea of relocating, she would only say—in a nod to my
grandfather's refuge in poetry—"I will only move to places that rhyme with
Tehran, such as Milan." This awkward relationship with reality also characterized her life in Iran, where she spent most of her time reminding us all
that "this is not a country, it is hell."

She thought if left to my own devices, I might forget we lived under an
Islamic regime and stride outside in a tube top. *Are your ankles covered? Elbows?* Khaleh Farzi would call out a checklist of body parts from wherever
she was in the house, as I headed for the door.

Mercifully, by the time I began living in Iran, the Khatami spring had made it possible to wear *roopoosh* (a long, loose coat also called by the French term *manteau*) that did not make one look like a great-aunt. Just one year before, going outside had meant draping oneself in banal and anonymous folds of cloth. Every morning, getting dressed had involved a *me* vs. *the regime* calculus. Shall I look remotely like myself, or shall I pass through all this unpleasantness as a ghost, invisible in a wash of grey or black? One's relationship to the veil had been a truly existential question: How important is it to be myself, to have my outside reflect my identity? When faced with this choice, only the true radicals and street warriors chose to flout the dress code. Because it was a fight, they applied war-paint— coats and coats of makeup—and aggressively risqué clothes. But ordinary women who just wanted to go to work, rather than be Rosa Parks through their choice of dress, simply accepted the erasure of their personality through the *roopoosh* uniform.

But by 2000, a *roopoosh* as concealing as the *chador,* the billowing, all-encompassing black tent that only very traditional women and government employees wore, was no longer required apparel. The middle part of the spectrum—between washed-out ghosts and angrily painted peacocks—had grown. The stark contrast between how one looked in public and private faded. Isn't it lovely, I said to Khaleh Farzi happily, we don't look like crows anymore. Come on, she replied, running her fingers over the rainbow of colors in her drawer, it's just a prettier cage. Like so many small freedoms that Iranians began experiencing that year, it registered as miraculous progress for about ten minutes, and then was deemed no progress at all.

Still, once the costs of disobeying the regime were reduced, people began steadily pushing the limits. My great-aunt, who had no patience in her dotage for purchasing something that would be confiscated the next day, went out and bought a banned satellite dish. We stopped carrying socks in our purse, reasonably sure we could bare our toes in sandals without hassle. My uncle stopped watching basketball on satellite television each and every night, and began reading the newspapers instead, stopping every ten minutes to read aloud a particularly amusing criticism of the ruling clergy. The changes were modest, and no one pretended they were nearly enough or nearly secure; but they made life, compared to the gloomy years of pre-Khatami privation, infinitely more livable.

My family in Iran still amuse themselves telling stories about the first weeks I moved to Tehran, in the early months of 2000. My patience for this humor is limited, because in the end, no one who feels imbued with serious purpose enjoys being mocked for verbal slips, such as confusing the Farsi words for "speech" and "cabbage," which were unhelpfully distinguished only by a twist of a vowel. But there was such an entertainment deficit in Iran that the bumbling first steps of a newly returned relative offered a welcome distraction from the dulling routine of daily life. I was like a running sitcom played for their amusement, *Azadeh in Ayatollahland:* Watch her accidentally insult powerful clerics! See her try to wear a beret instead of a veil!

My Iranian version of the exotic ethnic novels I read in college—my Persian *Like Water for Chocolate,* where I was supposed to discover the ancient myths of human civilization in a kitchen, in the ancient ritual of sauces or puddings three days in the making—was nowhere to be found. Where were the orchards, the old houses filled with evocative scents and closely knit clans who spent their days cooking together and puzzling the meaning of life over tea? Not only did this world not exist anymore, it had been replaced by something cynical and alien, familiar only through course of habit to those who had known nothing else. Iran, fountain of my memories, the leisurely black and white world of old films like *My Uncle Napoleon,* had been wiped away, replaced by the Islamic Republic.

Of course until that moment, had someone asked me, I would not have admitted to living most of my life under the spell of nostalgia, an emotion that disguises itself as healthy patriotism or a fondness for Iranian classical music or a hundred other feelings that are sincerely experienced as something else. The first, jarring chip at my romanticized view of Iran was inflicted by Siamak Namazi, a cocktail party acquaintance who quickly became one of my closest friends. Many of the U.S.-educated Iranians who had returned to Tehran were there because they had been mediocre in the West, and preferred to be big fish in a small swamp. "All the exceptional people have left," said a young Tehrani to me one night at a party. "They're the ones who'll never come back."

Siamak was one of the few exceptions. He helped start a business consulting firm in Tehran because he actually wanted to be there and build something that could make a lasting contribution. He was twenty-eight, a Tufts graduate, and the son of a U.N. diplomat, with wide brown eyes and the sort of endearing, chauvinist-tinged gallantry common to frat boys from the American South. Socially, he affected an image of rebel playboy, but he could strategize better than most Iranian ministers and was vulnerable to his mother's dictums.

He warned me, in the early weeks of our acquaintance, of the difference between nostalgic and realistic love. If you are a nostalgic lover of Iran, he said, you love your own remembrance of the past, the passions in your own life that are intertwined with Iran. If you love Iran realistically, you do so *despite* its flaws, because an affection that can't look its object in the face is a selfish one. I observed Siamak's life, its constant negotiations and self-interrogations, and took note, tried to set things in perspective. I had to reconcile with *actually existing* Iran; fate had determined that in the course of 2,500 years of Iranian history, I would live during this blip, this post-revolutionary second.

Most of my relatives lived uptown, in northern Tehran, in quiet back streets of leafy suburbs, behind tall gates that separated them from the loud, polluted, congested downtown that was home to the rest of the city's inhabitants. As a rule, I am not the sort of person who sees valor in discomfort. The *Vogue* down the pants was pretty much my threshold. But from the moment I arrived, I saw very clearly that I would not see much of Iran from my family's privileged perch.

Much of my extended family had left Iran on the eve of the revolution. One of my uncles, an industrialist with close business ties to many of the Shah's associates, saw his assets confiscated, while another uncle, who supported the revolution, saw his appropriated as well. The latter uncle was one of the few to stay in Iran and, with a great degree of effort and caution, managed to rebuild his petrochemical company in the course of the next two decades. I spent a great deal of time with him and his wife, but among all the relatives who had remained, including a few of my parents' cousins and the odd great-aunt, I was closest to Khaleh Farzi, my mother's sister who had returned a few years before me. This smattering of family lived in various corners of the city, and I shuttled between their houses for teas and lunches, but when it came to choosing a residence, I decided to move in with my grandfather.

My father's father, whom we called Pedar Joon, lived in central Tehran. Still the family patriarch in his nineties, his house sat off of Villa Street, in a middle-class neighborhood that forty years ago, when he moved there, had been a desirable location. It was near one of the few institutions the Islamic Republic did not rename after the revolution, the Danish Pastry Shop. Living downtown meant inhaling air thick with pollution, hotter during the summer than north Tehran and sludgy with dirty, melted snow in the winter, but it was worth it to be closer to the heart of the city, to Tehran University, to the cafés where Iranian intellectuals had sipped Turkish coffee and brewed politics over the years.

Though I hated parting with my long-cultivated fantasies, I began to accept that life in Iran was more a firsthand lesson in the evolution of a tyrannical regime than an ephemeral homecoming to a poetic world of nightingales. But there were enough moments of delicious poignancy that I could, for a time, postpone facing this reality. The first round of teas and lunches with relatives around the city were so atmospheric and idyllic, so overflowing was everyone's graciousness, that I felt like a character in a period drama.

An elderly relative cooked my favorite saffron rice pudding, *sholeh-zard,* and sent it over with my name written across the surface in cinnamon and slivered almonds. Another aunt mapped out the city for me, with the determination of Martha Stewart on a desert island, and introduced me to the family fruit vendor, tailor, candlestick maker. When I phoned up the fruit vendor for the first time, he greeted me like long-lost kin, trilling with courtly salutations for minutes. We're so *pleased* to hear you've come back. An hour later, the delivery arrived, and covered every surface of the kitchen with tiny mountains of my favorite fruits—bright green, sour plums; miniature, blush apples that taste like roses; fresh almonds in their furry green skins. The kitchen smelled like summer, and I sat on a barstool at the island in the center, enchanted with the abundance and the knowledge that generations of my ancestors had eaten this precise sort of apple, exactly these peaches.

My grandfather's house occupied the width of a short block, tucked inside high walls that separated it from the street. The airy rooms were a delicate, pale blue that softened the navy tones in the Persian rugs covering the floor, and were situated around a central dining room with a vaulted ceiling that reached the second story. A curved staircase, the sort designed for young boys to careen down, led to the upstairs bedrooms. Attached to the front house was a separate quarter, where the maid, Khadijeh Khanoum, lived with her husband and daughter.

Khaleh Zahra, my aunt, and her fifteen-year-old daughter Kimia (like me, born and raised in California) had moved back to Iran a year before me, and were also living with Pedar Joon. We formed a motley, impromptu family that became the nucleus of my first few months in Iran. We spent most of our time in the atrium that looked out onto the garden, and the small sitting room downstairs, because Pedar Joon, a widower in his nineties, did not interrupt his tight schedule of naps and herbal tonics to entertain.

Small elements in the house were familiar to me from my childhood summer. I remembered hiding shyly behind the dining room chairs, during the commotion of a family lunch, and perching on the cool stone steps leading to the garden outside. But beyond the walls of the house, lay miles of alien, traffic-clogged Tehran sprawl. I rose each day to a lingering fuzz of disorientation, and the unshakable sense that I was a stranger to my surroundings. Having no real desire to admit this to myself—the agonizing possibility that I would feel transplanted everywhere, just in varying degrees—I focused instead on the steady supply of comedy our household offered.

Of all my aunts, Khaleh Zahra was the most unlikely to have returned home. In her years abroad, from Swiss boarding school to Los Angeles, she had converted to Christianity, officially taken Clarissa as her middle name, and married more than one non-Iranian in poofy church weddings. My defining memories of her date to childhood visits to her house in Tiburon, where she would paint my nails crimson, and let me play in her fur closet with the lights turned off. She was fond of sensational effects, and had decorated the house in all-white, retired all the fur coats save the white ones (which she wore even during the summer), and acquired a mysterious Eastern European husband with a regal air and romantic accent.

Into this world, she brought a string of miniature Doberman pinschers named Badoum (almond), all destined to die when they raced into the blind curve behind the house. After each dog's death, she bought an identical one, and without bothering to dignify it with a new name, simply called the replacement Badoum II, Badoum III, etc. All these years later, she was still slinky slim, still leaned back with the same posture, legs crossed with a cigarette dangling languidly between her fingers.

When she moved to Tehran, Khaleh Zahra shipped the entire contents of her California house, bedroom furniture, washer and dryer, so convinced was she that she would love Iran, and that Iran would love her back. The move tore Kimia from all she knew and loved, namely the mall and Britney Spears, and she was wretched with homesickness, with a nervous, prancing Pinscher named PJ as her only consolation. They walked down Villa Street together each afternoon, she with a foot of light brown hair hanging out beneath her veil, he with his tiny legs working furiously to keep up, enhancing each other's oddity.

Pedar Joon was a devout secularist who mocked religion with an enthusiasm most old people reserved for complaining about arthritis. But dogs he considered filthy, in the ritual sense; a ghost of religious sensibility in an otherwise profane person and household. PJ disrupted his peace, trotting into his room at all hours, soiling the august atmosphere of herbal medicine and law books with paws still greasy from his meal of choice, French fries.

My arrival in Tehran had captivated the family's attention for weeks, until I was deposed in relevance by none other than PJ. One day, on a perfectly ordinary summer afternoon, catastrophe struck. PJ was dognapped. He was abducted while waiting in the car for my aunt, who was calling on her cousin in a neighborhood nearby. Probably he was sporting one of his dog accessories, which alerted the potential thief to his owner's excessive devotion. His disappearance both thrilled and devastated the household.

There's a *fatwa* out against poodles, I said the next day over lunch, which was served at precisely the same time each day, when the grandfather clock downstairs chimed noon. What's a *fatwa*, asked Kimia, poking a French fry into ketchup, and painting red circles around her plate. It's like a law, I said. PJ is un-Islamic. Maybe even counterrevolutionary. It was mean, but I couldn't help it. The clerics' hatred for miniature poodles, which they considered bourgeois lapdogs, was one of those ridiculous things about Iran. An aghast ayatollah in the provincial city of Orumieh had even devoted a portion of his Friday sermon to condemning canines. "Happy are those who became martyrs and did not witness the playing with dogs!" he had bellowed, referring to those killed in the war with Iraq, who had luckily been spared the lapdog trend.

Wobbly tears formed in Kimia's eyes, and she fled to her room. Khadijeh Khanoum, who had been instructed to wait on PJ as a "member of the family," hid a smile as she cleared the table. That afternoon, Khaleh Zahra, who had, by that time, mastered the skill of throwing money at problems, hired a pet detective to track PJ down. Dognapping, it emerged, was the hot new crime in Tehran. The thieves preyed on thoroughbreds and poodles—the kind of dogs that obviously belonged to women who could afford to indulge their whims—and subsequently held them for ransom, or sold them in the exotic pet bazaar on Molavi Street. To this smelly, loud alley, hopeful owners would come to root out stolen pets amidst monkeys and iguanas.

One lazy afternoon, in that hallowed space between lunch and tea when everyone is meant to be napping and it is exceptionally rude to call people's homes, the phone rang. "We've got the dog," said a deep male voice. "Oh, well I thank you very much for your help, but we don't want it anymore," said Pedar Joon. "Don't bother to call again; we won't be changing our minds." By that point, Kimia was high-strung enough about her nascent social life that she could hear the phone ring from several blocks away, and since it was common practice in our household to listen to each other's conversations, she intercepted Pedar Joon's attempt at exiling the recovered dog. After shadowy negotiations conducted by the pet detective, PJ was returned to our household, and for a few days ignored Kimia in a sullen, Patty Hearst–like manner, but then reverted quickly to his nervous, French-fry guzzling ways.

PJ's recovery, in all its glorious absurdity, revealed a great deal to me. I had suspected the regime's revolutionary Islamic ethos would be floundering. But I hadn't expected that mocking mullahs, long a cultural tradition, had become a national sport. Iranians felt a harsh contempt for the clerics, who had taken over an oil-rich country in the name of Islam, sunk its economy, and now spent their days railing against poodles. As Iranians saw it, the revolution had failed in most of its grand ideals—poverty persisted, the Zionist enemy thrived—and yet the clerics hung onto power, accountable only to God. In a hundred small ways, the bankruptcy of this extreme, Islamic ideology manifested itself in people's lives.

I reeled, not because the chaos of Iran was shocking, but because it was, of all things, terribly foreign. In the twilight hours of those early days, when we gathered in the atrium and played backgammon or cards till it grew dark, I made silent inventory of my conflicting reactions. In private places, inside homes, I felt perfectly at home as an Iranian. At dinners, I knew the ideal texture and color of *fesenjoon* sauce, a dish of walnut-pomegranate chicken; I could predict the tribal origin of a kilim; I could sing *tarof,* the flowery, elaborate expressions of courtesy native to Persian conversation. In California, these Persian sensibilities had distinguished me as Iranian. But in Iran, in the bosom of homeland, they were tangential, and reached not even a fraction of the savvy required to live in the Islamic Republic.

⭑

It was ten A.M. on a day like most, the hour I usually rolled into the BBC office, where I had a desk and often wrote my stories. I spread the newspapers out before me, traded story ideas with the other journalists in the office, and then started making phone calls. Between an analyst and a diplomat, I checked in with a student activist, and then hung up quickly in time for the official news bulletin. Throughout the morning, I tracked the news of Iran from the office, chatting with my sources and planning longer stories on the dissident clergy, the student movement, foreign policy, and social and cultural trends.

After lunch, a few of us piled into a car to drive to Tehran University, for a meeting of student organizers. Someone always stayed in the office, to alert us by mobile phone in case a newspaper was shut down or an intellectual was arrested in our absence. On the way there, I huddled in the passenger seat over my mobile phone, setting up interviews for the rest of the week. It was late afternoon by the time I got back, and editors in New York and Cairo would be at their desks, dispatching reporting assignments and considering story suggestions. The Cairo bureau chief and I conferred over when I should fly to Lebanon, because quickly my duties had expanded to include Iran's neighbors as well.

In all respects, it was a typical day, except for the phone call that came late in the afternoon. A mysterious voice instructed me to show up at a government office near the house the next afternoon. I left the office early that day, and arrived at the appointed time. For about fifteen minutes I waited in a stark office until two men entered and sat behind the metal desk. One of them promptly fell asleep, while the other leaned forward, and began dissecting my past with exquisite politeness. It was my security interview, required before the Ministry of Culture could officially grant me a press card authorizing me to work. I thought it was a one-time session, but it ended up being the first in a long series of meetings designed initially to ensure I was not a CIA agent, and later to control my reporting and torment me as a person.

Because I had no idea what to expect, and was covered in cold sweat, my rational brain abandoned me, leaving me prey to a scared and impish imagination. I wondered whether they had a folder of grainy black and white photos of me drinking cocktails and eating ham in New York. "Miss Moaveni, was this or was this not you, drinking a mimosa at an unknown location in lower Manhattan?" I imagined the awake one demanding, waving the evidence in the air. Silently I prepared my plea. "It was, Mr. X, a painful but ingenious strategy on my part, of promoting a tolerant image of Islam and Iran in America. I *pretended* to enjoy mimosas to gain the trust of influential Americans, to better enable me to defend Iran by stealth."

Lost in this imaginary defense, I didn't notice Mr. X had actually asked me a much more mundane question, like, What were you doing in Cairo? As I answered, I could see that he was disappointed in my Farsi, which was too basic for the sophisticated word play of his questions. Do you consider yourself Iranian? What would you do if you were asked to write a story that would damage Iran's reputation in the world? Do your editors change your work? How much influence do you have over your own coverage? Where are your parents? Why aren't they here?

It was fair enough that he was asking these questions. The media shaped public opinion, and politicians and powerful interest groups influenced the media, and it was natural enough to wonder how the mechanics of it worked. But couldn't they try to discover such things in a more subtle way? Couldn't they put some slick intellectual on their payroll, and send him out to ask these questions at a dinner or a conference? This Soviet-style questioning in a bare room seemed so dated and clumsy. And it was less effective, too, because it freaked me out and inclined me to lie.

The barrage of questions lasted for over an hour, and I stumbled through my Farsi to find words like ambivalence, editorial oversight, and spiritual reservation. Searching my Farsi vocabulary didn't take very long, I discovered, because it was tiny, limited to the domain of family gossip. I could have easily explained why someone had married above or beneath themselves, or whether the stew was seasoned properly, but the articulation of abstract thought was beyond me.

I searched his expression for signs of approval, but he was impassive, scribbling down notes at everything I said, leaving me with no sense of what was interesting or important. I tried to explain how the urge to return to Iran had come to shape my life, and that they shouldn't judge my family—the diaspora, for that matter—unpatriotic simply because circumstance had taken us to America. That I, too, wanted to see Iran strong and thriving, not isolated and imperiled. But the sentences came out wobbly and incomplete, in the language of an insightful but illiterate adolescent. His expression remained blank.

You haven't touched your tea, he said finally, and I obediently raised the cup to my lips. It was flavorless brown water, like all office tea. Finally, several tortured answers later, I saw a flicker of approval pass over his face, and tried to remember what I had just said. I had begun a sentence with "We Iranians think"—not in Iran it's thought, or just Iranians think, but *we* Iranians.

Soon after, he ended the meeting, and I rushed home, clanging the white iron door shut behind me. My unconscious choice of pronoun intrigued me, and just as my interlocutor had, I held it up as proof that my subconscious self considered itself Iranian. But that very night, while speaking English on the phone, I found myself saying "We should . . ." to make a point about U.S. foreign policy, and realized that my word choice was fickle. In truth, the language I was speaking directed my reference points, invoking a set of experiences and accompanying beliefs particular to an American or an Iranian context. In Farsi, the kitchen-table politics of my childhood rumbled quietly in the back of my mind; in English, the countless tracts of philosophy and political science I had absorbed as a student. Depending on what I did on a given evening, the company I kept and what I ate for dinner, I could spend the night dreaming in either language.

⚜

Just a handful of weeks after my arrival in Tehran, a cousin from California came to visit. Daria and I had grown up together in San Jose, and like me, he was convinced he was entirely Iranian. His friends in America included other second-generation children of Latin American and Middle

Eastern immigrants, Latinos and Lebanese, who were born and raised outside their countries of origin, and chose to identify with African-American culture in America. His friends called him Perz, short for Persian. They wore their jeans low on the hips, and listened to hip hop, the anger and alienation in rap music resonating with their own resentment at being the brown-skinned children of immigrants.

When Daria showed up in Tehran, he brought with him an Eminem-flavored American attitude toward guns and the streets—cops were bad, the muscle behind a racist system, and people who took their safety into their own hands were good. He noticed the *Basij* on the streets of Tehran, the Islamic vigilante thugs used by the regime to harass people, and concluded they were something akin to the Guardian Angels. He didn't know they were the regime's shock troops. Who would suspect that, really? Why should a regime that had a standing army, and considerable formal police and security forces, also employ a ragged, thug militia whose only purpose was the crude harassment of ordinary people?

One afternoon, Daria strode into Khaleh Farzi's living room, paced back and forth between the wooden columns that held up the high ceilings, and announced he wanted to join the *Basij*. "Those guys have it going *on,*" he said. "I went up to one of them today, and he told me they protect the streets. . . . I'm down with that . . . He was right . . . He said women get harassed . . . That's not cool. . . ."

"Stop. Stop right there. You don't get it. The *Basij* are the *bad guys.*" I said. "Everyone hates them. They don't protect people, they abuse them. They're the ones who break up parties, and raid malls. They sell drugs, take bribes, and run rackets."

Khaleh Farzi set a bowl of freshly sliced cantaloupe on the glass table, thanked God she'd never had children, and sat down to watch us argue.

"Listen, Daria. Can I just tell you what happened to me last night? Listen, and then afterward tell me if you still want to become a *Basiji.*"

I had been out with a friend, Nikki, her boyfriend, and one of his friends. Everyone had been raving about the new Chinese restaurant at the Jaam-e-Jaam mall food court, so we had gone over there for dinner. After eating, which involved much chopstick flirtation, we called a taxi to pick us up, and were waiting outside on the corner for it to come. As we chatted under the warm evening sky, one of the dark, menacing Land Rovers driven by the morality police, known as the *komiteh*, rolled up, and three officers jumped out. (The *komiteh* were different than the *Basij* but performed the same functions.)

The two guys turned to face each other, and Nikki turned to me, our body language giving no indication we knew one another. One of the *komiteh* walked up to Nikki's boyfriend and asked how they were related. I don't even know who you're talking about, he replied. The *komiteh* then stepped in front of Nikki, got up within two inches of her face, and repeated the question. I've never seen him before in my life, she said coolly, without blinking. Don't lie to me, he hissed, I just saw you standing here together. You must've gotten me mixed up with someone else, she said, it's a busy intersection.

He tilted his head back toward her boyfriend. So if he's not your boyfriend, if you've never seen him before, you won't care if I hit him, right? And he punched Nikki's boyfriend in the cheek. I felt her body tense next to me, but her eyes didn't flicker. The *komiteh* watched her reaction closely. From behind him, one hand pressed against his face, her boyfriend shot her a look of warning: Don't give us away. The *komiteh* turned back again, and this time he punched him on the other side, on the ear. Nikki exhaled slowly. You can beat him till he's bloody, she said coldly, but I've already told you, and now I'm telling you again, I have no idea who he is. Her voice didn't even quiver.

She turned her back on them both, and dialed a number on her cell phone. Hey maman, yeah, we're still waiting for the cab. Do you need anything from outside? See you in a bit. By this time, the *komiteh* was livid. Okay, so maybe he's not your boyfriend. Was he bothering you? Because if he was, just tell me, and I'll make him pay for it. He stepped closer again, so close he was breathing on her, and she moved back. He wasn't. And I don't need anyone, especially you, to hit someone for me. Deflated by his failure to provoke an admission from either of them, the *komiteh* got back in the Land Rover and shot up Vali Asr Street.

It was, to me, an encounter of shockingly casual violence. I thought Nikki would need months of therapy to recover, and that her boyfriend would insist on meeting indoors forever after. Not at all, it turned out. To them, it was just another Friday night in the Islamic Republic. Young people anticipated these sorts of incidents, and had confronted them so many times that they were almost taken for granted. They considered the morality police part of the geography of the city, like the Alborz Mountains and the long boulevards. They had perfected the art of inventing and synchronizing stories on the spot, how to predict what sort of policeman would take a bribe, and what sort would respond to a convincing argument.

As I recounted the story for Daria, he seemed genuinely puzzled. He made little rows of fork holes all over the slice of melon in front of him, morosely refusing to look up. That's fucked up, he said, a minute later. We had not been prepared to find the cosmologies of our universe so skewed. In California, where I was obsessed with Middle East politics and he was obsessed with the Iranian national soccer team, we had assumed here, in this country where people could pronounce our names, our world would expand. Instead, we felt constricted. Everywhere, it seemed, there were barriers. Of thought and behavior, of places and time. And most dizzying of all, a culture of transgression that could only be learned through firsthand experience. For women, there were eternal limits on dress and comportment, but they could be flouted easily—in the right neighborhood, at the right time of the day or month, in the right way. Young couples also faced endless prohibitions, but these too could be circumvented, with the right verbal pretexts, at the right times, in the right places.

Ignorance of this culture made you a victim, marooned at home with bad Islamic television. Knowing how to navigate its rules gave you freedom, to choose a lifestyle as sedentary or riotous as you pleased. As newcomers, Daria and I were only familiar with a simple, American sort of freedom. Confronted with an oppressive system, we instinctively viewed the Iranians around us as victims, because armed with only our knowledge of California highways and the mall, we had not the slightest idea how to exercise freedom, Tehran-style. We couldn't conceive of a life where you forcibly *took* your rights, through adept arguments and heaps of attitude. Where you lived "as if" the rules didn't exist, and took the skirmishes for granted. And so it felt that in Tehran, even the sky shrank, the streets twined in mazes, and the whole of existence retreated under imposing barriers.

Life in America came with its own set of frontiers, but they were familiar, and from the vantage point of Tehran, seemed more subtle, more bearable. As a Middle Eastern person, they were symbolic barriers placed between you and your culture, in the Islam-bashing and prejudice that seeped into everyday life, ephemeral barriers between you and your peace of mind, as you had to work to disregard the slights and political slander and ignorance that presented themselves so routinely, in so many guises.

The barriers here were overwhelming, in your face, physical and visual. There were walls and partitions, dour billboards and angry-looking *pasdars,* around at all times to enforce them. I wasn't sure which ones I preferred, or perhaps better, which ones I despised least. In America, I hadn't learned, really, how to scale the barriers. They were political and amorphous, and often I felt they existed only in my head, that I created and carted them about myself. For now, these Iranian barriers frightened me. They produced incessant confrontations between people itching to scream at one another, escalate, and let loose the brew of anger and resentment inside.

⁂

To conduct successful and active social lives in Tehran, young people devoted much energy to avoiding the police. These efforts created a sort of predictive science, similar to how people who live in traffic-congested cities try to plan their schedules around rush hour and congested neighborhoods. It was a complicated task. There were several different brands of police and militia, with distinct vehicles, dress, beat, and mandate. They sometimes behaved erratically, and made unexpected appearances at places like pizza parlors, with the obvious aim of keeping everyone in a permanent state of low-level anxiety.

One day, some enterprising Iranian-American from Los Angeles would move to Tehran and set up a radio with ten-minute updates on police flow around the city ("There's a heavy *komiteh* presence northbound on Modaress expressway, and a *Basiji* checkpoint on Aghdasieh Boulevard, but Mohseni Square is flowing"). Keeping this sort of thing in the back of your mind at all times was unpleasant.

It was the kind of emotional strain that I stopped thinking about consciously. Iranians didn't make a big deal out of it, and I didn't want to be like one of the strident European expatriates who perpetually complained about the harsh backwardness of life in Iran, as though they hadn't made the same comments ten times the previous day. Realistically, I should have admitted to myself that adjusting to Iran was tough. I had family around and spoke the language, but that didn't make life in Tehran easy. In retrospect, I'd have been better off talking about how nervous everything made me. That way, I might have defused the pressure as it built up, rather than waking up one day and finding myself unable to get out of bed. But I was too busy pretending to be cool and brave, like the urban Tehrani girls who sailed through the tensions with poise, managing to look fantastic the whole time.

More often that not, though, the police behaved predictably. This bestowed a small sense of control upon the young and social. It helped, for one, to stay vigilant about the dates of the Islamic calendar. If the regime was liberal with one thing, it was the official celebration of Shiite holidays. The births, deaths, and key events in the lives of various imams and members of the Prophet Mohammad's family were occasions for public commemoration. Public displays of piety involved leaving the house, and provided handy excuses to proffer at checkpoints ("Really officer, I was just out celebrating/mourning the birthday/death of Imam _____!") It also resulted in strange calculations, such as waiting for the birthday of a holy man born in the seventh century so you could throw a party.

A vivid illustration of how young people exploited the regime's Islam preoccupation for their social purposes fell each year during the month of Moharram. In this month in the seventh century, the prophet's grandson Hossein was martyred in the holy city of Karbala, a significant date in the early schism between Sunni and Shiite Islam. The Islamic regime took this holiday, called *Ashoura*, very seriously, and draped the whole of Tehran in black. Ubiquitous mosques blared sorrowful chants, and many other devices were used to produce a somber atmosphere that was roundly ignored.

Before the Islamic Revolution, people commemorated *Ashoura* tamely in their neighborhoods and went home by around nine P.M. But in recent years it had taken on grand, carnival-like proportions, with young people out in the traffic-jammed streets until two or three in the morning. Like everything else, it had been transformed into a battleground of wills between Iranians and the Islamic system.

I was still new to Tehran, dim to the social significance of *Ashoura* to hormonally fizzy teenagers, until one of my cousins informed me that the candlelight vigil marking its final night (called *sham-e ghariban*) was by far the most excellent night of the year to pick up guys. Young people from across the city congregated for what they called a "Hossein Party" in Mohseni Square, in a busy neighborhood of northern Tehran.

The traffic en route inched along, as though the whole city of ten million was attempting to converge on this snug square. Initially, the scene seemed decorous and tame. Teenagers and families peered at the displays of gold in jewelry shop windows, and milled about the sidewalks, which were lined with police.

As I inspected the young women more closely—they were touching and ethereal, floating through the night in their gauzy veils, with perfect, glossy locks poking out—I realized the conceit of "Hossein Party." Each one held a flickering candle in her palm, and had tucked underneath scraps of paper bearing her phone number; a great deal of preening went on, and lucky fellow "mourners" were slipped numbers as they passed.

The *Basij* stood aside and observed this decidedly unsorrowful behavior with surly faces. They are officially considered "volunteers," but they enjoy the regime's tacit approval for enforcing Islamic morals, usually with a great degree of violence. Many are impossibly young, no older than fifteen, but their eyes shone with the eager rage of unrestrained bullies. Some, with their untucked shirts and trademark beards, strode around aggressively, eyeing the crowd and deciding what totally harmless transgression would finally provoke their attack.

I walked up to one of them, astride an idling motorbike, and asked him who had sent him here. He didn't answer. What, then, was his purpose? "They sit around with their candles pretending to mourn Hossein, when all they really want is to let out their sexual desires. It's our Islamic duty to control this," he said, revving his engine and peeling off into the street.

I hid behind a tall, potted plant on the front stoop of an apartment building, from where I could safely watch the brewing confrontation. The *Basij* circled a street corner where a crowd of teenagers stood talking, bathed in the light of candles, and ordered them to leave. The crowd moved apart slowly, but some stood their ground. One, a young girl wearing clown-like make-up and a scant slip of veil over masses of long auburn hair, stuck a hand on her hip, and continued chatting into her cell phone.

A *Basij* raced up to her from behind, and cracked a baton over the back of her head. She doubled over, and hung like that for a full minute. Then she drew herself up, and charged headfirst into a line of approaching policemen. Her parted arms forced them to break rank. Behind her a chaotic crowd of several hundred watched her, stunned. Some of them started to run into side streets, to escape the *Basij,* who by that point were swinging their batons around at will and gunning their bikes up and down the street. Others lingered to see whether the vigil would go on. Twenty minutes later, the corner was deserted, and I crawled out from my stoop, tiptoeing around the cooling wax puddles left behind by the teenagers' candles.

I found a taxi to take me home, and as we inched through the clogged streets toward the expressway, the driver talked morosely about *Ashoura* past, and *Ashoura* present. No one has their heart in it anymore, he said, recalling the cathartic, sincere emotionalism of *Ashoura* during his youth. His sons had also been at the vigil. I told them to stay home, but they said they had to go, he said. Last year they called it a "Hossein Party," but this year they're saying "techno-*Ashoura.*" What's techno? he asked shyly. He was worried about his sons, so I lent him my cell phone to call home and check on them. Clashes between socially deprived teenagers and vigilante thugs were always volatile, and black eyes and broken arms were not uncommon.

Often their worried parents accompanied their teenagers out on such evenings, and when a riot threatened to erupt, matronly moms with gray hairs peeking out from under flowered headscarves beseeched the vigilantes—with the cultural authority an Iranian woman of fifty-five should have over a boy of fifteen—to put their clubs and chains (their weapons of choice) away. Their efforts met little success. The *Basij* were carefully selected in the poorest of neighborhoods and were cultivated to violence with a skillful balance of brainwashing and small incentives. I hated watching these scenes. I hated how I could scarcely recognize the traditions I grew up with in the Iran around me. I hated how the Islamic Republic not only dissolved the ties between exiles and Iran, but those between Iranians and their own culture.

⚓

A few days before the start of *Norouz,* Persian New Year, an old friend of Khaleh Farzi—my aunt from California who had moved back to Tehran a few years earlier—called to invite me over for *chaharshambeh-soori,* the night that opens the cycle of Persian New Year festivities. Come over, Azi jan, we'll talk a little politics, have a few drinks, jump over a couple fires. Bring whoever you want, he said. Of course I'll stop by, I said. I have to cruise around the city first, but I'll definitely come.

Unconsciously, I had internalized the nightlife-as-obstacle-course mentality of young Iranians, and I knew it could be an evening rife with both parties and raids. Once the sun set, I set out with two reporter friends in search of celebrations. Rumors had been circulating that the celebration would be banned this year, since it fell too close to *Moharram,* and we were curious to see whether the regime would dare sacrifice *Norouz* to *Ashoura.*

Norouz originates from ancient Zoroastrian rites, and falls each year on the vernal equinox, celebrating the arrival of spring. Persians practiced Zoroastrianism before Islam's conquest in the seventh century, and it irked the ayatollahs that people held Persian festivities, with their pagan origins, closer to their hearts than Islamic holidays. In origin and ritual, the holiday is delightful. Ancient Zoroastrians worshipped fire, for its purifying properties. To symbolize the regeneration of new life after a long winter, they lit a row of small bonfires, and skipped over them, singing a poem about fire. Traditionally, they also set out special *ajeel,* a colorful mixture of pistachios, dried mulberries, walnuts, and green raisins, in large bowls with delicately painted wooden scoopers.

As colorful and lively as it is all meant to be, as a child it filled me with dread. My father, ever keen to embrace anything the mullahs opposed, loved *chaharshambeh-soori,* and insisted we celebrate it in San Jose. He spent the week beforehand collecting tumbleweed from the deserted railroad tracks behind his house, arranging them in huge piles in the backyard. Without fail, the plumes of smoke from the fire would curl up high into the air, and some well-intentioned neighbor would call the fire department on us.

As we drove around the city, the neighborhoods looked like battlefields. Immense bonfires lit up the night sky, and young men ran about exploding fireworks that were more like Molotov cocktails. The streets were filled with smoke, and the women who were out cowered near buildings for shelter, afraid one of the firework-bombs would blow off a limb. Holidays like this gave young men, seething at the double humiliation of economic and social privation, an outlet to release some of their anger with satisfying loud noises and bangs. For one night, they would be the ones making things go pop and terrifying passers-by, not the militia.

We drove away from the wide Tehran boulevard, with snaps and pops and explosions going off on all sides, toward the family party, where only the embers of the fires remained. Inside, my aunt and uncle were standing with their friends at the bar near the kitchen, sipping pink drinks and smoking miniature Bahman cigarettes. Everyone held out their face for double kisses, and then offered me what happened to be in front of them: *ajeel?* Tea? Vodka? Potato salad? A joint? I want the pink stuff, I said, sniffing my aunt's glass. It was *aragh-saghi,* homemade vodka mixed with sour-cherry juice. Apart from a handful of *ajeel,* I hadn't eaten all day, and the drink quickly softened my jagged nerves.

Someone tried to engage me in a discussion about the speaker of parliament, and the cleric's name suddenly escaped me. Please, please don't make me think about clerics, I said, savoring the cool, sweet juice trickling down my throat. People still didn't know what to think about the reformists, and in all honesty, neither did I. At parties such as this, people lingered in each others' living rooms late into the night debating politics. The reform movement had awakened in Iranians two sentiments rare in the Middle East: hope and high expectations. That combination meant everyone—from grocery store clerks to snobby intellectuals—discussed the future constantly. The conversations, though peppered with the political squabble of that particular day, always ended with the same wistful conclusion about the reformists: They're not great, but we must back them, since they're our only hope.

What confused people, kept them up holding the same conversation night after night, month after month, was the knotty question of how much credit the reformists deserved for the tangible changes coinciding with Khatami's presidency. Whether or not to vote in elections (for city councils, for parliament, again for the presidency in 2001) hinged on this answer. At the top, within the strata of officialdom, the degree of change was slight—the mullahs had reshuffled their positions, improved their marketing by rebranding themselves as progressive or pragmatic, but the rotten structures and attitudes were firmly in place.

When Iranians stopped to scrutinize exactly how and where these transformations had taken place, they concluded it was from below—in people's behavior and dress, their ideas, spirits, and conversations, attitudes and activities. At some historic moment impossible to pinpoint, around the turn of the millennium, Iranians' threshold for dissimulation and constriction sank, and people simply began acting differently. Women started wearing lipstick, exposing their toes and curves, wearing their veils halfway back, "as if" they had a right to be uncovered. Writers and intellectuals wrote vicious satire and stinging commentary, "as if" it was permitted to criticize the regime. People of all ages turned up music in their cars, caroused with the opposite sex, "as if" people could listen to whatever they wanted, "as if" young men and women had the right to go out for coffee. All of these "as if" acts became facts on the ground, and the authorities knew it would be foolish and impossible to stand in the way. While they were still happy to appear comical, hysterically condemning "decadent, immoral, Western-ized _____ [fill trivial noun in the blank, e.g.: poodles, CDs, ties]," over time they recognized cultural rebellion as a force beyond their control.

Iranians felt they were the ones responsible for all of this, since they were the ones who began flouting the rules and speaking openly, waiting up worried while their teenagers tried to be carefree and adolescent on the streets of an unpredictable city. When the reformists were unable to fix the most urgent problems facing the country—from corruption to the poor economy, from lawlessness to urban traffic—the people dismissed them as spineless collaborators, and cursed themselves for ever having vested hope in Khatami, interchangeable with all his turbaned predecessors.

Reformists, in turn, reproached Iranians for being ungrateful and impatient, like children who demanded everything but understood the cost of nothing. They counseled that change would require time and patience, and predicted ominously that Iranians would regret the day they withdrew their support.

During such debates, I argued both sides. Yes, the reformists had serious and potentially fatal flaws. But they had also created an atmosphere hospitable to all that change from below. They were the ones who issued the permits for independent newspapers, and campaigned to redefine Iran as a relatively normal country, rather than a rogue menace. Beneath the flowery rhetoric, they were helping to dismantle the taboos of thought and behavior entrenched since 1979. They had inspired hope and active debate, and given people the sense (however mistaken) that their votes might count for something. In contrast with the flat despair and apathy that prevailed in the other living rooms where I had held such discussions—in places like

Cairo and Beirut, where change seemed so improbable, the leaders so unin-spiring, that internal politics was hardly worth discussing—the Iran of the reformist era seemed less bleak to me.

Around two in the morning, my feet started to feel like cement blocks, and I decided I had to go home immediately. Waiting for a taxi would have taken ages, and since home was just a twenty-minute walk away, I blithely put on my *roopoosh,* tied my veil around my head bandanna-style, and lurched toward the door. My friend Dariush was aghast.

Dariush was a photojournalist, an unrepentant snob, and attached to his cell phone by umbilical cord. We lived in the same neighborhood and often carpooled on reporting assignments. Eventually, we began dating, not be-cause we suited one another, but because he was a still a teenager in spirit, and I had to be an adolescent in Tehran before I could be an adult there. We were carefree and innocent together, scampering about the city drinking fresh juice, taking walks through old neighborhoods, hunting for antiques, and lunching in the garden of our favorite restaurant downtown. We were having so much fun that I didn't notice initially how little I liked him.

When he saw me ambling out, Dariush hung up reluctantly and spread his arms out in front of the door, blocking my exit. You, you who aren't standing so much as swaying, you want to *go walk down the street?*

Flopping home drunk, a regular ritual for young people all around the world, was a dangerous proposition in Iran; if you were unlucky enough to be picked up by the police, or run into a *Basij* checkpoint, you could spend the night in prison, or get beaten up on the street. The breathalyzer test was usually a Kalashnikov against your throat, and much suspicious sniffing by a bearded eighteen-year-old vigilante from impoverished south Tehran, who despised you for having all the economic and social privileges denied him. If you were a woman, urban legend held that you might have your vir-ginity checked at the local precinct. Equally horrid, and far more common, was one punishment for being found with a man not your husband: forcible marriage.

But I insisted on walking home, and so Dariush put on his coat too, in a rare act of gallantry. Open your mouth, he said. I parted my lips slowly, hoping guiltily he was going to give me a cigarette, since I was too uncoor-dinated to get out my own. Instead, he stuffed three pieces of gum into my mouth, to cover the smell of the alcohol.

As we ambled down the dark street, it became clear I would have a hard time walking unassisted; Dariush had to take my arm, which made us conspicuous. I remember finding the situation very funny, but he thought it was disastrous. A garbage truck was slowly making its way down the hill, and he flagged it down, pumping a frantic arm into the air. Can you give us a lift to the bottom? He grabbed my arm and hauled me onto the edge of the truck, our toes shoved perilously close to the wheels. We occupied the stinking, one-foot gap between the trash and the cabin, commanded by Afghan workers. Do. You. Realize. What. You've. Done. I screamed. This is garbage! I'm being transported with *refuse*. This is madness. Why don't you people revolt or something?

Shut up, Azadeh. This isn't the time for political analysis. I don't need you getting lashed on my conscience.

Throughout that jolty ride, through my concern for my shoes and my entertainment at Dariush's uncharacteristic gravity (he seemed like a boy trying to keep his pet safe), I felt a warm sense of security. With someone who knew the gaps in the rules, there was adventure to be had behind the grim, rigid façade of the Islamic Republic.

CHAPTER THREE

We Don't Need No Revolution

You will soon see.
Say a name.
Paint a profile.
Offer your hand.
Walk like anybody.
Smile.
Speak of sadness.
You will see.
This is not your country anymore.

—ADONIS

A couple months after I arrived in Tehran, my uncle charged his assistant at work with helping me through the country's labyrinthine bureaucracy. When I met Celine for the first time, she was peering into a compact, applying a thick coat of mocha-red MAC lipstick. Celine became my first new Iranian girlfriend, guiding me to the best manicurist, waxing lady, and private pastry chef in the city with the shared belief that these were urgent priorities. Of all my new friends, Celine's curiosity thrived the most; she was always on her way to learning something—Italian grammar, step-aerobics, puff pastry. She had lived in Tehran all her life and was still impossibly bubbly, ever enthusiastic about what Tehran had to offer.

Unlike most of my girlfriends, Celine still had lots of time for me. In the Tehran of my first visit, my female cousins and family friends were available to me all the time. We spent hours drinking tea, dancing in the living room, napping, and waking up to drink more tea and repeat the cycle. Now they all had boyfriends, and were constantly off at cafés, dinners, and parties, so I had to book them in advance. Happily, Celine was single and so was I.

A kinship blossomed between us, centered on leisurely afternoons sipping mochas at our favorite café on Gandhi Street. All week I looked forward to our coffee ritual with great anticipation. We had marvelous conversations, skipping from topic to topic and dissolving into malicious giggles, but communicating a complex thought took me so long I bored even myself in the process. One afternoon, as soon as we settled into our usual spot, I asked her why, given how talented, curious, and hard-working she was, she had never gone to college.

"I knew, from everything I'd heard, that there were *Ershad* groups active on campus, telling women to fix their *hijab,* asking them why they were talking to this or that guy, or telling them that their laugh was too loud." The verb she used, *gir dadan,* was common in the vernacular that evolved after the revolution, minted to describe the new realities of everyday life. It meant "to hassle, purely for the sake of hassling." *Ershad* means guidance, and these groups were charged with "guiding" students toward proper Islamic behavior.

They were interested in torturing people, not educating them, she said. They don't understand that young people need a relaxed and happy mind to be able to learn, and improve themselves. I didn't think I could stand it.

A slice of cheesecake later, she asked me why I had broken up with my boyfriend in Cairo before coming to Tehran. I tried to explain, dismayed to see notions like "I need space" evaporate into meaninglessness in Farsi. It was as though the soft, soap-opera lighting of English had been switched off, and replaced by the harsh, fluorescent glare of Farsi. I realized that lots of flimsy, disingenuous things I said in English ("I love you, I'm just not *in* love with you" or "Let's see other people, while we work things out") were codes. They stood in for feelings I didn't want to admit to myself (I just spent a really long time with someone I don't even like) or that were too harsh to air ("It's totally over, erase my number from your cell phone"). Breaking up, or explaining why you were breaking up, relied on a linguistic shorthand everyone understood, and that no one but a therapist or a best friend would challenge you over.

Celine sat listening through all of this, her hands patiently folded in her lap. She occasionally murmured "Hmmm." She was far too polite to tell me that everything I said sounded false. That I would be better off confronting reality, rather than obscuring the sadness of sad things through a hazy filter of language.

It wasn't always like that. Sometimes I arrived with straightforward stories of wounded pride. Those times I wanted nothing more than to be direct and talk about how humiliating it was to be molested during a security pat-down (by a *chadori* woman, no less), how I couldn't bear the thought of another session with Mr. X, or how weak I felt, letting it all get to me. I knew precisely how I felt and was bursting to tell her, eager to ease the hurt with mockery, and unravel it all over and over again, from a hundred different vantage points—the sort of deep, swirling conversation one has with one's girlfriends. But Farsi denied me the nuance I needed. Without those shades of gray, my descriptions and ideas came out as partial, crude sketches. In the course of these halting monologues, I realized that some of my most integral parts resisted translation. It was only in not being able to transport them into another language that I saw how much they mattered.

A couple we knew walked in, and sat down at the table next to us, so we steered the conversation toward a new topic, one that was frequently on my mind as I sought to decipher exactly what it was that made me feel, and seem, so different from other Tehrani women my age. Khaleh Farzi insisted it was all in my head, and repeated her frequent refrain: You're just not used to looking like a peasant. Originally, I assumed it was a simple matter of style and comportment: I walked too quickly, rushing in and out of stores and offices, and didn't wear lipstick. I felt eyes on me constantly, and I wanted to pinpoint precisely what is was that gave me away as a foreigner.

After watching me for several weeks as we rode in taxis and shopped and had coffee, Celine concluded that it was nothing so obvious. She leaned forward in her chair, as if to make a serious pronouncement. One, you laugh whenever you want. And two, you smile too much. This is very American of you. It doesn't really occur to you, to alter yourself in public. So I should smile less? I asked. I should be less nice? No, she replied, you need to be more selective about who you're nice to.

Celine was my authority on how to wear and subvert the veil, as well as my guide to delightful public places, such as our café. She was friends with the café owner, whom I dubbed Elvis, for his head of dark, wavy hair. As Celine outlined whom one should not smile to, Elvis placed a second slice of cheesecake on the brushed aluminum table. He ran the café as a cross between a living room and an art gallery—a place people went for his cozy hospitality, and to see and be seen. A series of abstract paintings or drawings always decorated the walls, and he redesigned the aesthetic of the espresso menu every month.

The pebbles underneath our feet—the slate and earth tone décor was minimalist, in the style of a zen garden—crunched as we crossed and uncrossed our legs. Young people sought Elvis's café as refuge from the relentless ugliness that pervaded most public gathering places. Even in the rainy winter, people would crowd outside in the drizzle for an hour, smoking soggy cigarettes and waiting for a table. It was the only café in Tehran designed with innovative elegance and attracted young people starved for aesthetic beauty—the artists, writers, and musicians whose sensibilities suffered acutely in a city draped with grim billboards of war martyrs.

Elvis's coffeehouse inspired imitations all over the neighborhood and then the city. In early 2000, when Celine and I first began to haunt the tiny, modern nook, it was one of a kind. By the following summer of 2001, dozens of tastefully decorated cafés dotted the city, but Elvis's remained the original. In the Gandhi shopping complex, where it was located, at least six others sprang up, and the area became center stage in a café scene of shocking permissiveness. By that time, the dress code was so relaxed that everyone buzzed with tales of "You'll never believe what I saw this girl wearing!"; the fashion spring was likened to a silent coup.

Girls dressed in every color imaginable—veils of bright emerald, violet, buttercup—and in short, coat-like tunics called *manteaus* (also known by the Farsi word *roopoosh*) that hugged their curves, Capri pants that exposed long stretches of calf, pedicured toes in delicate sandals. They sat at the tables outside, in mixed groups, alone with boyfriends, laughing and talking into the late evening, past eleven. For a few weeks, Tehran actually had something like nightlife in public, not just sequestered parties inside people's houses.

Not everyone was keen to exploit the new Left Bank café scene. Because of the ever-present specter of the morality police, young people with strict parents or more reticent personalities often turned to the Internet to socialize. Online, they could be as outrageous and indecent, tame or sensitive as they pleased. Chat rooms, Celine explained, were an easy way to showcase one's personality minus the clogging distractions of public space. At that time, before the crazed advent of the weblog, chat rooms were the preferred venues in the virtual sphere. You were on *all* night, I complained to her, your phone was busy for years. Sorry, she said sheepishly. I met someone last week I really liked, and we've been emailing back and forth ever since. He's the perfect age. Funny. Speaks Italian. But I don't know, he hasn't sent a picture yet.

Often, once we finished discussing work, men, and the new styles of head scarf we coveted, Celine and I would sit and people-watch. The throng of students and young professionals flirted brazenly, and the coquettish slipping of veils produced nothing less than social theater. The Tehran of the revolution was one of the most sexualized milieus I had ever encountered. Even the chat rooms, Celine informed me, were rife with erotic discussion. People really, really wanted to talk about sex.

The major social aim of the revolution had been to impose Islamic faith on Iranian society. But the catalog of restrictions—on dress, behavior, speech—meant to instill a solemn decency instead inflamed people's carnal instincts. Made neurotic by the innate oppressiveness of restriction, Iranians were preoccupied with sex in the manner of dieters constantly thinking about food. The subject meant to be *unmentionable*—to which end women were forced to wear veils, sit in the back of the bus, and order hamburgers from the special "women's line" at fast food joints—had somehow become the most mentioned of all. The constant exposure to covered flesh—whether it was covered hideously, artfully, or plainly—brought to mind, well, flesh.

The relaxing of the dress code encouraged this tendency, by breathing sexuality back into public space. Women walked down the street with their elbows, necks, and feet exposed, their figures outlined in form-fitting tunics. After two decades in exile, skin was finally back. And so imaginations flared, everyone eagerly thought about and talked about sex a lot, as though they were afraid if they didn't exploit the new permissiveness in dress and mood, they might wake up to find it had disappeared.

Perhaps the preoccupation had evolved gradually, so at no point did it seem remarkable that in a country run like an Islamic theme park, complete with long lines for bad rides and portraits of ridiculous characters everywhere, everyone was addicted to talking about sex. Sexual innuendoes, double entendres, and dirty jokes were commonplace in daily conversation, in taxis, among politicians, in formal meetings. Viagra had recently debuted in Tehran, and a day did not pass when I didn't hear a handful of fresh jokes about its powers. At the bank. During an interview. In line for pastry.

In such a climate, the country of my birth singled me out as a sexual target: a giant, blinking red light signaling availability immediately after a round of introductions. It fell to Najmeh, a fellow high-strung journalist-workaholic, to instruct me on how to discourage unwanted attentions arising from the clichéd belief that Americans exchange sex like handshakes. We worked from the same office, anchored by the BBC, and our desks sat across from each other. Each morning we took up our stations with a stack of newspapers and steaming cups of tea, and she educated me about Iranian politics—horrid vs. less horrid clerics, insignificant reformers vs. highly insignificant reformers—and social conduct. Najmeh admitted to assuming the worst about people's intentions but argued this was a function of the Islamic Republic's skewed gender relations, not an innately dire view of human nature.

You realize, don't you, that they taught us to despise men in school, she said one day, when I complained that her attitude was too harsh. In the third grade, we played this game. Knock, knock! Who's there? Your Uncle Hassan. Oh, come in Uncle Hassan, let me give you a kiss on the cheek. Knock, knock! Who's there? Your Cousin Ali. Aaaack! Ali, do *not* come in, you are *namahram* (forbidden).

So you see, we are conditioned to be base with one another, she continued. There are cues to show you are not receptive: You must be cold, arrogant, and extremely formal at all times. Keep your greetings curt and short, and stop *smiling* so much. But then people will talk behind my back, and call me a snob, I said. They'll talk about you no matter what. Better they call you a snob than worse names. It's unfortunate, but you have no choice. This is the world you're living in now.

I was skeptical, but on a snowy afternoon in Kermanshah, a city in the Kurdish province of northwestern Tehran, Najmeh proved herself right. President Khatami had flown the press corps up with him, as he toured the provinces in anticipation of the presidential election the following year, 2001.

From the airport we squeezed into a few unheated mini-buses, and were deposited at a frigid hotel to await the precise itinerary of rallies and baby-kissing. If the electricity goes out, we'll all freeze to death, I thought, surveying the grim lobby. Then I wondered whether Islamic law would forgive unmarried men and women for huddling together for warmth, if they were in sub-zero temperatures and threatened with frostbite or worse. Mentally I made a note to submit this question to an ayatollah, since they are trained to resolve such dilemmas of faith and extenuating circumstance.

There was even a television show devoted to such questions, and the presiding ayatollah responded to queries like: Say there's a two-story house, with a woman sleeping on the first floor and her nephew on the second. If there's an earthquake that brings down the second floor, and somehow the nephew falls on the aunt and she gets pregnant, is the child a bastard or not? Such urgent and sophisticated matters were often debated on state-controlled television. It was not a high moment for Islam.

Inside the lobby, where we were destined to spend long hours, I sat on a faded brown couch and lit a cigarette. Najmeh frowned. Smoking in public, she informed me with a dramatic look of recrimination, is a major public statement. You might as well announce your room number out loud. What am I supposed to do? I asked plaintively. Not smoke for two days? Besides, anyone who thinks less of me for smoking is an ass, whose opinion wouldn't matter anyway.

The next event was delayed, and we drank endless cups of tea, cuddling the cups in our hands for warmth. A rusty aquarium stood near the entrance to the hotel restaurant. Even the fish seemed cold. I was flipping through my notebook when a journalist I vaguely knew, a correspondent for an Islamist television network, wandered over, and asked if he could sit next to me. His beard, television affiliation, and collarless shirt marked him as a pious Muslim man. But months later, when he was hired to work for a non-Islamist network, the beard was swiftly shorn and he acquired a tie, so as is the case with many regime apparatchiks and hangers-on, the real extent of his devotion remained a mystery.

According to Najmeh's rules, I should have immediately risen to change my seat; proper Iranian women did not elicit men's advances by holding conversations in public. But I was not yet convinced that a mercenary frostiness was required to have a civilized encounter with the opposite sex. And so I nodded, and he sat down and began a predictable conversation about the president's popularity among young people. After making a handful of generic observations, he proceeded to talk about Iranian youth generally, and the social challenges they faced, from drug addiction to unemployment.

"How do you think young people deal with their physical needs?" he asked, leaning forward, lowering his squeaky voice, and answering his own question: temporary marriage. In Shiite Islam, when a man wants to sleep with a woman without marrying her, he can opt for a *sigheh,* a temporary marriage. Though sordid and unromantic, temporary marriage is convenient: the duration can be as short as fifteen minutes, and the vows can be exchanged in about fifteen seconds. The institution serves clerics, seeking a theological loophole through which to philander, and prostitutes, who need such a pretext to operate in an Islamic society. The revolution popularized *sigheh* among ordinary Iranians, especially during the years when dating couples were routinely harassed by the police and forced to show some form of relation.

"What do *you* think about that option?" he asked. I thought: It is a form of prostitution, which enables a patriarchal culture to cement the imbalanced gender relations in the guise of empowering women with a temporary and flimsy legal status that rarely works to their benefit. But I didn't know how to say all of that in Farsi, and while I struggled to find the right words, he leaned in closer.

"What do you, *personally*, think about that. Might you consider it, were we to make that suggestion?" he asked, using the formal plural that in Farsi means "I." I felt a thousand ants crawling on my skin at once. This! This is what I got, for not flitting away like a nervous schoolgirl?

I shot him a reproachful glance, as my fingers flew up to fiddle with my head scarf, pulling it over my hair, closer to my forehead, as though to impose a cotton barrier of Islam between us. I'm sorry, I need to make a phone call, I said, and rose to walk away, furious with myself for being so naive, with him for the hypocrisy of his beard and Islamist television network, and with my Farsi for being deficient, so I could not sear his ego with a devastating retort.

I drifted to the other side of the room, to the side of a photographer friend I always relied on for pep talks. "I know I'm not supposed to smoke in public," I said. "What would you do if you were me? Would you avoid doing that?" "Personally, I dislike lies," he said. "I find that if you act them out long enough, you begin believing them. You'll find that lies are natural for people here. Having a façade is normal, because being honest is such a hassle. You have to decide what bothers you most—lying all the time, or the consequences of openness."

What an impossible pair of choices: One would corrode your spirit, and another would bring daily aggravation to your life. This, I realized, was the central dilemma of life under the Islamic regime, and its culture of lies— whether to observe the taboos and the restrictions, or resist them, by living as if they didn't exist. What if your conscience and your spirit dictated the latter, but you didn't have the energy to live each day as a struggle? What did you do then?

‌⁂

To ordinary Iranians—people like my Khaleh Farzi, my Starbucks-deprived aunt, who wanted nothing more than to go hiking without a veil, or her husband, who wanted to practice medicine in a system not wholly contaminated by inefficiency and corruption, or my driver, who wanted a job that paid enough for him to get married—reformist political debates were arcane to the point of exasperation.

If the reformists had a wish list, at the top would have been to abolish the system of rule by the supreme religious leader—in Persian, *velayat-e faqih*—altogether. While to those unfamiliar with Shiite state formation and jurisprudence, such a question sounds understandably intricate and abstract, it is actually not at all. A state must be anchored in an identity of law and be governed by a leader accountable to something. Under the Khomeini model of *velayat-e faqih,* upheld by the hard-liners, the state was Shiite, the leader was a cleric, and both were accountable only to God. Most of the reformers sought a system characterized by democracy, with an executive as leader, accountable to his constituency.

The open schism between reformists and hard-liners centered on this question. In 2000, that first year I lived in Iran, Iranians elected a reformist parliament by overwhelming majority, and eagerly awaited the passage of more liberal laws. But hard-line–dominated institutions like the judiciary blocked even their modest attempts at tinkering with the Islamic system. A proposal in parliament to allow single women to travel abroad for study, for example, would become lost within the sticky, labyrinthine system of clerical checks and balances, and eventually sink.

The Islamic religious law *(sharia)* imposed by Ayatollah Khomeini in 1979, as the legal foundation for his Islamic state, made misery and repression official policies. Shocking acts (like marrying a girl of nine) became legal, and ordinary acts (like listening to Western music or showing your hair) were banned. The religious codes stripped women of an array of rights—traveling alone, divorcing with ease, retaining custody of children—and produced a judiciary ruled by chaos and brutality.

Because the structure of the Islamic state, written into the constitution, granted over-arching powers to the supreme religious leader and clerical state bodies, the elected branches of government—like the presidency and the parliament—had no meaningful authority in practical terms. Their policies were either vetoed, ignored, or contradicted.

Well into President Khatami's first term, late 2000, most Iranians were on the verge of losing patience. They considered the changes to date an upgrade to Taliban Lite, and wanted much more—a free, lawful, and efficiently run country, and an end to the corruption and Islamic white noise that were the system's trademarks. Some already deemed the reformists a failure, a judgment the majority of Iranians would only reach after the presidential election of the next summer, 2001.

In my familial sphere, Khaleh Farzi was the voice of Iranian frustration, the people who despised the reformists for their powerlessness, and their inability to tear down and reconstruct twenty years of Khomeiniism in five years or less. "They should resign, they should call for mass demonstrations, they should hold a referendum on the whole stupid mess," she would say, furrowing her eyebrows in contempt.

⋆

It was impossible to understand sexual relations in modern Iran without understanding the culture of the revolution, and no one knew this better than the reformists. Many had been fiery radicals in the days of Khomeini and, two decades into the ayatollah's grand experiment, found themselves baffled that their utopian vision had produced an oppressive, overly sexualized society. Although they sensed that something had gone desperately wrong and recognized dysfunctional social behavior when they saw it, they still refused to believe that women's oppression was among the Islamic Republic's central problems. Somehow, they could not admit that all these deficiencies shared an origin—the animating ideological character of the Islamic state. The clerics were bad planners for the same reason they were sexists. But the reformists thought that if economic mismanagement were fixed, if more "immediate" rights were protected, the matter of women would sort itself out.

I realized the depth of that misperception through talks with one reformist legislator whose office was just a few blocks from home. We were on friendly terms, and I stopped by to see him frequently. During one visit, the view from his office raised the question. We had been talking about universities in Tehran, and how, paradoxically, the ones that banned student organizations, and separated men and women most rigidly, were hotbeds of political activity and dating.

The sky darkened as we talked, and during a pause, he pointed a finger at the office building across the street. All the lights were off, save one room, in which the outline of two figures was visible. Do you see that? he asked. She takes a different man up there each week. A woman like that, a simple clerical worker, isn't educated or cultured enough to know why she's compelled to sleep around like that. She's not conscious of craving freedom, of finding it in the crannies where the regime's eyes can't follow.

So they do understand, I thought to myself. We continued to talk, and he displayed an advanced awareness of gender relations and their intersection with politics in an oppressive system. But as with so many reformists, his were private reflections. I never heard him air them in public and incorporate them into policy strategy.

Many of the reformists came from an ultra-traditional class that held more conservative social values than the majority of Iranians. Because they were enamored with Western philosophy and borrowed all their ideas about freedom and rights from thinkers such as Kant and Habermas, they were starting to see that their vision of an open society was incompatible with individual rights. But they were as yet too narrow to include women in the category of individual.

This was the Achilles heel of their movement, this foolish idea that they could take a Western concept, like democracy, alter it with Islamic attitudes toward women, and expect it to function properly. Siamak described it well one day, in a conversation about his antique, forest-green Mustang convertible. He had purchased it for what he called "Mustang therapy," which mainly involved gunning it up and down the expressways of Tehran, blaring Led Zeppelin. His mechanic kept installing old Iranian parts into the car, and declared himself shocked each time to find they didn't work. It's the same with our politicians and intellectuals, Siamak complained. They borrow Western concepts like democracy, stick in Iranian parts, and can't figure out why they've lost the juice.

My reformist and I sat smoking in silence, until the light in the office went off, and the streetlights cast shadows over the building. We were both trying to quit, and always fidgeted through the first minutes of every meeting, before sheepishly asking if the other had any cigarettes. In those days, the height of the reform movement's struggles with the establishment, such figures made themselves available to journalists.

Those were the days when we saw each other every other week, when the reform movement was on everyone's lips, the topic of lively dinner debates in homes across the country. When it had spark and momentum and people actually believed it could change Iran. As I walked home, I wondered how long it would hold together, this delicate alliance between a long-suffering people and a political movement without prospect.

The mysterious woman across the street continued to fascinate me. When I watched her turn that light off, I knew once and for all that skewed sexual relations were not confined to cosmopolitan, Westernized Iranians. They were experienced by two halves of a society, sliced apart by the regime's gender hang-ups, struggling to relate to one another in a toxic atmosphere of moralizing propaganda. I wished I could find her, and tell her story.

I imagined her walking out into the street, getting into a shared taxi to go home. She would be wearing a navy-blue *maghnaeh* (an Islamic bonnet that cloaks the entire head), a faceless public-sector employee, and melt away into the ordinariness of rush-hour Tehran. She probably did not speak English, and her evening would not be colorful or particularly interesting. Her promiscuity did not offer as striking and exotic a contrast to the Islamic face of society as the parties of north Tehran, awash in tequila, drugs, and designer labels. Had I found her, she wouldn't have made coolly detached comments about love and tyranny that would have made sexy quotes for a story. But her alienation was also Iran's reality, in all its drab desperation.

⁂

Even teenagers, at the high-pitched outset of adolescence, found themselves relating awkwardly across the gender divide. I spent a lot of time with teenagers, and was becoming somewhat expert in their mores. They were easier on my nerves than Iranian adults, smooth men who flirted in grandiloquent, high Farsi, or catty women whose skillfully masked insults I was unequipped to defend myself against. Instead of being reduced to a tongue-tied teenager, I figured, I might as well just hang out with real teenagers. They made me feel clever and interesting. And their conversations, though no material for literature, were a lot more edifying.

One summer Thursday afternoon (the Friday afternoon of a Thursday-Friday Islamic weekend), as I sat scrawling vocabulary flash cards at the office, my cousin Kimia called my mobile phone. "Pleeeease, pleeeease, Azi, you *must* come out with us, it's going to be so fun, and Kaveh might even be there, and you can meet my friends, and if Mom knows you're going I can stay out later," she pleaded in one breathless, run-on sentence. I contemplated my choices for the evening: going out as Kimia's chaperone (again), or yet another night with my faithful companion, the dictionary. For the last two hours I had been too distracted to absorb new words and had taken to comparing the Farsi and English for terms like "lust," in search of cross-cultural insight. A change of scenery was clearly in order.

Fine, I'll go, but I'm not going to stay out too late, and I'm not going to drive, I said. Driving in Tehran, with its exhausted and edgy taxi drivers and daredevil motorbikes flitting through miles of gnarled traffic, gave me backaches. The veil impaired my sideways vision, and I constantly feared it would slip off while I was driving. What do you do first? Uphold modesty or prevent an accident? I had meant to pose this conundrum to an authoritative ayatollah, after one day, while attempting to do a U-turn across four lanes of oncoming traffic, I found my head scarf down around my shoulders. A man crossing the street in front of my car noticed my confusion, and laughed. *Khanoum* (lady), you've lost your Islam!

Kimia shrieked with joy at my agreement and promised to share her strawberry Pop-Tarts with me and love me forever, in that order. As dusk turned into night, her two friends picked us up in a gray Peugeot. One's face looked like a cadaver, under what must have been a solid centimeter of foundation and powder. The other had glued little rhinestones around her eyes, and wore a smear of fuchsia where her mouth should have been. We piled into the car, and headed toward Shahrak-e Gharb, a suburban neighborhood in west Tehran, which is home to Golestan, a large mall popular with teenagers.

I assumed the mall was our destination, until Kimia informed me she and her friends had been caught at the mall by *komiteh* last week and couldn't risk going back there so soon. As we fermented in the awful traffic, the girls scanned the cars next to them, making eye contact, giggling furiously, and rolling the windows up and down. Who knew so much flirtation could be conducted while cruising? They finally located their crew of male friends, having traded coordinates by mobile phone, and a Jeep full of teenage boys drove perilously close to our sedan, trying to keep pace so the couples facing each other could talk, or rather yell, over the engine noise.

This continued for an hour, and I leaned my head back against the seat, trying to test myself on vocabulary (How did you say *supranational* again?). A*zi*, hissed Kimia, stretching my nickname into two syllables, you're not *talking* to anyone. I'm here to observe, not participate, I said. But she looked so tense that I relented, and stuck my head out the window, to answer one of her friend's questions about UCLA. That one could be Iranian, from California, and *not* from Los Angeles occurred to no one. Suddenly, the exhaust fumes, the crick in my neck, and the sad nuisance of it all got to me, and I caught a cab home, leaving the youngsters to pursue the only public activity they could think of—getting cantaloupe smoothies.

Late that night at home, Kimia padded into my room and asked me what I thought of the evening. It was very . . . I don't know . . . very Islamic Republic, I said. The phrase stuck, and from that day forth we used "very Islamic Republic" to describe any experience that was comically tragic, or tragically comic. Kimia and her friends were still young, in that stage of adolescence when drugs and sex loomed on the not-too-distant horizon. It wasn't long, I knew, before they would tire of cruising the expressways of Tehran, the highlight of their evening a pit-stop at the juice stand. Eventually they would say screw the *pasdar,* and the traffic, let's just stay at home. And teenagers home alone for hours on end do, well, exactly what you imagine.

The next afternoon, Kimia ran into my room, as I was transcribing an interview tape, and flopped down on the couch, tossing her *roopoosh* on the floor. Her green eyes sparkled, and for the first time since we had begun living together, she appeared happy. With the culture shock receding, she was delighting in the rich drama of her new life. Dealing with the *komiteh* was dangerous and frightening, but it made each weekend a unique adventure.

The brushes with the law, the exposure to a mainly authoritarian system, filled her mind with lofty concepts like power and freedom that in Palo Alto—where her friends stole street signs for stimulation—were abstract to the point of meaninglessness. But if she stays here, I thought, there will be bad times, and in those there will be no glory. If she gets stopped on the way home from a party, and gets whipped, or worse, gets her virginity checked, she will come home devastated, and we will not laugh it off as "very Islamic Republic."

Her mother has agreed to bribe the police at the Caspian this weekend, so she and her friends can play co-ed basketball at their villa. This is a great social coup, and will make up for the fact that she can't invite her friends over. I could *never* bring them here, she said regularly in mortification. Pedar Joon, our grandfather, filled the pool with cement years ago, and there was no space for her friends to romp around in bikinis, listening to Puff Daddy, sitting on each other's laps, and pretending they are at the MTV summer beach house.

Kimia herself wasn't wedded to this sort of behavior, because she had lived in the West and knew that life did not actually resemble television. Most of her friends hadn't, and worked fiercely to imitate music videos and Hollywood movies to every last detail. They assumed, with a touching naïveté, that all guys should act like Carson Daly, and that girls in the United States wore tight, revealing clothes at *all* times. Thus convinced, they would show up at any social occasion—yearning to feel worldly—in wildly inappropriate clothes, called *lebass-e mahvarayee,* satellite dress, after the inspiring TV medium.

So we sat and discussed what she would wear that night to her friend's birthday party, to show up all her overdressed friends with a relaxed, sexy cool. Skinny, low-slung jeans, a cotton tank top, and sandals. Her light-brown, honey-kissed hair down her back in waves. Only lip gloss and mascara. PJ sniffed morosely around the room as we dressed, lonely now that Kimia had a social life. At nine, we covered everything up, got in the car, and drove north. Other than the steady stream of cars that silently pulled up to the Kermanis' front door, there was no indication of the scene transpiring inside the darkened house. For their daughter Leila's seventeenth birthday, the Kermanis were throwing a "mixed party," which meant both boys and girls would attend and dance together to Western music, both activities officially banned by the regime.

Inside, the atmosphere was more Japanese hostess bar than a teenager's birthday party: a disco ball flashed against the walls, as erotically dressed girls and bored-looking young men prowled about self-consciously, oppressed by the pressure to have wild, illicit fun. Staging and attending such an event involved such elaborate subterfuge that nothing less would do. Leila worked the room in a white halter top that glowed in the flashing strobe light, trying unsuccessfully to lighten the edgy mood.

Everyone scanned the room furtively, carefully blasé, holding distracted conversations. The heels were high, the skirts short, and the corners dark. In shadowy corners, shots were taken, hash was smoked. A Toni Braxton song came on, filling the makeshift dance floor with couples swaying in close embrace—an intimacy out of place in an Iranian family home, especially with Mrs. Kermani yards away in the kitchen, clucking orders to the maid preparing birthday cake. Toni Braxton went over well. So well that the song, "Unbreak My Heart," was played three more times, and each time, the embraces got a little tighter.

I, spinster chaperone, sat in the kitchen with Mrs. Kermani, who cast forlorn, helpless glances at the spectacle in her living room. I don't know what's wrong with these kids, she sighed. Poor Mrs. Kermani. Five years ago, she had fretted over raising a daughter in a grim, socially oppressive society. Now, she seemed aware that social permissiveness carried its own knot of worries—strained sexual relations, drinking and drugs, a new range of emotional pitfalls. When I was a teenager, we would dance all night, she mused, fiddling with the stack of dessert forks. They're dancing, just *slow* dancing, I said. She gave me the Iranian parental your-generation-is-weird look, and I gave her the your-generation-made-the-revolution look.

Around midnight, Mrs. Kermani began finding quiet rooms where worried parents could be pacified on the phone. While she called taxis, the girls scrambled to pull pants under their miniskirts. The cloakroom was strewn with slipdresses, for coming, and veils and *roopoosh,* for going. Leila looked exhausted; she didn't sparkle or preen, as she might have, given that she was beautiful and young, that it was her birthday, and that she had just presided over the most glamorous party of the season. As she shut the door, a girl in five-inch heels traipsing toward a waiting car turned her head back, and cried "Happy *moharram!*" in a tinny voice.

Three years ago, parties such as this were unthinkable. President Khatami's election made them commonplace. Elite Tehranis threw parties where waiters in starched white shirts circulated cocktails in gleaming crystal. Less status-conscious Iranians gathered as frequently, though they drank homemade vodka instead and were comfortable sitting on cushions. Everyone celebrated this newfound freedom in whatever way made sense to their lives. Trendy teenagers hung disco balls over their parties. Shiny, exposed, pedicured toes. Political arguments in the backseats of taxis. Young families picnicking with music in the Alborz foothills. Small freedoms, admittedly, that appeared inconsequential from the outside, but here they were felt deeply. They were the difference between suffocating, and breathing very, very heavily.

As Kimia and I drove home that night, careening down the wide expressway that connected north Tehran to downtown, I wondered how many more of such parties I could stand. All the laconic airs, the premeditated exposure of so much flesh. It hadn't been a birthday party so much as a pushing and shoving match with the Islamic Republic; a cultural rebellion waged indoors against the regime's rigid codes of behavior. Those codes banned young men and women from interacting casually together, attending soccer matches, studying at the library.

When they were finally permitted a few free hours in each other's company, they scarcely knew what to do, or how to behave. They had never developed a sense of what normal behavior between the sexes looked like; not only were they lacking a template, they found the prospect of normality unsatisfying. Instead, they sought to contrast the oppressive morality outside with amplified decadence behind closed doors, staking out their personal lives as the one realm in which they could define their individuality, and exercise their free will. The realm where the system tried to intrude, but ultimately could not control. The Islamic Republic does not control me; see it in the layers of makeup I apply to my face, the tightness of my jeans, the wantonness of my sex life, the Ecstasy I drop.

⁂

One indolent, quiet Friday afternoon, after lunch, my flamboyant Aunt Khaleh Zahra gazed with such hostility at the tea Khadijeh Khanoum was serving us that I suggested we go to a nearby bakery for cappuccino instead. We walked up Villa Street, past the closed government buildings and handicrafts shops, talking about stocks. For all her eccentricity, Khaleh Zahra was a financial wizard who, even when her life was falling apart, stayed up all night trading online with steely alertness. Halfway up the street, her gauzy, sky-blue scarf slid off her head, leaving her hair fully exposed, its wine-colored streaks glinting alarmingly in the sun.

She didn't miss a step, or pause in her meditation, which centered, as usual, on the Islamic Republic's backwardness. Azadeh jan, in the U.S. people are wearing computers the size of a phone on their belts, she said, taking longer strides. Inches matter in terms of how small you can get a piece of technology—a camera the size of your palm. Here they care how many square inches of your hair peeks out under your veil, how many inches of ankle you expose in sandals. I couldn't concentrate on a word she was saying. Her bare head might as well have been a bare breast. The effect would have been the same.

Khaleh Zahra had taken permissiveness to a new heights, turning her Islamic covering into lingerie. She deliberately chose sheer fabrics edged in lace, and they resembled nothing more than delicate slips. The effect was infinitely more alluring and seductive than a pair of shorts and tight T-shirt could ever have been. And now, now she was going without a head scarf entirely. This was as unthinkable as showing one's face in the Taliban's Afghanistan. One probably wouldn't be stoned to death, but nothing could be more transgressive. I was unnerved but stayed silent. People had different thresholds for the Islamic Republic in general, and the veil in particular. Some people were so distracted by other ideas and thoughts, they stopped noticing. Some felt it like a radioactive hood, all day, every day. Khaleh Zahra fell in the latter camp.

She was clearly trying to say something, either to herself or to Iran, and it wasn't my place to obstruct that message. So I just keep walking, staring ahead as though the gleaming, bare head-breast at my side was the most ordinary thing in the world. As people passed on the sidewalk, they shot *me* disapproving glances, assuming that she didn't notice (knowing and not caring being inconceivable), and that I was the one at fault for not telling her.

This is how the regime eased its burden of repression: by conditioning people to police one another. If you had conducted a national referendum that very day, the vast majority of Iranians—men and women alike— would have voted to abolish the mandatory veil. But accustomed to being watched in public, people internalized the minding gaze of the regime, and turned it back outward. When we arrived at the coffee shop, she mercifully pulled it back, with a quick, disdainful flick of her wrist.

Our household was showing unmistakable signs of strain. Had I been paying attention, I should have noticed earlier, but I had been detached for weeks. The days slipped by more easily when I blurred my vision, obscuring the details. I knew I had grown distant, and assumed that's why Khaleh Zahra exploited my runs for conversation. The groaning whir of the treadmill—not the world's most advanced machine—was her cue, and she wound her way up the staircase, lay sideways on the sofa by the window, lit a cigarette, and talked and talked.

I think, like me, she yearned to articulate herself in English, to someone besides Kimia, in conversations that went beyond "You're grounded" and "I hate you." It didn't matter that I was panting, sweaty, and unable to respond, because mostly she needed to inhabit her mind in English, release all that emotional pressure with the outlet of words. Twice, going downstairs for a glass of water in the middle of the night, I had found her reclined on the couch, in her bra and underwear, eating ice cream cake from the box. Want some? Sit down! What's new? she asked me brightly, waving her fork in the air, as I rubbed the sleep from my eyes.

Kimia finally alerted me to the urgency of the situation when she arrived home from school one day in tears. *Everyone* is talking about me, and it's *all* her fault, she hiccuped. She was becoming known around school as the girl with the crazy mother who refuses to wear the veil. Besides being mortifying, she explained, it is dangerous. A few days ago an enraged driver chased them through traffic, and got out of his car at a traffic light, waving his arms menacingly, all because of Khaleh Zahra's uncovered head. Really? I asked curiously. Does she not wear it all, or just way, way back? Around her shoulders, she said. What is *up* with that? Whose mother does that?

A few days later Khaleh Zahra announced they were moving. To Connecticut. Why Connecticut? Because I don't know anyone there, she replied cryptically, flinging cookie cutters and cases of salon shampoo into giant cartons. She never explained what had drawn her back to Iran, but I had watched her struggle, swimming upstream against a current far stronger than her determination.

She was accustomed, after decades in the West, to controlling society's perception of her life. In California, she could transform herself from Cruella de Ville of Tiburon one year to a Palo Alto soccer mom the next. Here, in the lap of a culture liberal with affection but stingy with tolerance, she had had no such freedom. For my part, I had chosen to dwell on their sense of alienation here, rather than my own, and their day of reckoning arrived with implications for all of us. Khaleh Zahra was a fuller synthesis of Iranian and American than I could ever hope to be; the decades of her life had been neatly divided between the two worlds. With her leaving, the questions hung in the air: Could I last? Was my Iranian side developed enough to sustain the compromises of life here?

But as I sat on the floor cross-legged, watching them pack, I wondered whether I was even posing those questions properly. Now that I had met actually existing Iran, the Iran of the Islamic Republic, the question of Iranian identity had become infinitely more complex. That Khaleh Zahra could not cope with life in the Islamic Republic did not mean she could not have coped with a different Iran, a place more tolerant of privacy, and private life. Amidst all this haze, one thing was apparent.

All of us, Khaleh Zahra, Kimia, and I, had arrived in Tehran as Iranians of the imagination. We had Iranian identities, but they were formed by our memories and the Farsi-speaking parts of our soul—the part that responded, with years of accumulated references, when someone said "love" to us in Farsi, our first language of affection. But we could not navigate the Tehran of today, or share in the collective consciousness of the Iranians who never left.

Khaleh Zahra and Kimia's departure reopened a wound in Pedar Joon. Before their return, he had spent twenty years reconciling himself to a life away from four of his five children. In his old age, he had grown dependent on their presence quickly, and felt more acutely the pain of its being wrenched away. Empty of half its inhabitants, certainly the louder half, the house took on the feel of an abandoned fort. Khadijeh Khanoum was liberated from cooking for PJ, but her relief was short-lived, as Pedar Joon became more crotchety and demanding, buzzing her quarters at all hours with the little electronic button near his bed. Eventually, he moved his quarters downstairs, to avoid the daily ascents and descents that grew more labored.

For a man well into his nineties, his mind was impressively alert. He needed less and less sleep at night and assumed only sloth kept the rest of us in bed past five A.M. A few nights after Zahra and Kimia left, he floated into my room at four A.M., wearing blue striped pajamas and an angelic smile, and put a plate of Danish pastry on my desk. He took a rusted Swiss army knife out of his pocket, and put that next to the pastry for *yadegari*, keepsake, and floated back out. After he left I couldn't fall asleep again, and padded downstairs in my slippers to look through the stack of discarded old photos and papers in the living room.

I spread the faded images into a fan, and through the dim moonlight that peeked through the window, pulled out my favorite photo. It was of me and four of my cousins, sitting on the steps of this house, the summer I visited Iran as child. I wondered what my personality would have been like if the small girl staring back at me from the picture had never left. I tried to imagine her as a twenty-four-year-old woman, her worries and dreams and sensibilities. As I sketched her in my mind, filling in her thoughts, I saw so clearly that she was not me. Her challenges would have been different than mine; other strings would pull at her heart. She was the woman I came here thinking I was, and at that moment, sitting cross-legged on the floor of the dusty, dark living room, I knew better at last.

⚓

I practiced one main ritual of normalcy in Iran. Ally McBeal night. Every Wednesday, my Australian friends, diplomats from the embassy, gathered a group over to have drinks, chatter about everything and nothing, and watch the show, taped off of satellite cable. In truth, I disliked the banal adventures of this neurotic, frail heroine, but watching the show lightened my mood. Like a sedative, it dulled my sensitivity to the ugliness of the world outside—the show trials and arrests—and lifted me to a plane of yuppie American preoccupations: promotions and dating.

One night I arrived late, clenched up with anger. I had gone to a hotel, one of the old American-built chains taken over by the state and run with a Soviet-style disregard for service or quality, to interview a visiting delegation of Hamas, the Palestinian militant group. I walked into the lobby, called the elevator, and punched the number for my floor. As the doors were closing, a hotel employee rushed over and jammed his foot to keep them open. Women, he said in a scathing voice, are not allowed to enter hotel rooms. Can you please get out?

I explained to him that I had an interview with a guest, and that there were other journalists upstairs already. He wouldn't budge, and spoke to me with his eyes averted, as though I were a prostitute. Aren't you *ashamed* of yourself? It's *Hamas,* for God's sake, I said, and there are fifteen other people in that room. What do you think is going to happen? A spontaneous orgy? He looked away in disgust. The minutes ticked away while we waited for the hotel manager to resolve the situation.

In and of itself, the experience was wholly ordinary—being humiliated in the course of working as a female reporter eventually became unremarkable to me, like the layer of pollution that would settle on the skin by the day's end. Had I gone to my aunt and uncle's, my bitter retelling of the squabble would have elicited perhaps one minute of discussion. But I went to Ally McBeal night instead, ringing the doorbell softly, certain they had started already.

My friend swung the door open, a hanger in hand. *Azizam,* where have you been? At the sight of that dangling hanger, something fluttered with joy in my stomach. He knew me well, knew that I would have taken off my *roopoosh* and head scarf in the elevator. I held it out to him with two fingers and a wrinkled nose. Two minutes later I was happily ensconced in the buttery leather of their couch, warming a glass of red wine between my hands. A familiar scent wafted out from the kitchen. Ooooh, tacos.

We put off the show for another hour, as I recounted the mishap. It led us into a conversation, reflective and engaged, on how the culture of the revolution had seeped into the behavior of individuals. They let me ramble on for a bit, pulling disparate thoughts together, airing ideas. After a quarter of an hour, my indignation evaporated, and I saw that it was for precisely this I had come. Not for the familiarity of American television and tacos, but to speak with people who, like me, needed and wanted to talk about Iran, and in English.

For my relatives and friends, the aspects of Iranian reality that I found fascinating—fatigue with Islam, political cynicism, flouting authority—were routine. They knew the regime wasn't held together by a devotion to revolutionary Islam, but a clique of corrupt clerics driven by messianic ideology and greed. The failure of the revolution, the bankruptcy of its ideology, was the backdrop of daily life, manifested in state newspapers left in unread piles at the newsstand, official newscasts no one watched. For those who lived these realities, they were foregone conclusions, too obvious to discuss.

But for me, new to all of this, spinning in outrage, there was nothing I needed more than to talk it all through, to release the anger in English, so that it did not stay welled up inside me. It was part of a building awareness that I had stepped into this Iran partly as an Iranian, reading the grinds of coffee cups, burning *esfand* to ward away the evil eye, but also as an American, constricted by the absence of horizons (of so many sorts), genuinely shocked by the grim ordinariness of violence and lies.

Three years later, when friends or relatives would visit, I would see my then self reflected in them, agog at the grotesque propaganda that I had, by that time, come also to take for granted. And there was something else too, besides the need to narrate this journey in both languages. Inside the co-coon of their apartment, the very act of speaking English invoked a sense of freedom. It was the language in which I had fought many battles, but it was also the language of an alternate existence in which I had never felt fear. It was unpolluted by the brutality of the things I heard and spoke about in Farsi, like arrests of activists and the killings of dissidents. Of course I wrote about them in English, but exported across the border of another language, their horror was somehow muted.

Before I moved to Tehran, all of my relationships that were conducted in Farsi were either with family members who had known me since I was small, or with Iranians who also spoke English, and didn't mind if I sprinkled my Farsi liberally with English words and expressions, or vice versa. You speak kitchen Farsi, a friend told me dismissively. He was right. Gossiping with family and whining to my parents had required no special fluency, and left me ill-equipped to hold abstract conversations with the highly literate.

Here, the fusion of Farsi and English that we spoke in California was deemed vulgar and pretentious, an affectation associated with Iranians who left the country for six months and forever after used lots of English words to remind everyone they had been abroad. *Oghdeyih* people, with a complex about not being worldly or Western enough. I resolved to immediately banish all English terms from my Farsi, and in the process realized that without English, I, as I knew myself, ceased to exist.

If more than a few days went by without a single conversation in English, my spirits shriveled. Internal dialogue had become a bad habit. Stop making faces Azadeh, Khaleh Farzi admonished, smoothing my forehead with her cool fingers, you'll give yourself wrinkles. I disliked myself in Farsi. I couldn't debate philosophy, flirt with any originality, recount jokes properly, or spar in a formal interview. Unable to paint my personality with words, I came across blank, an empty white canvas.

The poverty of my Farsi definitively revealed my immaculate Iranian character to be a sham. Politically, though, I felt tainted by having an American side. A reactionary anti-Americanism reigned in the Arab circles I still moved in, as I worked around the region. One was expected to distance oneself as much as possible from the Zionist infidels, and being excessively American was the social equivalent of having a harelip.

People who were right-handed could learn to write with the left, I thought, so why should I not be able to recast my personality in Farsi? Only by being free and effortless in both languages, I decided, could I discover in which direction my true nature leaned. From the moment I arrived at this conclusion, I dedicated my existence to a sole purpose: learning Farsi properly. This desperation fueled many sleepless nights spent with a Farsi-English dictionary and a stack of newspapers, with cigarettes, and *lavashak*, Persian fruit roll-up, strewn about.

Assessing my existential Iranian versus Americanness was also a parlor game for distant relatives. It was a favorite of Mehri Khanoum, a relative from Pedar Joon's hometown of Mashad, who used our house as a hotel during trips to Tehran. This obese, distant cousin was a saccharine-coated authoritarian and commandeered the kitchen from the housekeeper, Khadijeh Khanoum, during her visits. She considered it inappropriate for one member of the family to consume a different meal from what everyone else was eating. What was wrong with collective fare? Clearly, the demand of a spoiled American, I overheard her whispering in indignant tones. After a five-second delay, I realized she meant me.

At lunch she would proudly place a steaming platter of something or other drenched in oil on the table, and wait expectantly for everyone to coo over how wonderful it was. When I reached for the watermelon that we were only meant to have before lunch, she shook her head, and heaped a pyramid of glistening rice on her plate. I'm sure it's delicious, I said politely, but I'll go into a coma eating all that rice, and I have an interview later.

She gave me a withering look, and crossed her ample arms over her chest. Have it your way, Ms. Los Angeles. But your husband will never enjoy eating with you, if you keep this up. In *northern California,* where I'm from, Mehri Khanoum, there is a service called takeout, which I'm sure my husband will be proficient at using. Saying that made me feel slightly better, but then I felt even more irritated for being provoked into discussion of an imaginary spouse.

After that, she began pilfering my energy bars from the hidden drawer in the kitchen, in what was a serious escalation of conflict. I considered sticking all the fruit knives in an onion, as retaliation, but then poor Pedar Joon would also have to eat onion-perfumed melon. Instead, I emailed my father in California to grumble about this egregious relative, with whom I could not believe we shared genetic matter. He, enemy of Persian etiquette, called up the house and told her to stop stealing what he sensitively called my "special foods," as though I were a diabetic.

From that day on, we didn't say very much to each other, apart from a cold good morning. The day she left, loading an ice-chest full of snacks for the trip back to Mashad (five hours, though she was packing food for a week), she perked her face into a smile, for the benefit of Pedar Joon, who was standing nearby, and asked me when I would be visiting them. This was *tarof,* the Persian practice of saying elaborate things you don't fully mean to keep up the pretense of enjoying sparkling, warm social relations with everyone.

Definitely soon, I said, I hear there're tons of prostitutes around the shrine. I'm dying to do a story on religious pilgrimage and prostitution. She got into the car with a huff and a puff, and I could almost hear her complain to her husband as they drove away, Thank *God* we didn't raise our children in Los Angeles.

Now I can look back, and see Mehri's food terrorism for what it was, a last-stop defense against the decline of tradition; the set mealtimes, and shared meals, were a ritual that symbolized a whole way of life that honored and gave her influence as a matron. My insistence on eating separately was a way of staking my own bit of power in a system that reminded me incessantly ("Don't you want to get married? . . . What is this always work work work? . . . Your expectations are too high. . . . There can be no alliances without allowances!") that as an unmarried young woman, I was a partial failure, without status. But at the time, it didn't seem nearly so obvious. Instead, my tremulous Iranian within shook, and I experienced such criticism as a crushing assessment of me as other, as American.

CHAPTER FOUR

My Country Is Sick

Our tears are sweet, our laughter venomous,
We're pleased when sad, and sad when pleased
We have broken every stalk, like a wind in the garden
We have picked clean the vine's candelabra,
And if we found a tree, still standing, defiantly,
We cut its branches, we pulled it up by the roots.

—SIMIN BEHBEHANI

Since low-grade depression was a national epidemic, most Iranians who were not opium addicts or alcoholics had some expertise in spiritual restoratives. A generation ago, people turned to religious gatherings and prayer rituals for serenity, but in modern-day Iran, it had become commonplace to keep Islam at arm's length. Unintentionally, the Islamic Republic had redirected the spirituality of a wide swath of Iranians toward the esoteric and the mystical.

One afternoon, I stopped by a friend's house to get the address of a homeopathic healer, famed for his herbal remedies. Tandiss, a young woman about my own age, paused as she cleared away the crumbs from a plate of pistachio-dense, flower-infused baklava we had just polished off with our tea. "Do you want to meditate?" she asked me, hovering near the table. "Not really, but you go ahead," I said, fingering the soft cotton of her saffron-colored, Indian tunic.

Tandiss and her mother were just back from India, where they had gone to visit the ashram of a Hindu guru/mystic named Sai Baba, in a place called Shirdi outside Bombay. Each time I saw Sai Baba literature or a photo on someone else's mantelpiece, I clapped my hands together and exclaimed at the coincidence ("You follow Sai Baba, too?!"), until I discovered that Eastern spirituality was a widespread trend among the middle class as well as the educated elite.

The doorbell rang, and I raced to answer it, before it rang again and interrupted the meditating Tandiss. It was my cousin, picking me up for lunch. "Shhhhh," I hissed, opening the door. "Tandiss is with the guru." He tiptoed in, giving me a dirty look. Kami also followed Sai Baba and didn't appreciate being teased about "Guruji." He too had visited the ashram outside Bombay ("Even heads of state were kissing his feet") and returned with stories of Sai Baba's miraculous feats. Apparently, with nothing more than his touch, gaze, and blazing internal holiness, Sai Baba had: turned dirt into gold dust, healed lepers, moved a piece of paper across the table, cured blindness, banished tuberculosis from lungs, and rid a village of cholera. Mocking my cousins' faith in Guruji's miracles, I reminded myself, was insensitive. They respected Sai Baba, and respect was an important cornerstone of faith.

It was impossible to respect the Islamic Republic, and for many Iranians, contempt for the system tainted their traditional esteem for Islam. Everyone agreed that official Islam was a perversion, but this rational recognition didn't preclude them from emotionally wanting to distance themselves from things clerical and Islamic altogether.

People relished making their distaste for Islam—the tool of their subjugation—and its self-proclaimed custodians—their oppressors—known. When I lived downtown with my grandfather, our alley was right off a busy street, and I took public taxis frequently. Even at unrushed midday, when the taxis were half full, drivers took a special pleasure in ignoring clerics standing in turbans and robes trying valiantly to hail a cab. They were pariahs, an untouchable class. Clerical robes had come to symbolize one thing: corruption.

Eastern spirituality, with its internally directed, pacifist sensibility, was the ideal antidote to the militant, invasive brand of Shiite Islam imposed by the regime. And that is the story of how Iranian housewives, unadventurous by nature, began turning East, rather than toward Mecca, to nurture their belief in a higher power.

*

Since the sixteenth century, the era of the Safavids, the dynasty that instituted Shiism as the state religion of then Persia, the clergy have wielded significant influence over internal affairs. Though they never formally took charge until the revolution, their intimate relations with pious, powerful merchants, *bazaaris,* and moral authority at Friday prayers made them a major political force for centuries. Consecutive governments had been careful to accommodate the mullahs, or at least disguise their efforts to curtail clerical authority.

Resistance to injustice is the central theme of Shiite Islam, and during times of political unrest or oppression, clerics traditionally raised their voices against the imperial or local oppressor of the moment. In times of chaos, when emotions flared and events spiraled, few could calm or incite masses of Iranians like the mullahs, who spoke in the familiar tones of, and on behalf of, ordinary people.

Though there was a long tradition of mocking the clergy for gluttony and sloth, they were at heart venerated by traditional Iranians. Even my grandmother in California, sitting upon the ruins of a family dispersed and dispossessed by a clerical revolution, had refused to curse Khomeini, who like it or not was still an ayatollah. Loath to destabilize his government by alienating the mosque, the Shah of Iran, like his father and predecessor Reza Shah, had been reluctant to modernize and secularize Iran at the same time, as Mustafa Kamal Ataturk had done in nearby Turkey.

Raised on this history at home, and again at university, I chronically underestimated the decline of religiosity evident all around me in Tehran. Every branch on both sides of my family is ardently secular, and if the revolution taught us anything, it was not to assume that two-thirds of Iranian society felt and thought as we did.

Eventually, though, I came to see how two decades of mismanagement by mullahs had perhaps definitively squashed the clerics' historical prestige. Most societies that have flirted with Islamic politics, where religious parties win votes in elections, have not had the chance to watch their Islamist crush play itself out. A full and lasting conversion to secularism could only be reached after clerics were permitted to rise to power—as in Iran and Afghanistan—and make a gigantic mess of things. History had shown that this, ultimately, was the only way to test and discard the religious model.

Though Iranians alternately loathed and pitied themselves for their ill-fated revolution, they had at least come full circle. A secular government, a full separation between mosque and state, they were able to conclude, was the only answer. This conviction could be traced informally through voting records. Politicians who talked about a more accountable, less ideological government roundly won elections. But it was such a palpable truth, so implicit and freely discussed, that it scarcely required documentation. I absorbed it fully on my first visit to Qom, the power capital of the mullahs, the seat from where Khomeini ruled Iran.

Qom, a somber, dusty city 120 km south of Tehran, is the Vatican of the Islamic theocracy. Most Iranians—who derisively called it a "mullah factory"—did not bother to visit, and thought of it only as the place where *sohan,* a buttery brittle of pistachios and saffron, originates. As a child, I thought the name of the city meant "gham," the Farsi word for gloom, and heard it discussed as the epicenter of clerical evil, the Death Star from which the mullahs plotted their takeover of Iran.

When I told Khaleh Farzi I was going there with Scott, the *Time* magazine correspondent, to talk to dissident clerics who opposed the Islamic regime, her face pinched with worry. Hamid, she's going to Qom, she called out to my uncle. What if they steal her? Promise you'll head back before sunset!

I pulled my inkiest, roomiest *roopoosh* out of the back of the closet for ironing, and wondered whether I was sick, looking forward to a trip that should instill a normal person with dread. I wasn't, I decided. It was actually a very positive sign. It meant I preferred the distraction of work (fat clerics and all) to staying home all day feeling sorry for myself. The pace of a weekly magazine meant the last three days of our production week were a flurry of activity, and the first two or three of the next week a dead zone, too early to predict or begin chasing the next issue's news. Inevitably, these days at home meant lying on the couch with a bowl of cherries watching Oprah on satellite television, then feeling great remorse for such indolence, when I could have been interviewing freedom-fighting student activists or visiting my father's high school or learning how to make baklava, or some other edifying activity.

So often, my days off didn't measure up to the lofty, soul-enriching life I had expected to live in Iran, and this was depressing enough that it made me stop taking days off altogether. If a story demanded four interviews, I did ten. I typed up my handwritten notes, printed them out, and filed them with pretty page markers. Then I made a thimble of Turkish coffee, sat down to read the papers, and made a list (typed with bullet points) of more story ideas. Work had no equal as a balm to anxiety. I even took my laptop to family lunches, where relatives looked at me pityingly and remarked that American journalism was really a form of indentured servitude. Then they asked for the hundredth time why I didn't become a broadcast journalist (better for finding a husband), as though newspapers were pastures for unattractive reporters who didn't make the grade aesthetically for television.

No, Qom was an excellent idea. Between the drive, the reporting, and the filing of notes, it would consume two whole days.

The road from Tehran was flat and dusty, as was the city, which from the distance appeared like a few bumps in the desert, with splinters poking out into the sky. If a world beyond existed, there was little evidence to prove it—no colors, just lots and lots of mosques.

On this winter afternoon, Qom seemed very much an antique land, its streets filled with turbaned clerics of all ethnicities, carrying religious texts under their arms, as they had for centuries. But the debates inside those brown walls were current—secularism, democracy, Shiite militancy and jurisprudence. Unlike most other parts of the Middle East I had traveled, where hardly anything of note was debated in public, let alone Islam, in Qom the clerics were busy fighting about the soul of the religion, and the future of the Islamic Republic.

Many believed that Iran would only survive as an Islamic Republic if it embraced a democratic tradition of Islam, one that tolerated political dissent and freedom of speech, and granted full rights to women. They said that over the years Iran had swayed too far into the realm of Islamic theocracy, and that it should be returned to the original vision of a true Republic, loosely based on the spirit of Islam, but functioning as a modern democracy. The roots of all these debates extended into Shiite political and religious philosophy, and the rather central question of whether rulers should derive their authority from God, or the electoral mandate of citizens.

We visited one of the city's computer centers, elaborate places designed by the clerics to prove that Islam's seventh-century ideology can coexist with modernity. The government loved to promote the centers, and every foreign journalist who visited Qom was dragged through one of the fluorescent-lit rooms where turbaned clerics stared at screens and listlessly clicked away at mice. Scott wanted to know if Qom's clerics were trying to export Shia revolution by CD-ROM. The immense cleric who was showing us his archive of *hadith* was puzzled by the question and asked me to repeat it.

"So, are you trying to export revolution by doing this?"

For a minute he just looked at me, squinting through the fleshy folds of his sleepy eyes. He was clearly not used to sitting up straight. His work, as he might say, taxed the mind, not the body. My father always said clerics were the laziest species on earth. But this one in particular, oozing out of his chair like Jabba the Hut, one slipper hanging off his toe, seemed to prove him right. The thought of exporting anything at all, let alone revolution, seemed to tire him.

I tried again.

"Er, my colleague here would like to know, if perhaps these tools could ever be, or do you conceive them as possibly ever being, helpful in the export of the Shia Revolution."

"Um, no, they're just for Muslims to study with. So, you said you live in Cairo?"

"No, he says no exporting going on," I told Scott in English and turned to hiss at the cleric, in Farsi: "No, I *used* to live in Cairo."

"Because I come to Cairo occasionally for conferences. Maybe I could call you? Do you have a phone number?"

"What's he saying?" demanded Scott, pen poised above his notebook.

"Oh, the same thing. That these are study tools for the faithful."

The cleric walked us to the door, readjusting the black turban—which marked him as a direct descendant of the Prophet Mohammad—along the way. "Did you say you live all alone in Cairo? No family there or anything?"

I brought my scandalized account of this encounter to the dinner table that night. My aunt and uncle both snorted with laughter, as they typically did when I came home and breathlessly pronounced an insight that was, apparently, a cultural platitude. My father had taught me that clerics were lazy; more specifically, that they were unsuited to run a country because their work kept them in seminaries, sipping tea in robes, and that sort of languid profession did not lend itself to the more challenging task of administering a government. Convinced their worst sin was sloth, I had not assumed they were equally lecherous. One really could not have a proper conversation with a cleric. They were absurd. A one-hour interview with a mullah inevitably cycled like so:

First fifteen minutes: Gaze averted, stares at own feet, wall, space, anywhere but two-foot radius around opposing female.

Second fifteen minutes: Slowly casts glances in direction of head and talking voice.

Third fifteen minutes: Makes eye contact and conducts normal conversation.

Last fifteen minutes: Begins making googooly eyes, smiling in impious fashion, and requesting one's mobile phone number.

I didn't understand why they did this with me, since they are supposed to favor round women and fair women, and I was neither. Some actually complained about this, with mock concern for my health ("Miss Moaveni, have you been ill? You've lost so much weight. . . . Don't you like Iranian food?"). How they could detect a body underneath the billowing tent I wore, let alone its fluctuations, was beyond me. I asked Khaleh Farzi, who explained that clerics had x-ray vision. That was why they didn't mind keeping women veiled.

It was only over time, after repeated exposure to womanizing clerics, clerics who stole from the state and built financial empires, who ordered assassinations like gangsters, who gave Friday sermons attacking poodles, that I came to understand the virulence of my father and my uncle's hate for the Iranian clergy. Perhaps their flaws were no greater than those of ordinary mortals, but ordinary mortals did not claim divine right to rule, ineptly, over seventy million people. As the gravity of the Islamic Republic's hypocrisy revealed itself, I came to the slow, shocking realization that Iranian society was sick. Not in a facetious, sloganny way, exaggerating the extent of culture wars and social tensions, but truly *sick*. The Iran I had found was spiritually and psychologically wrecked, and it was appalling.

★

By winter, when Ramadan, the month of fasting, rolled around, I had no idea what to expect from this nation of ambivalent Muslims. During its first week, the most active student organization organized a pre-*iftar* (breaking of the fast) lecture at a university in central Tehran. Undeterred by the chill, and the oppressive, gray sky, the students huddled in patient bunches outside the main auditorium, waiting for the speakers to arrive.

In the several months that had passed since the pro-reform parliament convened in the middle of 2000, the reformists had suffered setback after setback. The hard-line judiciary had shut down at least twenty-five independent newspapers and magazines, under the pretext that their strident criticism of the ruling clergy jeopardized national security. Several key reformist intellectuals had been dragged before the court on similarly empty charges and sentenced to lengthy prison terms for their ideas.

The already fractured coalition of reformists was in full disarray, and the student movement was equally split about how to proceed. Many believed the reformists were moving too cautiously, and accused them of abandoning their vision for sweeping change (full civil and political rights) in favor of micro-progress (a few degrees less of international isolation). They too, by that point, had concluded that no real progress could be achieved without severing the mosque from the state. But with fundamentalist mullahs heading the judiciary, the armed forces, and state institutions, they saw no way of realistically moving this agenda forward.

The film being screened at the university was produced by the most radical student organization, whose members had started calling on President Khatami to resign. It was simply a stark, silent sequence of footage: vigilantes attacking student meetings, activists being driven to prison, bustling newsrooms suspended by a judicial decree, culminating in a shot of the smiling president waving at a crowd, a beauty queen's wave, at a pageant of persecution.

After it concluded, the auditorium remained dark for the opening scenes of the play to follow. The auditorium was pitch black and silent for several moments, until a powerful flashlight cast a beam of light down the aisle. "I'm going to find you," growled a scratchy, furious voice, as the light hunted through the rows of students. Everyone stiffened visibly, unsure whether this was part of the play or an actual raid. I looked for exit signs and saw none.

Finally the light shone onto the stage, on a desk where a bookish young man sat writing. The bearer of the flashlight came into a view, a bearded, angry youth meant to represent in his speech the rhetoric of the hard-liners, and in his bearing the thuggishness of their vigilante shock troops. The play was one long encounter between a reformist journalist and the hardline vigilante—a parable for the deadlocked state of the country—and at the very end, the writer turned to face the audience. "I know this is the part in the plot where a poem should be read to give people hope . . . but the end hasn't been written yet."

And then the lights went on. That line, I thought, best captured the mood of Tehran in 2000—a fundamental uncertainty over how to view the future, whether to consider the system immune to change, or simply averse. At the sound of the call to prayer, the auditorium emptied into the university cafeteria, where long tables were set with dates, bread, and tea for the breaking of the fast.

The next afternoon, Khaleh Farzi phoned me to suggest we meet at her cousin's house for lunch. Back in California, fasters were rare—apart from the occasional old lady or depressive middle-aged woman, the community conveniently forgot Ramadan existed. But I assumed this was a Western-ized diaspora habit and had resolved to fast, naively expecting to spend the month in harmony with the daily rhythm of the millions of Iranians around me. I imagined that, as it did in Egypt, regular life would slowly grind to a standstill, interrupted by disturbed sleep and work schedules and a flurry of *iftar* socializing. Eating on the street for the duration of the month was illegal anyway, and there were psychedelically colored bill-boards celebrating the month along the expressways. But the first couple of days were disappointingly like any other. Some schools forced students to fast, but often their parents weren't, and so observance felt like a public/bu-reaucratic duty—what students had to do to get their report cards, or civil servants to pick up their salaries, unmolested. I resolved to persevere.

As it turned out, not eating all day was actually not that hard, once you got used to the idea of being a being that did not eat. But to not eat, *and* not smoke, *and* not drink coffee was a human rights abuse. There was clearly a conceptual problem with this holiday, which essentially imposed a month of calorie, caffeine, and nicotine withdrawal on a half-hearted na-tion ambivalent about its Islamic faith. Without any hint of festivity or communal spirit of fasting to brighten the days ahead, the holiday loomed like one long rehab program. I snipped at everyone, returned to bed at noon, and whimpered into the pillow, willing the sun to set.

It didn't help that *no one* else was bloody fasting. I suspected at first that my family was unrepresentative in their flip disregard for the fast. But then I began to notice that Iranians of all walks of life, of all levels of education, were sneaking sips and bites during daylight hours. The guy at the corner shop hid a cup of tea behind the cash register. My driver, Ali (a believer whose favorite holiday was *Ashoura*), took back roads and shortcuts the whole month, so he could smoke behind the wheel. The ratio of non-fasters to fasters was something like 6:1. When I realized this, my resolve faltered. What was wrong with this place? Everything was inverted. Observing Ra-madan was in bad taste, the revolutionary class (champions of the *mus-tazafin,* the oppressed) lived in white-columned mansions, and young people planned raves in chat rooms.

I calculated the hours of daylight remaining, and traffic, and figured this would work. Before leaving, I surfed the Internet for an hour in search of the ayatollah who had decreed that smoking was permissible during the fast. Tobacco was not a food substance, this enlightened cleric argued, as it was not being consumed, but inhaled. If I could just find him, I could declare myself his follower, and puff away for the rest of the month. In Shiite Islam, extremely learned clerics eventually ascend to a rank called *marja-e taqlid* (source of emulation) and develop their own set of approaches to piety and religious observance. Individual Shiites have the right to choose which *marja* (senior cleric) they wish to follow (often members of a single family will follow different *marjas*), and whose particular scriptures they will be bound by. I needed to find my nicotine-friendly *marja*, and make him my source of *taqlid* (practice). But I found nothing online but a bunch of preachy Sunni anti-Ramadan-smoking rhetoric and gave up.

I can't come to lunch, I said to Khaleh Farzi, I'm fasting, thank you very much. She laughed merrily. All this time you spend with mullahs is going to your head, she said. I gritted my teeth. What was the point of enduring this deprivation, if it wasn't even a community ritual? Why don't you just come over, take a nap, and then break your fast, she suggested.

The nap appealed, so I changed my mind and called a taxi. On the way there, a good two hours before the call to prayer, the taxi driver did the unthinkable. He *lit a cigarette,* holding it low near the gearshift so it couldn't be seen from the other cars. Ahem, agha, I cleared my throat. Aren't you fasting? No, I haven't had anything to eat all day, but it's accidental. I overslept and missed breakfast. Clearly, I concluded, in modern Iran not fasting was as authentic a tradition as fasting. And then I asked the driver for his lighter, took a protein bar out of my purse (an emergency reserve, in case I changed my mind) and split half with him, and two days into Ramadan called it a month.

Toward the end of the month, on the anniversary of the death of Imam Ali (Shiism's central figure), a handful of the non-fasters observed the one day and fasted. Ali, my driver, showed up for work that day wearing all black, and fasted grumpily. Even I fasted. Don't you have a family *iftar* to attend, I asked him, as the sky darkened and we grumped our way through the city. No, he said, me and my dad both have to work late, and my sister isn't fasting. We stopped at a grocery store, and held *iftar*—chocolate milk and cigarettes—amid the twinkling lights of the highway's stalled traffic.

As we sat on that highway, it occurred to me that ironically, and against all odds, the Islamic Republic had actually served to make a huge segment of Iranian society more tolerant. Before the revolution, millions of newly urbanized Iranians, still traditional in their provincial mindset, had been offended by the modern mores of the city-dwelling, secular classes. By taking rigid moralism to such a bloated, extreme level, the regime had shown definitively that minding thy neighbor's religiosity was an ugly way to live. During a month like Ramadan this remarkable tendency for broad-mindedness was evident. It was one of those many ways in which Iranian society was evolving from the bottom up, becoming more sophisticated and progressive, while the mullahs on top remained exactly the same.

⁜

When I went to visit Ibrahim Asgharzadeh, one of the reformist candidates who would run for president in the 2001 election, all I knew about him was that he was a former city council member and a former hostage taker. Like many reformists, he was ready to embrace democracy as long as it ensured that men like him would be at its helm. Democracy as it furthered his political future, not democracy as it benefited the country.

As we sipped tea in his elegant, modern office, his polished manner impressed me—a fusion of Bill Clinton and the Ayatollah Khomeini. The birds chirped in the park outside his window, *bagh-e ferdows,* garden of paradise, and I started imagining how someone like Asgharzadeh could guide the Islamic Republic out of its reactive, ideological posture in the world. Someone like him stood a chance, even more so than President Khatami, who at the end of the day still symbolized the clergy more than the future. Asgharzadeh's Westernized style—beige tweed blazer, frameless glasses— would appeal to young people who instinctively distrusted men in turbans, and his militant credentials would help him maneuver within the system.

As he droned on, I daydreamed about quitting journalism and becoming his press aide, writing speeches for his trips abroad. I could be the female George Stephanopolous, and he could devise a Clinton-like "third way" for Iran, assembling a team of clever, savvy young Iranians who would work exhaustive hours, trying to rehabilitate Iran's image in the world. My American side would stop being a mark of difference, but an asset to the nation. But as I translated his Farsi in my head, and jotted down notes in

English, I noticed most of his sentences began with a strange phrase: in my country. Not words one would use in conversation with another Iranian.

As we wrapped up the interview, I asked what he thought about the closing of a newspaper that morning, and he made a smooth reference to this being natural, one of the many pitfalls "his country" would face evolving into a democracy. It's hard for foreigners to understand these kinds of growing pains, he said with an oily smile, turning to the mutual friend who'd arranged our meeting. I stared at him in shock. Foreigner! How could Mr. Hostage Taker, ruiner of Iran's international reputation, call me, an upstanding citizen, a foreigner?

He turned to an oak bookshelf, and reached for a glossy book of photographs of Iran, the sort that's sold at the Tehran airport to tourists. For you, he said, beaming in the manner of a tourist guide, and holding the book outstretched. Talk about nerve, I thought. What sheer audacity. No matter how many ideological twists you take, I wanted to say, no matter how modern and reformed and improved you appear to be, you with your tweed and your spectacles, you will always be considered a thief. Iranians will never trust you, because you—not the nation—are your own first priority. People know this, and they despise you for it. Do you think people have ever forgiven you for what you did twenty-three years ago? For the people you executed on rooftops? The only reason you are in a position of influence, sitting here in this office you neither earned nor deserve, is because everyone is exhausted and terrified and can't think of a way to bring you down without turning their lives inside out all over again. You ruined my country. And you stand there, calling *me* a foreigner?

Are you ready to go, my friend Reza asked me with a quizzical look. Yes, I said, let's get out of here. His answers were way too long, weren't they, he said apologetically, as we walked out into the park. He doesn't know how to talk in sound bites yet, but don't worry, we'll get him media-trained. I looked up at the sky, tugging the ends of my veil to hold my head back.

Reza had arranged the interview, as he often did for journalists working in Iran. He worked for the Ministry of Culture in some capacity that I never quite understood, though it was clear he had to have influential friends, because functionaries of the ministry came and went, but Reza stayed put. Whatever it was that he did for the ministry was his day job, but he was an intellectual and scholar at heart and was working toward a doctorate at Tehran University. Reformist politicians and editors, like Asgharzadeh, were his friends, the liberal Islamists with whom he bantered about Western philosophy.

Reza was in his late thirties, lanky, with a brooding manner. He was obsessive about privacy, spoke in a low voice, and was convinced that intelligence agents were following his every move. Within the reformist clique, the one-time revolutionaries who had undergone a change of heart and decided they liked freedom, Reza was particularly broad-minded. Many reformists didn't really care about Western thought, they just learned the theorists (John Stuart Mill for dummies) so they could say the fashionable things and be invited to conferences in Europe.

Necessarily, their intellectual inquiry, their appreciation for notions such as the rights of the individual, was utilitarian and only marginally sincere. But Reza explored out of a deep and generous curiosity, and actually applied the logical extension of his explorations to the breadth of the world around us. He saw how the political conservatism of the Islamic regime was bound up in its fear and hostility toward women and their sexuality. He was alone in this. The other reformists refused to discuss such matters, and teased Reza like nervous schoolboys.

He offered to give me a ride home, but I said I'd rather walk. I couldn't bring myself to go back yet. My aunt would be tossing a salad for dinner, and my uncle would arrive with a stack of newspapers, eager to discuss what had been said that day by the men, like Asgharzadeh, who ran the reform movement. The movement. I wondered when we would stop calling it that, this movement that didn't move. I walked loops around the park, past the old men sitting on the benches, and the young couples on the grass. I told myself reformists, just like any other politician in this regime, had to call people like me foreigners because it was politically necessary for the future of the Islamic Republic. And it wasn't just me, I reminded myself. Secularists, nationalists, anyone who was not with them was against them. Dividing the country in this way made it easier to rule authoritatively, neatly sidestepping criticism by labeling critics anti-revolutionary or un-Iranian.

Mr. Asgharzadeh was not the first or last person to call me a foreigner. Most of the time, I smiled patiently, pretending not to care, but one day, tightly wound up from another "interview" session with Mr. X and Sleepy, my interrogators, I burst into tears at the lunch table. Why do people keep saying this to me? Khaleh Farzi looked startled, and rose immediately to pour me a cup of hot tea from the samovar. At what point, I asked her, will I stop being considered an outsider? I live here, I breathe the pollution, I suffer the bureaucracy, I carry the passport, both my parents are Iranian, and I know more about Shiism and Iranian poetry than half the girls my age.

Khaleh Farzi tried to console me. "Do you suppose people mean to hurt you, by saying such things? Look at it from their perspective. They think all the exceptional people have left. Can you see it's almost a compliment?" But I refused to understand. If I felt alienated in America—considered to be from an imagined land of veils, harems, suicide bombers, and wrathful ayatollahs—the only fair compensation was that somewhere else I would be ordinary, just like everyone else.

The day before, my photojournalist friend Dariush and I had argued bitterly over foreignness. Since our neuroses complemented each other with perfect, destructive harmony, we managed to argue grievously over nearly everything, but our most serious confrontations were over Iran. I knew when Dariush called me a foreigner there was no subtle compliment lurking behind this categorization. Don't demand what's not yours, he told me peevishly. You weren't here during the war, when Iraqi warplanes were flying over Tehran. You didn't have to run into bomb shelters, or duck when windows shattered, or call around to see if your relatives and friends were alive, the mornings after. You don't know what we *endured*. So don't show up here and start calling yourself Iranian.

Stop being such a victim, I hissed back. So there were occasional bombing raids. Do you think you're the first people to deal with war? What if you were Lebanese? In Beirut, the fighting was *street to street*. You had to pass through ground combat zones to get to school.

Worried by the noontime outburst, my long silences, and my growing tendency to disappear for afternoons without explanation, Khaleh Farzi asked me to stay the night. The evening wore on, and time slowed to drips, as we shuffled through the newspapers, and watched a German travel show on mute. Time behaved capriciously in Tehran. Sometimes successive days would click past each other rapidly. Sometimes the minutes and hours seemed to swell, their passage slowed by the blurring sameness of cloistered days inside.

Khaleh Farzi lived in the leafy neighborhood of Elahieh, in the northern half of Tehran called Shemroon. Tall trees shaded the narrow streets, still lined with graceful two-story villa-homes, surrounded by gardens and lattice or stone walls. A few blocks away, there was hidden an old house with an expansive garden where people gathered on summer nights for my most beloved pastime—smoking *ghalyoon*, a water pipe filled with fruit-scented tobacco. On summer evenings, an accordion player wound his way through the alleys, intoning mournful old songs to the rich, organ-like wails of his instrument.

That night, as I lay awake with my regular nocturnal companion, the dictionary, I thought I heard noises outside the window—a suspicious cacophony of barking dogs, banging drawers, and moans that began around one or two A.M. Khaleh Farzi had mentioned hearing odd sounds in the middle of the night before, but her husband and I had both ignored her, dismissing what seemed just another grievance to level against the Starbucks-lacking Islamic Republic. We had discussed the noises one morning over breakfast, after Khaleh Farzi, convinced of her own hearing, had proceeded to investigate. She began by asking the gardener next door to whom the old, deserted house belonged, and returned with eyes sparkling with bemused mortification.

"Azi, can you believe it, his son is the Iranian consul in *Milan*, . . . the son . . . of a gardener. . . . Milan! . . . His wife asked me to stay for tea. . . . She was really nice, poor woman, . . . but I said no." Snootiness momentarily distracted her from the haunted house next door. "Do you think his wife wears *chador* on the streets of Milan?" she continued, envisioning the consul's wife tripping down the Via Montenapoleone, past the couture houses, in house slippers and a *chador* smelling of stew.

"But what about the house?" I asked.

"Oh, the house. It's in the hands of the Ministry of Intelligence."

Like many of the old villas still standing in Tehran, the house had been confiscated from its owners during the revolution and was now officially owned by the regime. Khaleh Farzi made it her business to know exactly who the old houses in the neighborhood had once belonged to, and could give expert, narrated walking tours ("Here lived the under-secretary to the ministry of petroleum . . . "). She acquired such information by approaching whoever happened to be outside during her daily walks, and brightly asking, "Excuse me, who was this house stolen from?" One day, she posed the question, rather unwisely, to a man quite clearly pious, and quite clearly not a descendant of the original owners. He screamed at her. "*Stolen?* What do you mean *stolen?* This house was *liberated,* and we'll keep on liberating and liberating until we liberate them *all!*"

In the early months of that year, 2000, an investigative journalist writing for reformist newspapers was slowly revealing the details of an important series of murders. Two years ago, four dissident intellectuals had been brutally killed. The Ministry of Intelligence, the public was now learning, had sent death squads that butchered them in their homes. The journalist had also disclosed that it was in the old houses of north Tehran, in the hands of the ministry, where the torture sessions, forced recantations, and planning sessions behind these schemes were conducted.

The dictionary fell closed, as I recalled this conversation and tried to pretend I heard only silence. My heart jumped into my chest, as the door to my room creaked open. Khaleh Farzi, looking like a schoolgirl in her flannel nightdress, stuck her bobbed head in. "Azi, pssst, get up and come to the window, I think they're torturing someone," she whispered.

"Er . . . no . . . let's just leave it." I turned to my other side, and stared down at the knots of the carpet.

"No really, come," she insisted. And so I relented, climbing out of bed, and following her to the windowsill, where we perched, peering through the thin white iron bars, over the overgrown weeds, into the backyard of the house.

The barks of the dog were unusual—frantic and angry—and through the dimly lit, dirty window came long, sustained moans, the unmistakable sounds of a human being in pain. Khaleh Farzi stared at me, smug and horrified: "See, didn't I tell you . . . ? I told you it was haunted, . . . that it was a government safe house." I tried desperately to control the fear sloshing inside me, and I came to speak, but my tongue was paralyzed, as in dreams where one is being murdered, but cannot scream.

"We have to call 911," I spluttered, grasping about in the dark for the rotary phone. "Hah! The police? Listen to you! They're already there. Those *are* the police," she said triumphantly, all her resentment unhappily avenged by that hopeless moment when we faced the grim possibilities: a) we were mad and paranoid; b) next door a man was being tortured, or dealt with cruelly, with the sanction of the state; c) if b, then it must perforce go unnamed, uninvestigated, untold. It was unreal, unnerving. We released our tight knuckles from the window, and returned to my bed. Staring at the ceiling, we clasped each other's hands, and lay silent until the barking ceased, the sun rose, and we finally fell asleep.

After that night, I began to turn inward, doing most of my interviews over the phone, relying on journalist friends to alert me when important news broke. The weight of the world outside, on top of my own interior interrogations, threatened to overwhelm me. Categories of experience that had previously existed clearly in my mind—like "unbearable," "unacceptable"—lost their meaning, when everyday I saw the unbearable being borne, the unacceptable being accepted. Concepts that had previously obsessed me, like East and West, became so intricate and layered that they inflated into swollen constructs, and floated away.

It wasn't just that one incident at Khaleh Farzi's, it was the accumulation of layers of strain. The stories I wrote about most frequently—newspaper closures, arrests, show trials, crackdowns—were pockmarked with sadness of the sort that lingered with me always. My interrogators, Mr. X and Mr. Sleepy, were a shadowy, unnerving presence in the backdrop of my life. Tehran was difficult, a city that like a minefield demanded a constant, intense vigilance, and I wasn't so set on denying that anymore.

That summer, as the dry, heavy heat descended on central Tehran, I decided I couldn't live with Pedar Joon anymore. The BBC office, where I had a desk and worked out of, was a nearly one-hour commute each day during rush hour. Most days, after sorting through the newspapers and talking to sources on the phone, I moved about the city—attending student demonstrations at universities and reformist lectures or stopping by a newspaper that was about to be shut down. Half my days were already spent in the car. When time came to make evening plans, I contemplated the long trek back to north Tehran and usually opted to stay home. Since I was already in my hermit phase without the added excuse of traffic, and since socializing at Pedar Joon's wasn't comfortable for anyone involved, getting my own place seemed like a good idea all around.

Once I calmed Pedar Joon's concerns about my living alone, as well as my ongoing spinsterhood (no longer considered a joke, but a serious affliction) I moved to a cozy one-bedroom apartment in Kamranieh. There were two reasons why I chose it. First, it had a magnificent, oak-lined walk-in closet, and to me ample closet space equaled fabulous apartment. Second, the bathroom had atmosphere. Deep tub, antique turquoise tiles, soft lighting.

But my bitter sense of displacement followed me everywhere, to the bazaar, in the expression of the merchant who sold me pillows to decorate my new apartment, to my new neighbors, who watched me move in, with looks of pity and curiosity on their faces, eyeing this girl from America who had chosen to live alone. I gave up searching for myself, and for what constituted the real Iran, whatever that meant. Instead, I dedicated my days to one task alone: decorating my apartment.

My relatives came to visit, and admired the traditional architecture, built around a central garden courtyard. But they all said I was paying too much. I countered that I would probably expire in Tehran without a nice apartment, and given that I didn't have medical insurance, it was probably worth it.

My American friends got suspicious when I told them. They sent emails demanding to know how a young, single woman could live alone in Tehran. They didn't believe half the things I told them about Iran, which they assumed was a slightly more cultured version of Saudia Arabia, and began to suspect that I was holed up in Rome spinning elaborate fantasies with a Tehran dateline.

The apartment soon became my world—a substitute for the world outside, to which I seemed not to belong, unfit to understand—and so I figured, it might as well look sublime. I bought plants, chose fabric for bedspreads, hunted for antique tiles in the bazaar, commissioned a table, and mounted track lighting on the ceilings. I put a bronze statue of Antigone on the mantle, and stared at it from every angle for an hour, then moved it across the room, and stared at it there. The objective was to create an interior space where East and West fused with elegance, and the apartment became a canvas on which I could endlessly practice different combinations.

When friends called, I refused to go out. The heat of high summer made the dangerously high pollution especially toxic, and I hated coming home caked with sweat and dust, my veil scented with car exhaust. Come visit me, I suggested to the dwindling number of friends who continued to phone me, long after I had ceased returning calls. Reza was one of those friends, though our friendship perpetually surprised me. We never acknowledged being on close terms publicly. At events where we encountered one another, we nodded stiffly and walked in separate directions.

It took him a long time to trust me. His advice, especially in those early months, guided me through a system of mysterious, potentially dangerous, unknowns. It was from him that I learned most Iranian journalists were routinely interrogated by intelligence agents (Mr. X was not just my cross to bear), and that they were all constantly forced to rat on one another. That I should never let down my guard even with my closest journalist friends, because they would lose their jobs if they didn't inform, and because they had families to support they had no choice. Certain things I already knew, like watching what I said on the phone. But Reza suggested I get a second mobile number and keep it on reserve, so I would have a clean, untapped line in case of emergencies. The sort of thing that wouldn't occur to me until I needed it, when it was too late.

He taught me how to recognize a "plant"—a person who casually inserts himself into your life, discreetly offers you tantalizing scoops or sources, or who seeks private information, all with the purpose of entrapping you, or securing material to fatten the file with your name on it, in the event that one day it would be used against you. Evading such people, knowing in what public situations I would be assessed, and how, were not instincts that came naturally to me. But they were required for reporting in Iran without triggering suspicion.

Speaking over our mobile phones, which were certainly bugged, we used a code. "I've printed out an article for you" meant I need to see you immediately. "I'm not that busy today" meant I'll be home in the evening, come by. In person, after exchanging a few pleasantries, we both turned off our phones, and removed the batteries—supposedly the phones could be used as listening devices. I thought he was paranoid and treated all his cautionary measures lightly, until his friends—reformist editors and intellectuals—began getting rounded up.

The hard-line judiciary started arresting activists, and intellectuals whose opinions were considered criminal, on a regular basis in early 2000. The process was methodical. Among the first to be arrested were the influential thinkers whose work inspired and propelled the reform movement. Once they were behind bars, the judiciary moved against the prominent editors and journalists in the pro-reform press, who discredited the conservative clergy each day in their newspapers.

The campaign was designed to make the personal cost of political opposition untenable, and it worked. The prison sentences varied between one year and ten. And then there was the blackmail. The hard-liners collected intelligence about their targets' private lives—extramarital affairs, old scandals—and threatened public humiliation unless the activists in question agreed to sign documents confessing to and apologizing for their "crimes." This systematic abuse eventually crushed the reform movement. Many activists simply gave up their political work, in return for promises that they and their families would be left alone. Others went to the West for year-long fellowships that became permanent.

Reza watched this all happen to his friends with a coolness I could not fathom. Sometimes he would drop by, and only an hour into the conversation would he mention that he had just come from dropping a friend off at prison, or visiting one in hospital. For the most part the regime had dispensed with brutal physical torture, but the emotional harassment, solitary confinement, sleep deprivation, and strange drugs administered in prison wrought a physical toll.

When I saw exactly how these reformists suffered in the process of a movement so many of us mocked as ineffective, I felt terrible. Iranians of all walks of life called them so many names—collaborators (for working with the mullahs), cowards, incompetents. But they were doing what no one else was willing to do. They were exposing themselves, making their families vulnerable, for the sake of making Iran a tiny bit more open. Yes, many of them were Islamists. Yes, many of them had supported, or still supported, the revolution. But were they not asking for the right things? For the right to free expression, fair trials, and free elections? It was so easy to sit at home and be pristinely secular over cocktails in the garden in north Tehran, or Switzerland, or Washington.

As the months passed, Reza and I became easier in each other's company and stopped being so formal and Iranian about everything. It wasn't easy. He was from a more traditional social background than my family and was unlike all the Iranian men I had ever known. Because he was not suave and

Westernized, I was initially suspicious when he talked freely about everything, even sexuality. I worried it was a clever, drawn-out, intellectual ploy to seduce me.

Sometimes he made me squirm, because he saw right through me and I wasn't used to that. Typically, Iranian men were too self-absorbed (forever princes of their mother's domain) to pay close attention to the emotional makeup of a woman they were not related to or sleeping with.

"You're Iranian in a superficial way," he said one day, after I rescheduled one of our meetings for the eighth time. "You come across warm, but your affective nature is really Western. Eastern affection involves generosity with time. You drench people with warmth and charm, to distract them from how miserly you are with your time. You handle minutes like an accountant."

Reza was my favorite audience for monologues of alienation. He said I was too intelligent to waste my time rotting at home, wallowing (his word) in my sense of exclusion. "Stop asking if you count as an Iranian. By asking you just make it seem like a question that other people have the right to answer. If you were confident about yourself, instead of tip-toeing around, no one would challenge you."

This made lots of sense. Probably my accented Farsi would be less noticeable if I didn't make such a point of apologizing for it. For hours after a talk with Reza, I'd stop tormenting myself and walk around feeling quite okay about things. But sooner or later, something would distress me (a call from Mr. X, a failed attempt to execute a bank transaction on my own) and I felt shattered and tentative all over again.

I thought of my family in California and superimposed the question onto them. What if they woke up one day, and decided they were really American? Even if they felt it with all the force of their being, did that mean Americans would suddenly stop considering them foreigners? Maybe identity, to an extent, was an interior condition. But wasn't it also in the eye of the beholder? It seemed delusional to go about convinced you were a peacock, when everyone treated you like a bear. The contradiction bounced around my head. What percentage of identity was exterior, what percentage self-defined? Was it sixty-forty, like a game of backgammon, sixty percent luck, forty percent skill?

That winter, when the holidays rolled around, I looked forward to a complete break from all existence, including work. *Time* scheduled its Man of the Year double-issue for the last month of the year, which meant a long dead stretch for far-flung reporters. For two blessed weeks I could ignore my ringing mobile phone, and retire the tight, fake smile I wore in public, when forced out for an interview. I considered staying somewhere besides my apartment, mainly to escape my maid, who thought it decadent and inappropriate that a young woman should live alone, not work (she thought the laptop was a cousin of the espresso machine), and stay in bed most days. She had started casting me baleful glances and making oblique jibes: "Azadeh Khanoum, what a sweet and kind girl you are. Really, how much I adore you. May God grant you everything you want. May he provide for you, so that you can keep on relaxing at home forever." Then she would massage her lower back, and ask if I had any *khareji,* foreign, creams that would heal the ache in her old bones.

I retreated to Shahabad, the old family home high, high up in the north of the city, almost out of Tehran. My uncle and aunt lived there, but it had a special place in my heart, as the house where my parents once lived together, in the early days of their brief marriage. The house was tucked in the back of a narrow, winding alley off the main road, and its wraparound terrace looked out on the orchards in the back, the line of willows, and the glittering, dark surface of the pool in the front.

The distance from the cruel, draining hustle and bustle of Tehran was quieting, and the day I arrived, with a small suitcase, I found my aunt, Khaleh Mimi, making jam. Goli Khanoum, the clever and kind woman who had been their servant for decades, walked around purposefully with vats of this, and canning jars of that. The scent of sweet quince wafted through the house, and a great copper pot simmered on the oven, full of the sticky, burgundy brew. The transformation of raw quince into jam was fascinating. The heat turned the yellow, fibrous meat of the fruit into soft red slices that melted in your mouth.

Khaleh Mimi's long, light brown hair was pulled back into a ponytail, and she wore a white button-down cardigan over a long, caramel pleated skirt, like a silvery cheerleader. They were driving up to the villa at the Caspian, and after much reassurance that I did, yes, truly, prefer to stay in Tehran all alone, by myself, agreed to leave me behind. My relatives could not fathom a thirst for solitude, and they continually tried to tempt me away to dinner parties, the hair salon, any little outing so I could "just get some air," as though wanting to be alone made me brittle and sick, like a nineteenth-century hysteric.

Khaleh Mimi showed me upstairs to my little room, with arched windows that overlook the garden, and the adjoining bathroom with the yellow cupboards my father installed years ago. There was a round tin of Nivea creme by the sink, and I smoothed some over my hands, inhaling the familiar scent, rapping my nails against the blue tin lid. It smelled like my grandmother and every other Iranian woman over sixty.

Iran was beginning to exhaust me. And like Reza, I was becoming paranoid, wondering whether my emails were being monitored, or if my apartment was bugged. It didn't help that Mr. X and Mr. Sleepy, the intelligence agents/interrogators assigned to monitor/recruit me, were making me meet them every few weeks. I couldn't tell anyone, because they had made it clear I should *not breathe a word.*

They would phone my mobile an hour before we were supposed to meet and give me directions to some secluded spot, sometimes an empty apartment in a quiet back street. The sort of place where no one could hear you scream. They didn't like some of my stories, especially the ones with anonymous sources, and demanded I tell them about everyone I had seen, everything they had said. They insisted on knowing who the unnamed sources were, even though I explained again and again that I couldn't betray their confidence.

Mr. X, the lead interrogator, was beginning to behave like a jealous boyfriend. He insisted on knowing when I was leaving the country, where I would be going, what I would be doing, and when I would return. When I was in Tehran, he asked what parties I went to, whom I talked to, and who else was there. To show me he knew when I was lying, he portrayed himself as omniscient, fully aware of the fine points of my social life. "Oh, is that the Jon who Hossein introduced you to at Babak's party?" he would say casually, to show me in one swoop that he knew I was friends with Jon, better friends with Hossein, and a frequenter of Babak's home.

When he didn't hear from me for a couple of weeks, he would telephone and announce himself with a strange intimacy. "Don't you know who this is? Have you forgotten me already? You never call. If I don't call you, you forget about me completely. What sort of friendship is this?" He tried to convince me that I needed him, by planting fears in my mind so he could then offer himself as defender ("By the way, if God forbid you happen to get arrested at the airport or held captive anywhere you can always call me").

He cracked mean jokes ("Now, you'd never try to commit suicide, would you?") and smiled at his own humor. He forbade me to tell anyone of our association, and when I admitted to having told the vice president (hell, you figure if it's about national security, it's okay to tell the vice president), he was furious. He held it against me for weeks ("How can I tell you're really telling the truth this time, since you lied before?"). He hinted at blackmail ("How would your editors feel if they knew you were meeting us all the time?").

In all fairness, he did not try to make me feel like a *taghooti,* an old regime slut. In the clumsy good-cop/bad-cop routine they played, that was Mr. Sleepy's job. Mr. Sleepy looked me up and down as though I was coated with filth, and then looked away in disgust. Mr. Sleepy was the one who asked if my jewelry was real and raised his eyebrows when I mentioned male friends (in their universe, such a category did not exist) and gave me a look that said, I cannot believe this Americanized, decadent, godless whore actually has a respectable career.

Worst of all, they made references to my family, casually mentioning where a cousin or an uncle worked, to show me they knew even my distant relatives, implying that even they were vulnerable through association with me. Every session was a battle of wills. I lectured them about journalistic ethics; they lectured me about national security. In the end, I was always shaking and drenched with sweat.

I had established a routine with my driver, Ali, to call me exactly one hour into these meetings. We had a code. If everything was fine, I said, "Yes, I'll be home for dinner." If I said, "No, actually I can't make that appointment," he knew to go get help.

I lived with my memories of these encounters, furious with myself for picking the wrong tactic, for being pliant when I should have been firm, for allowing myself to be goaded. I didn't budge from Shahabad for days, the longest stretch of my life I have worn pajamas continuously. I was still there when, to my wan dismay, the year 2000 ended. That, unfortunately, involved New Year's Eve. In the West, staying home alone on New Year's Eve was tantamount to admitting one was a romantic/erotic failure with no friends. Despite this implication, I could not drag myself out of bed, especially given the range of options: a diplomatic party that would inevitably lead to everyone getting very drunk, and at least one trashed European making the unoriginal confession that he thought the veil was sexy, and could I please keep it on in bed; or a chi-chi Iranian party where the women would be catty and pretend to admire my job, while secretly resenting me for having an independence they never had.

Unable to sleep, I descended to the kitchen, to find some fruit rollup to suck on while reading. As I peered into the refrigerator, Goli Khanoum accosted me, blocking the entrance with her stout frame, and let loose the lecture that had been brewing inside her. "Why are you always moping about? Are you the first person to be away from her family? . . . Are you the first person to think too much sometimes? No? Everyone praises you so highly, and says you have such a great job. . . . So what's wrong with you? You're going to really irritate your husband if you continue like this. . . . He'll want to come home, and enjoy himself, and what! . . . There you'll be on the couch, slumped over a pile of books. What about me? What should I say, if I was going to be like you? I've lost *four* children . . . and I'm making do. . . . Don't you think if we all let ourselves think as much as you do, we wouldn't end up the same way? The point is, we don't let ourselves."

I didn't know what to say. So I tried to make housewife talk, to appease her.

"Goli, don't you think it would be *so* much more convenient if the refrigerator door opened out *into* the kitchen, rather than away?"

"So everything has to be just the way *you* want it? You don't like eating dinner. Does that mean your husband doesn't get to eat dinner either?"

I couldn't believe I was standing in a dark kitchen on New Year's Eve discussing a hypothetical husband. I burst into tears and fled upstairs.

Tap, tap. It was Goli, knocking at my door. She felt bad for making me cry and knelt down next to me, pushing the ashtray aside. "It's all this pressure you put on yourself," she said. "Maybe you can get a nicer job. Don't any of the ambassadors need secretaries? You would be an excellent secretary!" I leaned my head against her shoulder, inhaling her scent of soap and leaves. It wasn't really fixable. The act of probing deeply, I realized, was an ingrained part of my California life, a telltale sign of an American consciousness. To not think so much—the stock local prescriptive—was simply not an option.

⚘

I remember with great clarity the day I stopped "claiming" authentic Iranianness. It was a frosty and overcast Thursday afternoon, and the streets were empty, because the official weekend—the second half of Thursday, and all of Friday—had already begun. I dressed carefully, in a simple black *abaya,* for my appointment with Mr. Abtahi, the president's chief of staff. He had chosen to meet in one of the Shah's old palaces, in the Saad Abad compound, and I arrived early, allowing me to wander around the elaborate foyer, examining the inlaid paneling.

His assistant led me up the winding staircase, into a corner room with windows on both sides, overlooking the gardens. As usual, the table was set with a gleaming bowl of fruit, and a tray of sweets. I flipped through my notes, waiting, and finally heard the rustle of his robes at the door. He settled in the chair next to me, and flashed his playful smile, eyes dancing irrepressibly. He smiled precisely the same way, whether exchanging favorite stories about Beirut, or divulging some explosive bit of news off the record, and sometimes I doubted my own hearing, so at odds was his expression with his words.

I started with women's rights, the subject of a piece I was working on, and when we paused to gossip, I asked him, half teasing, half serious, when I might hope to become Iran's first female ambassador. (I have since learned that one should not ask questions the answers to which one is not prepared to hear.) I expected him to say *"Inshallah,* one day in the future," or any other of a hundred polite phrases that would have meant nothing, but acknowledge the validity of the question. He looked embarrassed, and his eyes said: "Why did you have to go and ask me that?" He said nothing. I waited. *Say something, anything,* I willed him silently.

It was our ritual, enshrined in our roles, for me to ask unanswerable questions, and him to dance around them, with elliptical half-answers that pointed me toward the truth. But to this question, for the first time in our long history of questions and answers, he made no reply at all. He had always been advisor and friend, as much as a source. Through the best of times and the worst of times, inside the country and out, on weekends and evenings, he answered his mobile phone, agreed to interviews, because he believed in friendship and the importance of being accessible to journalists as a rule, not simply when he needed to spin a point or promote the president. He got me on planes, into private meetings, arranged introductions with senior officials around the region. I knew what he said, or didn't say, in answer to this question, was for my own benefit.

And the answer was: No, Azadeh Khanoum, in your lifetime, you will never be an Iranian ambassador. If there are any female ambassadors at all, they will be Islamist, *chadori* women, certainly not you, a secular, partial Iranian. I don't say this to hurt you, but because it is the truth, and you should know it. His silence cut me deeply, and I felt foolish for having opened my mouth.

His position elevated one man's opinion to an official pronouncement. I tried to detach myself from the moment by writing a headline in my head. Sympathetic Envoy of Vile Government Delivers Horrifying But Irrefutable Proof That Azadeh Is an American. The disappointment must have been written on my face, because he made some kindly remark, and held out a plate of green grapes, as though to distract a child gearing up to fling herself to the floor and wail.

CHAPTER FIVE

Election

Someone's coming,
someone different,
someone better,
someone who isn't like anyone . . .
And his face
is even brighter than the face of the last Imam
—FOROUGH FARROKHZAD

As the clamor of the crowd grew louder, the toy store clerk put the pink box of Barbie beach accessories on the shelf, and stepped out of his shop to investigate. We had been discussing the ban on Barbie, his best-selling product and birthday gift of choice for Iranian girls between four and ten, when we first heard the cries outside. Thirty yards away in front of the store, about 400 people were gathered, gaping at the sight of a young man, stripped shirtless, with his arms tied above his head to a tree.

A bearded man in an untucked, long-sleeved shirt, his voice distorted by the echo of a loudspeaker, shouted: "This man is guilty of possessing and selling alcohol." Then a second man raised a leather whip and cracked it across the young man's back as he counted, "One! Two! Three!" With each lash, the young man screamed, *"Ya Ali"* (the name of Shiism's most revered imam), then of his repentance, and his howls of pain. After the seventeenth lash, his hands were untied. With his head hung low, he quietly dressed himself and leapt aboard a passing minibus. Several other young men in line for the same punishment were tied face down to narrow wood planks for their whippings.

Every few months, a drug smuggler was hanged in public, a woman murdered for dressing immodestly. Sometimes the system staged and managed the spectacle, as it did with the public lashings, other times it bore responsibility obliquely—by fostering a culture of vigilantism that encouraged individuals to punish "offenders." A passage in the Koran exhorted believers to be proactive in maintaining the purity of their communities. The dictum *"Amr be marouf, va nahi be monker"* (Promote virtue and contain vice) was embraced by the regime, and gave powers akin to a citizen's arrest to pious, local bullies.

That day, the crowd was composed mostly of older people tense with disgust. Teenagers ducking into the mall, or in and out of the nearby coffee shop, chose to ignore the grotesque spectacle. If they must do this, seethed an elderly woman who stood watching, why not to thieves and murderers? They're the ones who menace society, not young people who

drink. She gripped her handbag tightly as she whispered, as though re-
straining herself from smacking the "volunteers" meting out the whipping.
Old women were circumspect in Tehran. Gone were the days when they
could say anything, do anything, cross the street anywhere, and be treated
with cordial courtesy. In the Iran of the Islamic Republic, the deference to
the elderly so central to Persian culture had collapsed, along with general
civility. People didn't hold doors for one another, mothers heaved strollers
up and down stairs unassisted.

Since the middle of the summer of 2001, Tehran had witnessed a baffling revival in the practice of public flogging, a form of punishment prescribed by Islamic *sharia* (criminal law) but abandoned by the Islamic
Republic for over two decades. In the parks and squares of the capital,
young people found guilty of petty social offenses like drinking alcohol, attending parties, and selling pornography were being rounded up every few
days and lashed before crowds in busy squares.

The Tehran police released a statement meant to explain: "Regarding the
spread of decadent Western culture in the society, police have seriously
risen up against the propagators of corruption." The corruption described
included: shop owners selling pets such as dogs and monkeys; clothes bearing pictures of Western movie and rock stars; coffee shops serving women
dressed immodestly and wearing heavy makeup; malls playing "illegal"
music; and shops that displayed women's underwear or nude mannequins
in their windows.

The head of the judiciary declared "an all-out fight against social vices"
and said "the people" had thanked the judiciary for carrying out the punishments. Both the police and the judiciary were run by hard-liners, while the
Interior Ministry, which was loyal to President Khatami, publicly opposed
the floggings. The standoff illustrated how the Islamic Republic worked, or
more aptly, did not work: one powerful semi-official body implementing a
policy that another sphere of government opposed and tried to obstruct.

Privately, reformists said Islamic criminal law, with its seventh-century
origins and arcane punishments such as stoning and lashings, should be
abolished. But discarding Islamic law would definitively secularize Iran.
What sort of Islamic Republic, after all, could be run without Islamic legal
codes? How else could Shiite clerics justify their divine right to govern
without religious law?

The hard-liners were anticipating the upcoming presidential election and feared massive voter turnout, which would bolster Khatami—the bee in their turban—with a second popular mandate to carry forward reform. Somewhere in some dusty, dirty-carpeted room in Qom, some wily hard-liner understood the psychology of electoral politics. Television attack ads—or in this case, public floggings—disgusted voters enough to keep them at home. Khatami's opponents staged such spectacles to discourage fence sitters, already unsure whether to support a maimed-duck president, from voting.

In the weeks that followed, the lashings sparked an open debate about the role Islamic law should play in modern society—a crucial and thorny question many Muslim societies are facing today. On many important issues in Islamic law—like stoning as punishment for adultery, or the killing of apostates, or a woman's blood money equaling half a man's—the Koran is largely silent. Historical records of the Prophet Mohammad's teachings, called *hadith,* offer some guidance, but because they are open to interpretation, the calculations depend on the philosophical and moral worldview of clerics. A skillful cleric can convincingly argue that a given punishment, like stoning, should be abolished, or upheld. Purely in theological terms, it can be argued either way.

The progressive clerics in the reform movement searched for a way out of the impasse. They argued that since Islam is silent about 95 percent of the matters people face in daily life, people should be free to determine their own behavior, adjusting to the changing times. But the hard-liners interpreted this domain of the 95 percent as their own, a chance to shape society in their own image, by prescribing rules by *fatwa.* This debate, obscure as it may sound, was the basis for the political battle over the Islamic Republic's soul, if not the role of Islam itself in modern life: In the realm of the Koran's silence, are people free, or subject to the *fatwa* of clerics?

While the debate was significant—unique in a region that as a rule stifled candid talk on sensitive religious issues—it couldn't have mattered less to ordinary Iranians. They were light years ahead of such conversations (the need for secularism being as obvious to them as the blue of the sky), and it only irritated them to watch the country's rulers engage in esoteric theological bickering.

Young people were busy launching weblogs (by 2003, Iran ranked number three in the world in number of weblogs); intellectuals were writing innovative, sparkling satire, graphic designers were creating websites for the West. Their interest was turning intensely outward, to the world of ideas outside, and they didn't have the patience for this conversation among men of religion.

Although the reform movement had a far more intimate sense of people's actual desires than the conservative clergy, its leaders were still disconnected. They made the same miscalculation that the conservatives had, and it was ultimately this that cost them people's support. They assumed people would always back them, simply because there was no better alternative. In a competition between violent, fundamentalist ayatollahs, and religious-minded moderates, surely the Iranian people would choose the latter. For a couple of years this logic held, but as the regime stayed the same, and as it became more and more apparent that official change would be slow and undetectable, the distinction between religious conservatives and religious moderates (both functionaries of a dinosaur regime) ceased to matter at all.

They're all the same, complained student activists who had once passionately delineated their difference. In the end, reformists and conservatives had more in common politically with each other than with ordinary Iranians. The gulf between a mullah and an Iranian civilian was far wider than between a mullah and a reformist.

That much became clear when I began reading the daily newspapers in earnest. Each day I had to skim at least ten, because the political cliques that lined the spectrum from hard-line to reformist each had their own mouthpiece. They included the Super-fundamentalist But Non-Violent Clerics of Qom; the Pragmatic Anti-U.S., Pro-Europe Technocrat Hard-liners; the Fascist Anti-Western Hard-liners Prone to Assassinations; the Classical Anti-Western, Pacifist Clerics; and the Society of Combative Clerics, not to be confused with the Society of Clerical Combatants.

These factions had risen up together through the ranks of the Revolution, studied together at the feet of the Ayatollah Khomeini, ordered executions and then dined on chelo-kabob. They were the architects of this system, and now they were bickering over its structure and its spoils. "Reformist" and "conservative" were the labels they used when fighting amongst themselves—and though they fought each other like cats, they still considered themselves *khodi* (insiders) and everyone else *gheir-khodi* (outsiders).

⚓

The eve of the presidential election, held in the summer of 2001, was a turbulent season for reformists. Nearly every day, the hard-line judiciary banned one of their newspapers or arrested a pro-reform activist. This was bad for the country, and bad for dinner-table conversation. Before the regime made brutal assault of the reform movement a daily ritual, Iranians followed politics like Americans follow baseball—as national pastime.

There were so many newspapers to read that neighborhood businesses bought a morning stack as a pool; in my neighborhood, the butcher, the florist, and the baker each bought different papers, and traded them over the course of the day. Their radios were tuned into the news, and you could pass in and check on the day's political developments, as you would the score of a game. Because at that moment most people still cared—it felt like a shared, national journey—and read the same satirical, critical papers, the news sparked flavorful and deep conversations.

But as the life was slowly pummeled out of the reform movement throughout 2000 and well into the spring of 2001, once reformist leaders lost nerve and direction, no one felt much like talking politics anymore. Though I now lived on my own, I was too lazy to cook and still went to dinner at Khaleh Farzi's most nights. The number of newspapers she brought home had dwindled from five to one. Its fate was to end up on the tub, its crossword puzzle half worked out. Dinner debates, the one regular feature of our lives, ceased altogether.

Thus disillusioned, families stopped talking about the thrilling national journey, and returned to topics more familiar, like whether or not to emigrate to Canada. Sooner or later, most Iranians lost faith that this particular reform movement would achieve sufficient or imminent change. It was the inevitable conclusion that followed round after round of defeat—the steady hard-line process of banning, vetoing, arresting, intimidating, and torturing. The disillusionment was not terminal. Everyone knew the present system would come to an end. It might not collapse overnight, or collapse at all, for that matter, but it would slowly evolve until one day the revolutionary Islamic Republic's ideology would die, in an age where ideology itself was outmoded. It was just a matter of time, the years it would take for the rancorous, powerful ayatollah-dinosaurs—mercifully an endangered species—to die off.

The shift in thinking, from a specific hope vested in recognizable figures, to the distant, abstract conviction that things would change because they must, occurred differently for everyone. It came for Siamak the week he stepped out onto a busy street with his baby niece and toddler nephew, and a car actually sped up.

He told me about it the next day, as we were having lunch at his office. He just stared at the feta cheese and cucumbers on the table, and I felt panicky at the grave look in his brown eyes, the disillusionment etched all over his face. "It doesn't make a difference who takes over," he said. "It doesn't matter whether Khatami is cloned or granted three more terms, or whatever. It doesn't matter who comes, because fixing the culture created by the system is now the problem. I used to take such pride, Azi, in my Iranian identity. I don't see that culture I was proud of anymore, that respect for elders, for children. These are the effects of lawlessness. If you do business and don't take bribes, you're considered strange, behaving outside the norms. Being corrupt is normal. The country's ethical code has gone mad. It's going to take so much more than politicians to fix that, this culture of lying, deception, and corruption." He pushed his lunch away in disgust. I had never seen my friend so dejected.

My own creeping loss of faith fell on a late spring afternoon when President Khatami registered his candidacy for re-election. It was meant to be a short photo opportunity, a few words, and a smile as he dropped the formal paperwork into a box at the Interior Ministry, in a basement room stuffy with reporters, and other hopefuls, including a dairy farmer whose opinions were disturbingly saner than those of the mainstream candidates. Khatami walked behind the table that served as a makeshift podium, and from the folds of his auburn robes removed a scrap of paper with notes. He began by addressing the obstacles the government had faced during its first term, and the importance of working toward a religious democracy.

Like most Iranians who voted him into office in 1997, I had fallen under the spell of his difference from the ruling ayatollahs: a smile over a frown, an Italian loafer over a flip-flop, a belief in lawfulness over anarchy, talk of dialogue rather than martyrdom. To understand how easy it was to fall for Khatami, you had to view him in the trajectory of his predecessors—a long line of slatternly, corrupt, unworldly clerics, with village accents and scant ambitions; they had held meetings on the floor, sat slouched before the cameras, and mumbled about "foreign enemies."

Khatami was the benign face of the clergy. He spoke three languages, studied Western philosophy, stood up straight, and spoke eloquently about rights and individual dignity. He wore the same clerical robes, but immaculately tailored, in refined fabrics and colors like pear and chocolate. He promised that Iran was for all Iranians, and even drew the attention of the diaspora, which was immune to taking Iran's clerical leaders seriously. No one thought him charismatic, but he radiated charm, and left everyone he encountered—from pedantic scholars to swooning schoolgirls—with the satisfying sense of having, finally, been understood.

For most of his first term, from 1997 to 2001, Khatami was a speck of light in over two decades of revolutionary darkness. The millions of Iranians who had lost a relative or several to exile, to war, to prison, to firing squads, projected their hopes for change onto this mid-ranking cleric with the sweet smile. Young girls showed up at campaign rallies as though for rock concerts, decked out, breathless, and screaming his name. When we traveled to the provinces, wizened old women, clutching their *chadors* close, came out to see him.

Once, when the press traveled with him to Khorramshahr, a desolate town on the western border that was bathed in the blood of young soldiers during the Iran-Iraq War, I saw just how far and wide his appeal extended. Under the crushing assault of the summer sun, a group of hunched, ancient women swathed in black, who had been unable to approach his motorcade, came up to me, and pressed their wrinkled, hot hands against mine. You're a good girl, you came here with him, you'll talk to him for us, won't you? And they sat there for the whole of his speech, hanging onto my *roopoosh* all the while, stuffing letters they had written him into my pockets, and detailing their troubles—water shortages, daughters widowed by the war struggling to raise sick children. A little girl in a white head scarf, who couldn't have been more than six, trotted over, and cupped her hands around my ear. Can you tell him, please, my baba needs a job.

I thought of all this, as I leaned back in the metal folding chair, waiting for him to start. It had become clear, by the twilight of his first term, that he was neither a leader nor a strategist. By nature, he was risk averse and deferent to clerical authority, the last person capable of the ruthless jousting that regime politics demanded. His notes fell to the table, and he began to speak freely, abandoning the speech.

"If I had it my way, I would try to serve Iran outside government," he began, his voice low without a microphone. I lifted my eyes from my notebook in surprise. "My assets are limited. I have a tiny bit of capital, and that's people's regard for me." Mullahs rarely spoke like this, clearly and proudly. They usually lost themselves in whorls of rhetoric, and atmospheric, labyrinthine thoughts empty of meaning.

Khatami's voice was scratchy, and tears welled up in his eyes, then overflowed down his cheeks. When he came to office in 1997, he infused his speeches with visions of an Islamic democracy, tributes to freedom, and the civilizing force of art. With bright eyes and his head held high, from podiums around the world, he repeated his belief that the revolution could be rescued, its nobler sentiments resurrected. Now, four years later, his body language radiated defeat. He had put on weight, and his face looked puffy and tired. It was as though he was acknowledging—internally and for the first time—a double failure: that of the revolution and his attempt to salvage it. On that day, the day he registered (against the urgent advice of many he respected) for re-election, he did not campaign so much as grieve.

"The road ahead is difficult, but as long as I feel a step forward can be taken, I will be at the people's service. When I feel that is no longer possible, then I prefer to serve them, and the revolution, elsewhere," he continued. As he uttered these words, it was evident how scarcely he believed them, and a moment later he began crying in earnest. I found myself crying too. For all the pain and sacrifice—the families torn apart, lives wrecked and a generation traumatized, a diaspora permanently displaced—that had achieved nothing, arrived at no place more significant than this moment. Khatami stepped away from the podium.

Embarrassed to be brought to tears by a mullah (what would my father say?), I pulled my head scarf forward and lowered my head. Looking sidelong and back, I saw that most of the women in the room were also crying. The men stood rooted, staring into space in shock.

I fumbled in my bag for a pack of cigarettes, and hurried to the back of the room, where Mr. Abtahi, the president's chief of staff, stood against a wall, all trace of his usual merriment wiped from his face. I flashed him a look of I told you so, and crossed my arms, waiting silently for an answer. I always teased him that a tsunami could wash over Iran, and he would predict a sunny outlook for reform. Mr. Khatami messed up, he said. He's too emotional. He gets carried away with himself.

⊥

Finally, the week of the election arrived. It would be the sixth presidential election since the Shah was toppled in 1979, and unlike most countries in the region—where elections were such shams that they passed with little remark—people actually discussed whether or not they would vote. The question was on everyone's lips, though, ever mercurial in their political outlook, most would only really decide the morning of the election.

I felt no such ambivalence. To vote in the presidential elections, it seemed to me, would be committing treasons against my family, and a lifetime of principled exile. The cat-shaped country my father taught me to draw was our Iran—secular and proud—not the Islamic Republic, and the sanctity of that distinction was the foundation of our lives in the diaspora.

Why else would we choose to be strangers in American and European cities? There was something bigger at stake than patriotism—the desire to live freely. In honor of this value, the diaspora had abandoned Iran. In opening myself up to accept this Iran, in the implied legitimacy that voting entailed, would I not be turning my back on my own community? Did I want to normalize my relationship to this regime—reduce it from the Death Star of my childhood imagination to a regular country whose citizens showed up on the appointed date and checked off boxes on ballots?

I had not been in the country in 1997, when Iranians first elected Khatami. Many who had voted for him the first time around were voting again, despite the disappointment of his first term. Friends and family unanimously said I should, and that en masse, it would be registered as a protest vote. By voting for Khatami, you're not really voting for *him;* you're voting *no* to the Islamic Republic, most people said, when I solicited advice. I suggested to Khaleh Farzi that we go vote no to the Islamic Republic together, but she was busy buying *sohan* and *gaz* and other Persian sweets to take back on her visit to California, and her head was already at the Starbucks counter.

As election day approached, the question ballooned in significance, and I was still undecided. The thought that I might, with a check of a ballot, help legitimize the system, help wash away its evils, made me feel dirty and complicit. But so did holding myself apart, declining to be a part of the decision because I had an American social security number. Not voting meant drawing another line in the sand, separating myself from the Iranians who were part of my world, and who would vote because this was the country they would spend the rest of their lives in. They didn't have the option of leaving; their lives were entangled in the system and dependent on its stability. They had prepaid for cars, bought apartments, made investments, and they had a stake in its evolution.

For them, voting was not a sign that they accepted this regime, but that they were stuck with it and had to make do. These charged, absolutist attitudes—never shall I vote, never shall I taint myself—were forged and held mostly in exile. They weren't wrong so much as irrelevant. At least to daily life in Iran. Who was I to sit here, absorbed in my private doubts, arguing with my outraged inner secularist? Really, who cared?

I tilted back and forth for days, until the afternoon I visited the atelier of a painter I knew, Khosrow, down near the old parliament building in the center of town. He worked in the cool basement of an aging, old-style house that smelled of cool old *lahaf* (quilts), cigarette smoke, and paint.

Khosrow had fought in the eight-year war with Iraq and, like most of the soldiers who returned alive, was bitter and cynical about the regime. He channeled all his pain at the carnage into art so haunting that it could not be exhibited in Tehran, where the official myth of war martyrdom still held that the sacrifice was glorious, that the hundreds of thousands of slain young men were happy martyrs, thrilled to give their lives. Khosrow painted body bags as ghosts, abstract cemeteries with rows of war dead—unflinching, raw renderings of how the war devastated a generation of young men. Looking at his paintings was like looking into the face of a sixteen-year-old who had just watched his best friend blown up on a mine. He served me a cold glass of sour-cherry juice.

After sipping its dregs, we locked up the studio and went out into the alley. I needed a ride to my next appointment, and Khosrow nodded his head toward a motorcycle parked outside. I don't have a car, he said. I hope you don't mind. He turned on the engine, and I sat behind him, wrapping the folds of my abaya tightly around me, so its ends wouldn't catch in the spokes.

A minute later, we were careening through the streets, darting perilously through unruly traffic, and I buried my face in his back, terrified that we would be mangled (motorcycle riders routinely lost limbs all over the city), trying not to think about how strange it was to be smushed up against a man in public, in broad daylight, but invisible.

Driving through the city one could sightsee the puzzling inconsistencies in the policing of gender relations. Motorbikes were cheap and a popular way of getting quickly through horrible traffic, and Tehran was full of them, their riders often couples, sometimes whole families who seemingly fell outside the social code by virtue of being on a bike. Even though buses were segregated, even though there were separate lines for men and women at the passport office, no one thought twice about women flying through the city with men of indeterminate relation literally between their legs. The further north we drove, the stranger and stranger it seemed, passing buses, passing policemen, slicing through lanes unobserved, utterly inconspicuous, in this public embrace. My thoughts turned to the strangeness of a system that permitted such contradictions, a system that was so fixed, yet flexible.

When I finally got home, I grabbed a pomegranate from the refrigerator, slipped the dust-covered *abaya* off on my way down the stairs, and stepped straight into the shower. I sat down in the tub, my back against the cool spray, and popped the ruby seeds off one by one, watching the water wash the crimson juice off my skin. When I was little, my mother used to bring pomegranates into the bath—because the juice would stain everything otherwise, but also because when she was little, they used to serve pomegranate in the public *hamam* she went to with her grandmother. Since then, whenever I'm struggling with a decision, I take a pomegranate into the bath, and mull the issues over as I pop and chew the tangy, glittering seeds.

Buoyed by my thoughts during the afternoon's ride, I was more willing to believe in the possibility of change; not in the simple, facile way I had imagined before—that a heroic president would work miracles overnight—but a longer process, unpredictable, but made possible by the fact that the regime had cracks, and that social momentum would one day broaden them.

And the more I thought about it, the more the decision to vote resonated with the person I was discovering myself to be. When I first showed up in Tehran, brimming with assurance that I was just as Iranian as the next person in line for pastry, I figured assimilation would take a month, at most. Eventually I saw that my character had developed in response to other challenges, not the Islamic Republic's special perversions. I hadn't done what so many of my Iranian peers were doing, retreating into the mountains to make out with boyfriends, numbing myself with drugs because a chemical haze was more bearable than the stark reality of daily life.

As my sense of Iranianness simultaneously diminished and altered, my American consciousness grew—not in proportion to anything, or larger than before, but in my awareness of its existence. The more I tried to superimpose my Iranian identity on Iran, on the distresses and contours of my life there, the more I saw that it did not match up. In unguarded moments, the knowledge worked its way into me, until finally it became shiningly obvious: Of course I was partly American. It was strange, how this question of once agonizing importance became unremarkable.

Ironically, it was my American side that was helping me cope with Iran. As an American, I believed in unconditional love, not the contingent affection one had to earn as an Iranian woman. Iranian-style love, though extravagant, poetic, and intense, came with a prenuptial agreement. You had to promise to adhere to tradition, respect boundaries, pretend a great deal, and keep yourself decently coiffed at all times. You were not entitled to love, it seemed, simply by being who you were; but by fulfilling expectations. Or at least pretending the substance of your life until that point had been an accident, and that deep down you really wanted to be married to a software mogul named Payman, driving your Ralph Lauren–baby–line–clad children around the suburbs in a BMW SUV. If you strayed too far, dropped the pretense of harboring such wants, you risked perpetual criticism.

American-style love, in contrast, seemed more tolerant, with a more gentle approach to the individual at its core. My American friends pretty much lived their lives as fresh endeavors, unburdened by the feeling that résumés and relationships should make tribal or dynastic contributions to the family. Their decisions were often private, not witnessed by the amorphous community of *mardom* (people) under whose watchful eye Iranians seemed to exist.

I loved this Iran, with all its dysfunction and unruliness, just as I would one day love my child, even if she had had a baby out of wedlock, decided she wanted to be a musician, or told me she was a lesbian—all things that would have made my mother say "From today you are dead to me, no longer my daughter" and mean it. I cleared the dregs of pomegranate skin from the drain, and dried myself off, twisting my hair into a towel. I had made up my mind, and called Siamak to make my announcement. I'm going to vote, I said proudly. Let me call the Interior Ministry, and tell them they can now proceed with the election, he replied drily.

⚹

There was no mystery surrounding the election; the question was not who would win, but the size of Khatami's landslide. Still, the imminence of the election hung in the air, because suddenly there were *Basiji* checkpoints all over the streets. The *Basiji* style of moral policing—aggressive searches of cars, interrogations of their passengers—had for the most part been retired as part of Khatami's drive to keep the regime out of Iranians' private lives, but on exceptional occasions, like holidays and elections, the militia reappeared on the streets of Tehran. They set up checkpoints, the kind that had once been a regular feature of urban life, to remind Iranians that they existed, and that their patrons, the hard-line ayatollahs, were still in control.

The memories of what used to happen at those checkpoints were still acute for most people, who reverted to the cautiousness of life pre-Khatami. "There's no way I'm leaving the house after dark until after the election," a friend said to me. "Stop being so neurotic," I scoffed. "You know things are better now." With no memories of harsher times, and after months of navigating the night without trouble, being waved through the rare checkpoint, I was blithely sanguine.

Two nights before election day, I was heading home after a day's reporting (Me: Why are you voting for Khatami? Everyone: Because there's no one better to vote for), intending to drop off Dariush, who had been taking photographs, along the way. As I approached the square near my house I thought there must be some sort of neighborhood bomb threat.

Cars were pulled along the side of the street, and everywhere men in commando fatigues strolled about, kalashnikovs in hand. Inching forward I saw it was a massive *Basiji* checkpoint, where "suspicious" cars—either expensive models, or those containing men with long hair, or both men and women—had to pull over and their passengers submit to verbal interrogation and possibly a search of their car. Being young, having a member of the opposite sex in the car, and an inch of hairline showing under my veil rendered my car a beacon of immorality. "Pull over," growled a bearded man.

I glided my aunt's grey sedan onto the side of the road. Oblivious, Dariush continued yabbering away on his mobile.

"We're being stopped by police," I said. "Can you please hang up?"

"How exactly are you related," the man demanded.

I explained that we had been working together, and both of us got our official press cards out.

"If you're a journalist, shouldn't your *hijab* be more proper?" the *Basij* asked, scanning the cards.

"Should it?" I asked. "I don't see why." I really didn't.

Dariush nudged me. "Shut up. Don't provoke him."

Soon enough, our interrogator spotted the word "America" on my press card and became alarmingly animated. He strode over to his friends and flashed the card at them.

"We have nothing to say to an American magazine but 'Death to America,'" he yelled, and soon his fellow *Basijis* chimed in.

In the middle of a suburban avenue, in front of a fruit stand, this gaggle of scraggly, armed men began screaming "Death to America" in my ear. It was a very stupid, Not-Without-My-Daughter sort of moment, not to mention embarrassing. "Ohmigod, what if we see someone we know?" I whispered to Dariush.

Our interrogator returned, and I reminded him primly that the *government's* Ministry of Culture had issued the press card. "Did you read that little line on the back where it says, 'Please cooperate with the bearer of this card'?" I asked.

"We reject the Culture Ministry," he replied, as though this was a rational answer, as though ministries, official institutions, were something an ordinary person could simply reject. All right. Not much you could say to that.

Ten minutes later, we hadn't budged. Dariush fiddled maddeningly with his mobile. I still thought the whole thing was a joke. Reporters and photographers working for foreign media were often held like this while out covering stories. It happened to us all the time. Usually you were released after about an hour, though sometimes you had to put in SOS calls to Mr. Shiravi, the deputy at the Culture Ministry press office, who patiently tracked down who was holding you, and got them to stop.

The interrogator came back and made himself comfortable leaning against the hood of the car. I tried to make small talk, thinking that at least I could use the time to do some more reporting.

"So, who are you going to vote for?" I asked.

He said he didn't know, and when he asked me, I said I too was uncertain.

"What do most people say when you ask them?" he asked.

"Well, most of them say they're going to vote for Khatami," I replied hesitantly, debating whether it would be more stupid to offend him or to tell a preposterous lie.

"Hey listen," he began yelling. "She's says she's voting for Khatami, and that I should too. She's posing as a journalist, but propagandizing for him, out to collect votes. Take them in."

I was dumbfounded. In the instant it took to begin sputtering a denial, the rear door of my car had been opened and a severe, bearded face appeared in the rearview mirror. "Drive," it ordered, from the backseat.

I steered through the summer night, following his directions, to a nearby apartment complex for retired military officers. The two twin towers bore immense, scowling murals of Ayatollahs Khomeini and Khamenei. Not a single question—"Where are we going? Why? What are you charging us with? Who's in charge here?"—was deigned with an answer.

We arrived at what looked like a *Basij* barracks, and the scattered shoes outside, dainty sandals amid Adidas sneakers, attested to the presence of hapless young people somewhere inside. We were placed in a room reeking of dirty socks, lit by a glaring fluorescent light, and ordered not to talk. Every five minutes, a man entered and confiscated something. Within half an hour my notebook and Dariush's camera were gone.

I sat crosslegged on the floor, and stared up at the walls. The room was an ode to Palestine, covered in the Palestinian black-and-white checked scarves called *keffeyehs* and decorated with photos of Al-Aqsa mosque. The militia's job, technically, was to promote virtue and prevent vice *(Amr be marouf, va nahi be monker),* in the Islamic tradition of guarding the ethics of the community. Because they were loosely affiliated with the Supreme Leader's office, they carried ID cards, but they acted with impunity, often unaccountable even to the police.

They were notoriously corrupt. They operated in neighborhoods mafia-style, taking bribes from local shops, in exchange for allowing them to sell banned CDs. They took cuts from local drug dealers.

"Please tell me this isn't happening," I said to Dariush in English. "Please tell me we are not in this room." Our new captor heard me speaking English and yelled.

"If you don't shut up," he threatened, "I'm going to put you in separate rooms."

My hands grew clammy. If anything truly horrifying could happen to a female journalist, it would be in precisely such a situation, alone in a room with a *Basiji* interrogator.

"Can you tell me what's going on?" I pleaded.

"We're taking you to the Intelligence Ministry," said an unshaven man in a shabby green suit and bloodshot eyes. By that time it was one in the morning of a public holiday. He sat in front of us, dialing a number, supposedly the Intelligence Ministry. "If you're going to take us somewhere, you have to tell us first," I insisted.

If they actually planned to take us there, we would have to put up some sort of fight.

Once you were detained by the Intelligence Ministry, God only knew what would happen to you. If you were passed to Judiciary Intelligence, there could be endless interrogations, possibly a beating, possibly a sexual assault, and possibly a charge of espionage. And no one could get you out. I had seen it happen before. Seen a photographer get taken in, seen the president's office itself make official inquiries, only to be told their interest in the journalist's case would only make things worse.

"Why should you be told anything? Should you know where the Intelligence Ministry is? Do you know where CIA headquarters are?" he said. "Actually, you probably do," casting a significant glance my way. At that comment, my gnawing nervousness turned to panic, and I reached for my mobile phone, to dial Mr. Shiravi and beg for help. "Take out the SIM card," he ordered. With hands shaking, I removed the tiny chip, my lifeline to the outside world.

Finally, a more senior *Basij* member arrived and took over the situation. I heard him arguing with the two men who had been handling us up until then, who had clearly been waiting for approval to take our case to the next level, whatever that might be. But he seemed reasonable, and unlike the others took no petty, sniggering pleasure in the fear on our faces, when he came in to talk to us.

"I swear, I wasn't out promoting Khatami, that man put words in my mouth," I explained, the minute he entered the room.

"President Khatami is the light of our eyes," he replied. "Let me sort this out."

From outside the room I heard his voice crackling over the walkie-talkie: "No, they have press cards. She's covered properly. . . . Yeah. . . . Her veil is simple. . . . No, no makeup." In moments our things were retrieved, and I was left explaining various terms I had jotted down in my notebook. Another search of the car produced nothing incriminating. "Nothing? Not even a tape, to justify the trouble?" teased our moderate savior. As I thanked him, and prepared to drive off, he asked a parting question: "So, who do you think is going to win?" I nearly choked. "Well, opinion polls conducted by impartial observers suggest Khatami. But what do I know?"

Leaving the barracks, we saw that the shoes were still outside. For ordinary Iranian teenagers, the evening could prove far worse than it had for us. We were picked up because we were Iranians, but released with no scars more lasting than shock, because we were journalists. As counter-intuitive as it might seem, I had the weight, however contested, of a government ministry and a foreign publication behind me. The crimes of the others there—playing music, showing hair, consorting with the other gender— could carry fines, whippings, and, always, humiliation. For all of us, the outcome was capricious.

As we drove away, I asked Dariush whether it was not a relief that under Khatami, such run-ins happened a couple times a year, instead of every weekend. He gave me a searching look. "However infrequent, I do not find any consolation in the fact that my fate is determined by the whim of an armed sixteen-year-old."

About six months after I came to Tehran, I put my labors of self-interrogation to rest, happy to nominally consider myself Iranian from America, but mostly happy to just live, and not consider myself so much, the more the Iranians in my world treated me as one of them. At last, I was normalized. And like any proper immigrant, I celebrated my fresh assimilation by criticizing new arrivals. Did you hear that girl's accent? I would whisper odiously about some harmless visiting Iranian-American at a party. Did you know she can't even read and write Farsi? Iranians from abroad were coming to visit Tehran more frequently, and I observed them from the vantage point of those who had never left—an experience more illuminating than a hundred meditations on identity might have been.

The evening after Dariush and I tussled with the law, Khaleh Farzi hosted a dinner party for a relative visiting from Los Angeles, who had Americanized his Iranian name to Fred (Fred, Mike, and Alex being the triad of names Iranian men in the U.S. typically resorted to). She asked us both to come over and recount our adventure for Fred's entertainment, and as she had promised to serve pomegranate tart for dessert, I consented. I could predict already that Fred would be crass, tedious company. He had left Iran fifteen years ago and, on his first trip back, made sure to speak in affected California tones that emphasized how far he had ventured. "Do guys and girls, like, date here?"

Fred fit an identifiable type—the smarmy, awkwardly assimilated Los Angeles exile exhilarated by his return to Iran, where his dollar had brawny buying power and his passport magnetically attracted young women. He would spend his month here at parties, dangling the possibility of a ticket to America as bait, dallying with women far more beautiful than he attracted in the U.S.

He would remark during regular and cliché sermons that Iran was a vile place, unfit for civilized existence, a trash bin of mosques. He proclaimed the reform movement hadn't changed Iran at all, yet he was happy to show up and get trashed at the parties it had made possible. Driven by guilt for having left, or by traumatic, early encounters with the regime, or by some nostalgic loyalty to the monarchy—or some combination of all three—he was keen to portray Iran as *exclusively* static, declining, and repressive.

For many Iranian exiles, this image of Iran was both useful and necessary. For the monarchists, it provided the cultural and social definition of Iran that made calls for regime change (or overthrow) more expedient and attractive to hawkish Republicans in Washington. For artists of Iranian origin, based for decades in New York or London, it lent an air of authenticity to tired, exotic images of women prostrate in pain, stranded on mountains in *chador,* in all sorts of positions in which most Iranian women—busy working and getting on with their daily lives—rarely found themselves. Because this sort of visual imagery was deemed authentic, depicting the "real" of modern Iranian existence, it was elevated to high art, celebrated in sophisticated, urban settings by important cultural institutions, and always billed as Iranian art, though none of it ever came from Iran. Inevitably, when I visited New York or Europe, someone would suggest attending a performance, or visiting a gallery of this genre, and I generally passed. Was Iran not already considered exotic enough in America and Europe? Why were Iranians, who knew better, producing art that made Iran seem like Saudi Arabia, a place where women actually *were* covered in black all the time?

In California and New York this dated, self-serving vision was irritating, but in Tehran it infuriated me, because it ignored all the vibrant, important ways Iran was changing. Up close, it meant watching people like Fred condescend to my aunt, to my friends, with his saccharine tone of pity, inquiring after their challenged lives. Because Dariush and Fred were both single men under thirty-five, etiquette dictated that Dariush offer to take him out to a few parties or to cruise Jordan Street (the crowded, social artery of northern Tehran) on a Thursday night. But Dariush ignored Fred all evening, preferring to drink homemade vodka in the kitchen with Khaleh Farzi's friends. I bugged him about this as we left.

"Would it have been possible to exchange more than three words with Fred?" I asked. At first I thought he suspected some matchmaking scheme on my aunt's part (visiting Iranian men were often introduced to a slew of suitable girls) and had pouted all night in remonstration. As usual, I attributed the basest possible motive to him and then felt guilty, realizing it had not been that way at all.

"Azi, do you know how many fucking times I've been in that situation? With my own best friends from elementary school, who come back from

UCLA and want to scam all summer? With my cousins, who treat Tehran as a summer playground, that's barely palatable for some exotic diversion, then back to the real world where they'll get on with their real lives, real educations, and real jobs?" he said, shaking his head. "This is my goddam life here, for me this is it, there isn't anything better lined up. This is the totality of my existence, and I can't stand being the tour guide of its limited use."

It was two in the morning when we got back to his house, and all the lights were still on. By that time, it had become blindingly clear that Dariush and I had nothing in common (he didn't care about Middle Eastern politics; I didn't care for action movies), and that we found each other insufferable (I thought he was a snobby child; he thought I was a fickle neurotic). Our conversations rapidly degenerated into battles, where we competed for the role of premier victim—he punched walls and screamed about the revolution; I chainsmoked and hissed about exile. It was insipid theatrics, and we should have ended things after the second episode. But shared strains like our recent arrest were dragging out our demise. In the interim, we hung out together around our relatives, whose presence enforced a measure of civility.

His family, the Moghadams, were among the few old, aristocratic families remaining in Tehran. When the revolution blundered across Iran, it brought their charmed, hallowed world crashing down. They *literally* had not left the house since, if visits to relatives were excepted. In twenty-three years, they had not dined once in public. They saw no one but the oldest friends, and close family. By withdrawing into themselves, they tried to protect the cultivated grace of their lost world from being tainted by the Islamic Republic.

Inside, time stood still. Visiting them was like dropping by Miss Havisham's, the character in Dickens who sat in her house and collected dust in her wedding dress for years, refusing to put away the cake, or change her clothes, after the moment she was jilted at the altar. Unable to live in the present, with an almost physical will, they kept scraps of the past, like yellowed invitation cards to brunch at the American ambassador's, close at hand. In the intervening years, they had become reactionary conservatives, coming to view the revolution as a black hole of evil, Islam as violent and anti-modern, and life in Iran as uniform, uninterrupted oppression. They were blind to the realities that helped produce the revolution, blind to even its minor accomplishments.

Dariush's parents and grandmother were all insomniacs, playing cards or backgammon late into the night to amuse themselves. Because they despised the Islamic Republic and had confined themselves to the house, they channeled all their mental and physical energy and disappointment into domestic squabbles, which predictably strained the household. Inside, the air smelled like roses, dust, and rancor. Walking through the garden, we passed two vintage European sports cars in various states of decay.

Dariush's father spent countless, fruitless hours on these cars, tinkering with their rusty engines, trying to locate parts. Every few weeks, he managed to resuscitate one long enough to drive it around the block. His wife thought he was mad to fritter away his life with these cars, but most of the time she was, like so many Iranian women of her age whose lives were turned upside down by the revolution, too zoned out on antidepressants and sleeping pills to care. Thirty years ago, when he was an influential administrator, her husband drove cars like these to work, tennis, and lunch with American friends. His cars were to him what that sad patch of garden was to my grandfather in San Jose—a tender ritual that paid homage to a lost world, a task that kept the hands busy, while the apathetic spirit lived in the past. It was a self-imposed exile, but exile nonetheless—isolating and melancholy, an island in a strange, hostile society.

Under usual circumstances, I didn't pay much attention to Dariush's deeper thoughts. They were typically narcissistic in a dull way and involved rating other people's ancestral lineage and finding them lacking. But that night, he had stopped to have real emotions, and I realized half of what he said about me being too American—in fact, half of what *most* Iranians said about me in this regard—had nothing to do with me. I supposed I could have paused and tried to pin down what was going on inside him, why it made him feel better to pick on me as an American. But I was honestly too tickled at being able to throw away that brand of criticism, to stop letting it provoke and depress me, that I couldn't be bothered. It was basically over, anyway.

⚓

Election day fell on a Friday, and voting stations around the country extended their hours three times. In Tehran, people lined the streets well after midnight, waiting to cast their votes. The expatriate television networks broadcasting from Los Angeles called the election a sham, since the candidates had been vetted by an unelected clerical body, effectively allowing the system to handpick the ballot. But the millions who stood in lines to vote, babies on hips, toddlers in tow, couples hand in hand, apparently thought it was enough of a non-sham to be worth the effort.

The results were released Saturday evening. Khatami won by 78 percent, and a remarkable 66 percent of eligible voters had turned out to vote. It was nothing approaching pure democracy, but at least people were engaged and believed their vote made some sort of difference. Relative to the rest of the region, this was somewhat significant. In Egypt (an American ally), the sitting president had been re-elected for two decades by a farcical 99 percent margin, and no self-respecting Egyptian would ever conceive of going to the polls. Saudi Arabia (an American ally), a country named after a *family*, didn't even bother with elections.

That night thousands of Iranians—families stuffed into cars, couples with babies, teenage girls wearing several extra layers of lipstick for the occasion—turned up on Vali Asr Avenue to celebrate. The traffic barely budged, but no one cared. People turned off their cars, honked their horns, turned up their stereos. Those on foot strolled through the stalled traffic, holding hands, licking ice cream cones, chatting between the lanes. Everyone seemed to be wielding something high up in the air—a gladiola, a balloon on a stick, a flag with Khatami's face—jabbing it around like a triumphant foil.

I had stepped out of a dinner party for a quick drive through the city, and decided to park my car for a stroll among the crowd. As I walked north, the traffic began to move again, toward Mellat Park. People retracted their arms and gladiolas into their cars, and rolled up the windows. The symphony of horns died down, and I could hear the distant gunning of motorbikes. A block ahead, a group of vigilantes surrounded a car with a Khatami poster on its back window, and shattered the glass with a club.

They belonged to the paramilitary group Ansar-e Hezbollah (referred to as Hezbollahis), whose members were the most ruthless of all the hard-liners' foot soldiers. Fundamentalists with a brutal streak, they performed tasks—such as beating up students, terrorizing activists, carrying out gruesome assassinations—where even pedestrian thugs like the *Basij* and the security forces drew the line.

Suddenly the *Ansar* were everywhere, chasing people on the street with batons. I ran back down the boulevard, past the brightly lit juice and ice cream shops, toward my car. Every few yards, I ducked down a side alley or into a shop, sliding my loose sandals back on, cursing myself for being dumb enough to wear flimsy shoes. If you are caught and clobbered, I thought, it will be social Darwinism at work and you will deserve it. I finally reached the car, slid behind the wheel, and wrapped tissue around my swollen, torn-up feet. I scanned ahead to see where the vigilantes were coming from. They were descending down out of the park in waves. A sea of bearded men dressed in all black, standing shoulder to shoulder as though marching into battle, repeating the name of the supreme leader Ayatollah Khamenei in scary, cult-like intonations.

Once they reached the street, they broke ranks and fanned out, kicking in car doors, screaming all the while. They called the women whores and threatened to tear-gas the crowd, full of children, if it didn't disperse. At one point, I couldn't see out my windows, there were so many of them pressed up against my car, their faces contorted. I clicked the power locks and prayed.

Finally, riot police showed up to restore order, but they took their time. First they watched the vigilantes terrorize people for a good twenty minutes, and then they only half-heartedly intervened. Whispering into their mobile-phone headpieces, the militiamen attempted to regroup, but the riot police dispersed them down side alleys, finally clearing the way for traffic. Broken glass and trampled flowers littered the street.

I dragged my shocked, sweaty body back to the party I had left two hours ago, to find my friends sprawled on the sofa watching *Friends,* the smell of hash heavy in the air. Someone get this girl a drink, one of them said. History rumbled around them, literally right outside the door, and they were more concerned with what Rachel said to Chandler. Iranian television had recently debuted a new sitcom, a sort of *Friends in Veils,* and they were arguing over how directly the plots had been lifted.

I took my drink into the bathroom, filled the tub with water, and let my feet soak as I tried to understand why some of my friends were so indifferent to the changes unfolding around them. Years of failure and layers of stale rhetoric had emptied the revolution of meaning. The war with Iraq and a decade of bombs and privation had turned them cynical, detached from the doings of the system. To them, upgrading from one brand of mullah to another was not a compelling enough reason to forsake this inner domain, free of pretense and false slogans. Why stand up for the revolution as it lurched to find itself? They would rather stand up for themselves, living in a way that might, after many years, indirectly force some modicum of change on the system.

✢

I'm Too Sexy for My Veil

✣

I will rise in slow increments.
I will make my face beautiful
like a mirror held to the wind,
let my silk scarf flutter in abandon . . .
I will find myself suddenly in full bloom
and you doomed to rot.

—SIMIN BEHBEHANI

"The first half of the day, from nine until two o'clock, is reserved for ladies, and afternoons and evenings for the gentlemen. Fridays [the only full day off in the Islamic work week] are men only," explained the manager of the Farmanieh Sporting Club, who clearly catered to a society of women who had nothing pressing to do before two on the average weekday. Since the monthly dues were the equivalent of a government worker's yearly salary, it was taken for granted that if you could afford to work out there, you did not work, and therefore didn't mind being relegated to the margins of the "gentlemen's hours."

On most mornings, women in dewy, immaculate makeup marched leisurely on a long row of treadmills, arranged close together to facilitate chatting. They wore an abundance of jewelry while doing this, and the tinkle of their gold bangles created as much background noise as the Kylie Minogue CD that was always playing. The spacious gym had the only properly functioning treadmills in town, and so I went ahead and signed up, despite the peculiar atmosphere, absurdly high prices, and sexist hours.

The gym tried desperately to imitate the sort of gleaming, vast health clubs that dot urban America, but it was run by managers whose only nod to fitness was the velour track suit, and its priorities ended up all wrong. Upon entering, a sycophantish "helper" began following you around, attempting to be your valet through the complicated task of changing into gym clothes. Then there was a nonsensical fixation with hygiene, that required the wearing of four different pairs of slippers in *four* separate areas. With all this scrupulous attention to detail wholly unrelated to the act of breaking a sweat, the exercise balls were deflated, and the air conditioner malfunctioned regularly.

To me, the oppressive minutiae of rules made working out at the gym stressful in itself. Clearly, it was not a place where people emotionally strained by life in Tehran went for the relief of exercise. So whom did it serve? After a week or two, I realized the club was created by and catered to Tehran's nouveaux riches, the clerics and revolutionary elite, and their business cronies, who made their fortunes by reserving lucrative state monopolies for their families, and controlling the Islamic charitable foundations that had absorbed the vast assets of the Shah's government. In the early years of the revolution, they shunned Western lifestyle habits as decadent, but in the last decade, thirsting for the admiration of Iranians and a closer resemblance to the status elite of other countries, they relaxed this attitude.

They began disfiguring the graceful old neighborhoods of northern Tehran with gaudy, white-columned mansions. Suddenly, a little swankiness was okay. A revolutionary cleric could buy an estate in rural England and outfit his daughter in Armani without an overtly guilty conscience. Though it was politically prudent to be discreet about such "decadent" habits, preening was half the goal. And so the Farmanieh, Tehran's first post-revolutionary, posh health club, was born and kept exclusive enough that the masses could not see how the clerics were living it up with their money.

Many of the women there were obviously the mistresses of these rich men because they were too young, breathtakingly beautiful, and middle class to afford the place otherwise. They carried themselves with a defensive, haughty brazenness that only kept women would think to affect. Others were simply high-end call girls, a trainer eventually explained to me, when I asked why they were taking photos of each other doing erotic leg lifts on the machines. They exercised with small movements—crossing and uncrossing legs, retouching their makeup, and sipping tea. If they broke a sweat, it was because they had gone up to the roof to tan, or sat in the sauna after a massage, their activity of choice. On those rare occasions they moved quickly enough to actually raise their heart rate, they rushed immediately afterwards to the club café for a reviving, dainty three-course meal.

For some reason, they hated me. Maybe it was because I spurned the cloying ladies' maid/valet, or dashed in and out without the requisite fifteen minutes of languorous small talk. Maybe because I was young, like them, but a non-mistress, unlike them. Perhaps if they knew that I worked, that my life included more pressure than leisure—deadlines and all-nighters, indecent clerics, and a perpetual fearfulness of Mr. X—they would be less resentful. But they clearly believed I rushed home every day to be fed sugar-dusted grapes and fanned with a palm frond, and they tortured me with incessant, niggling assertions of their authority over the world of the gym. It seemed the less power women had in the world out-side, the more they sought to flex their influence in the small universe in-side. In the non-mistress-run gyms, as I would discover, people pretty much left you alone. But here, each day it was something new: "Ms. Moaveni, can you please put your flip-flops *inside* the cubby holes, and not *next* to them? Can you please change in the dressing room [there was no one around, *ever*, and I used a towel]? Can you place your mobile on the left of the treadmill rather than to the right?"

Two impulses drove my obsession with finding the just right gym. One, which I tried to ignore, was that I had been raised in California, and there-fore had an incessant tape playing in my head about the religious impor-tance of exercise. I could sit there pretending to be as Iranian as the heavily madeup girl next to me, but the tapes would whir on, urging me to keep running, keep eating tofu, keep washing my fruit sixteen times to rinse off the pesticide. The second was the need to calm the chaos inside me with a steadying routine and the sedative effects of exercise. At the time, I could-n't, or wouldn't allow myself to, see that life in Iran strained everyone. I felt only that there must be something wrong with me, to be experiencing Iran so painfully, with a constant sense of suffocation and gloomy dread. Clearly, I must be a spoiled, self-absorbed, consumerist foreigner, to be suf-fering so much. Every day, I put myself on trial, and ruled myself guilty as an American, instead of a resilient, roll-with-the-punches Iranian. Restless within myself, I worked longer hours, and those longer hours—spent over somber, distressing stories—made me even more prone to melancholy.

And so I kept searching for less aggravating ways to work out, and ded-icated a whole week to the task. Tehran, a city more palpably tense than any other I had ever known, a city that generously gave all of its ten million res-idents so many causes for distress, must surely contain places where people could cope with the physical manifestations of the strain.

The first afternoon, I resorted to an aerobics class, despite the off-put-ting Richard Simmons/Jane Fonda associations. The instructor had built a private studio, complete with wall-to-wall mirrors, in the back room of her house, and cavorted about in sparkly leg warmers, blaring Madonna. Aer-obics appealed to Iranian women—it was indoors, so it solved the problem of sweating under a head scarf—and offered plenty of opportunity to talk while exercising. Had I been into coordinated group exercise, Tehran, with its abundance of aerobics classes, would have been a fitness paradise. But all that energetic shouting and synchronized stomping was not for me. I was a runner at heart, and decided to try jogging in the park.

The next morning, I drove through the whitish haze of city smog to Qeytariyeh Park. Scores of exercising women filled the park, power-walking laps around the perimeters, their arms pumping vigorously, or splayed out on the lawn, stretching. Though I had put on the lightest cotton veil I owned, I began to swelter, once my body warmed up. There must be something wrong with me, I thought, all these women are doing just fine, what's my problem? Running, I concluded, must raise your body temperature higher than walking, and the head scarf prevents your neck and ears from cooling you down. I tried to stick it out, tried to get to that point where I forgot I was running, absorbed in the smell of the grass, the rhythm of my strides. But the whole time I imagined portly ministers treading water in the Farmanieh pool (the latest thing for the *aghayoon,* the gentlemen, was swimming lessons), and I overheated as much with irritation and resentment.

With outdoor exercise out of the question, I went back in search of non-mistress gyms, where one could work out unmolested, and discovered they were *everywhere.* They were more modest and worn than the cavernous, well-equipped mistress gym, but functional, and more importantly, filled with women lifting weights and sweating, rather than reclining supine, popping dates—the gym as harem. The one I ended up joining opened at seven A.M., and minutes after that, women overran the locker room, undressing quickly, talking about their jobs, their families. They were young women and older ones, new mothers and college students, housewives and university professors; some had stunning figures, others were almost spherical, but they all showed up regularly, before work, class, or after dropping their children off at school.

I relied on that non-mistress gym, that glorious, precious realm of normalcy, as an escape from not only Tehran but my personal Tehran. No one talked politics. No one knew I was a reporter for an American publication and asked me if the country would be saved, as though I was a magic eight ball. No one took me aside and recounted in wrenching detail the tale of a student relative who had been beaten/arrested/disappeared, because I was an outside witness, and a repository for such testimony. No one knew I had an American passport and asked if I could get her daughter/cousin/cat a visa to a freer life. My mobile phone didn't get reception (the gym was in a basement), so no editor called to send me off on impossible, terrifying tasks ("Can you drive by the alleged nuclear weapons factory this afternoon, please?"). It was a sweaty paradise.

Since for so many women the sisterly atmosphere of the gym centered on stress reduction, the place was a live bulletin board for other ways to make one's life feel less constricted. One day I overheard a group of young mothers discussing a yoga class, and one of them pulled a Farsi-language yoga magazine out of her bag to show the others. She let me peek at the table of contents, which listed articles about ayurvedic medicine and vegetarianism, and, best of all, a long index of the various yoga centers and classes around Tehran.

At dinner that night, I raved about my discovery to my aunt. "Why didn't you say before you were interested?" asked Khaleh Farzi in exasperation, spooning sour cherry rice on my plate, poking through the fluffy, saffron-specked mounds for extra cherries. "Everyone we know does yoga. But I thought you didn't like it."

As it turned out, not only did everyone do yoga, but Lily, a distant relative, even held classes at her home in Aghdasieh, a neighborhood near the tip of Tehran. We called her after dinner, and she invited me to attend the next day.

Sandalwood. The plumes of the sweet-smelling incense overpowered the snug apartment, lined with tatami mats and decorated with portraits of multi-limbed Hindu gods and goddesses. I walked in to find the class, composed of a cult of women dressed identically in snowy-white tunics and pants, drinking tea in the kitchen. They looked like martial arts practitioners or a Mormon sect of housewives, until Lily dimmed the lights, clucked them into silence, and took her place at the front of the room.

At the end of class, we lay on our backs, hands and feet spread apart, as though poised to make angel imprints on a field of snow. Lily instructed us to curl our toes and then tighten our calves, and we tightened and released each muscle working our way up the body. I ran my hands back and forth over my stomach, willing my internal organs to cooperate, to produce an egg and be done with it. I hadn't menstruated regularly since leaving Cairo, and four months had passed since my last cycle. Unless I had immaculate conception to add to my worries, something was definitely wrong with my ovaries. The worry turned to alarm one night, when a tingly heat welled up from within my body, and I woke up to find dusky-red hives growing all over me. The doctor detected nothing perceptibly wrong with me, and suggested I eat less sushi. But I knew what was wrong. Iran was slowly making me sick.

The women in the room rested peacefully, with blissful smiles on their faces. I could not recall ever seeing such a relaxed crowd of Iranian women, who typically began to provoke one another in groups larger than five. The general stressors of Tehran life—toxic smog, traffic jams, fundamentalist theocracy, inflation, unemployment—together with the special burden of the veil made Iranian life particularly wearisome for women, who were depressed in large numbers. The depression had a major, physical component, in that it was compounded by the clothing regulations of the regime.

Ayatollah Khomeini probably did not consider the damage the veil would inflict on women's hair, when he mandated Islamic modesty. Besides split ends and a perpetual lack of volume, the veil intensified the general sadness many women were prone to feeling over all the things that were wrong in their personal lives, and in the country at large.

Why do your hair if it's going to be covered all day? Why watch your figure if it gets lost in the folds of a cloak? And in fact, it really *didn't* make sense to spend half an hour blow-drying your hair only to cover it up. And in the heat, as well as in the cold, it was exponentially more comfortable to wear sweats or leggings or nothing at all underneath the *roopoosh*. As a result, women often found the fine line between a practical approach to Islamic Republic grooming and slovenliness blurred. Before you knew it, you had devolved into a sloppy version of yourself, with unkempt hair (oh, skip a washing day, no one'll see it anyway), alternately clad in mumu-like *roopoosh* outside, and messy house clothes inside. On the occasions when Khaleh Farzi and I tended to our appearances for dinner parties, we would check each other out and exclaim, ahhh! I forgot what you looked like!

This phenomenon afflicted younger women much less dramatically. They were more inclined to exploit the fresh permissiveness in the dress code and quickly adapted to the new reality of being able to wear whatever they wanted, as long as it skimmed their upper thighs. Since they were coming of age in a *roopoosh* that revealed, instead of cloaked, they had the dubious privilege of becoming preoccupied with body image. The fret of their mother's generation ("Am I letting myself go under this tent?") was replaced with a more universal, modern concern ("Is my butt too big?"). Perhaps in its own strange way, this counted as progress.

⊥

I sat in Khaleh Farzi's living room, munching on roasted chickpeas and dried mulberries, pondering the nature of change. It was all a matter of perspective, I decided. To me, Iran's future looked bleak. Bad economy, spineless president, pissed-off populace, entrenched hard-liners, spiraling heroin addiction. It was fashionable at the time, in the West, for analyst types to say Iran's demographic time bomb made change inevitable. I had trouble buying that. As far as I could tell, the Islamic Republic could experience a succession of baby booms and stay exactly the way it was. Obviously not for fifty years, but easily for ten or fifteen. The only way in which a huge and young population could directly destabilize the system would be for everyone to go stand outside on the street at exactly the same time, and that wasn't about to happen.

Looking at the big picture—the laws and policies and grand structures of state—the political situation had not altered in a truly meaningful way over the past five years. But from the vantage point of the living room and the park, life was different in the ways that mattered most. My friends now had the freedom to sit around watching American television, give each other rides home at night, sneak pecks on the cheek in public, and dress as fabulously or dowdily as they wanted. No longer forced to fret about things that should have been irrelevant (to wear or not to wear lipstick), there was now mental space for more interesting matters, such as choosing one's weblog pseudonym.

As this kind of change became ordinary, the gulf between Iranians of my generation and those of Khaleh Farzi's widened. She belonged to a type of older Iranians I came to think of as purists, because they applied the Purity Test to every facet of life in the Islamic Republic. Every time a lifestyle choice presented itself—Should I have lunch at the new Italian restaurant? See the new comedy everyone is raving about? Buy a new linen buttondown shirt to wear as *manteau?* Try the homemade wine made by the local

Armenian vintner?—they asked themselves how it compared to its equivalent before the revolution.

The answer usually failed the Purity Test, because of course the restaurants were now mediocre, the comedy banal, the wine sour . . . and the *manteau* question was not applicable. Picky and scarred, the purists estranged themselves from the rhythm of the younger generation's life. It was as though the intolerable years had left a mark on them, and now they resided permanently in that old state of mind—a powerful assurance in the bottomless awfulness of being in Iran.

The purity business always led to arguments between Khaleh Farzi and me. Often, the disagreement centered on lunch, and whether we should go out or not. "I don't have the patience to eat wearing a veil; you know I don't enjoy it," she would say. I hated eating in a veil too, worried the ends would fall in the soup, unable to get past the odd sensation of chewing with my ears covered in cloth. As annoying as it was, I still occasionally wanted to go to lunch. Unlike Khaleh Farzi, recollections of vintage, veil-less Tehran lunches did not color the decision for me.

Khaleh Farzi settled in next to me on the couch, and dialed the rotary phone with a pencil. Ever since she had moved to Tehran, she had developed a habit of directing her contempt for the Islamic Republic at inanimate objects, as though they were contaminated by the regime. She opened car doors with a handkerchief, poked squash at the vegetable stand with a gloved finger.

That afternoon, we were planning to address a major crisis: my wardrobe. One of Khaleh Farzi's chi-chi friends, a woman who spent her summers in the south of France and the rest of the year in a Frenchified bubble in Tehran, knew a designer who made swishy, smart *roopooshes* inspired by that season's couture collections. Khaleh Farzi was calling to get his address and held the receiver away from her ear as soon as it was answered.

"No, I said, pluck in the *direction* of the feather . . . *with* the feather! . . . *imbecile!*" Her friend was screaming at her cook for improperly cleaning the bird that would become that evening's duck à l'orange. She gave Farzi directions to the designer's atelier, a second-floor apartment on a back alley in Elahieh.

I owned exactly three *roopooshes,* and I had worn them so frequently they had become uniforms. The standard, black *roopoosh* Khaleh Farzi handed down to me the day I arrived in Tehran was spectacularly frumpy. It reached my ankles, and when I wore it I hallucinated that my thighs were expanding and that my hair smelled of fried onions. If I were unfortunate enough to catch a reflection of myself in a window in that *roopoosh,* I had to go immediately to bed and stay there for the rest of the day. The indignity of this *roopoosh* was even worse for being unnecessary. It made me look like one of those poor, shrouded tourists, who had clearly packed according to the dated advice in a Lonely Planet guide, and gazed in amazement at Tehrani women scampering around in stiletto sandals and short tunics that cinched at the waist.

The designer's atelier was nearby, so we walked over through the sycamore-shaded back alleys and rang the bell. An assistant opened the door and led us down a tangerine hallway into a bright studio space with custard-colored walls and a vaulted ceiling. A broad antique oak table stood in the center, strewn with fabrics and European fashion magazines, and there was a sitting area to the side with plush sofas and a glass table set with yellow roses floating in a bowl. Arash fluttered in, wearing a lavender linen shirt and khakis, apologizing for keeping us waiting. He turned down Ella Fitzgerald, and immediately began fussing over my aunt.

"I've heard *soooo* much about you," he said to Khaleh Farzi. "I hear you love to hike . . . just like me. . . . I adore nature. . . . People who like nature are usually very sensitive, don't you think? . . . You're so adorable!"

An assistant tottered over with a tray of tea, served in slim, gold-rimmed cups, and Marie biscuits. Arash talked for a good half hour about how much he missed Paris (he had moved back to Tehran two years before), the Louvre, and how much he adored the new "know thyself" classes he had just started.

"By nature," he explained, "I'm a pacifist." But in Iran, he was a foot soldier in the struggle against the regime's assault on beauty. He wanted to reclaim the *roopoosh,* make it exquisite and flattering, turn the Islamic uniform into a garment of aesthetic resistance. Khaleh Farzi nodded her head politely, and then buried her face in French *Vogue.*

"That's really great, Arash. I really respect what you're trying to do," I said. "I need something functional, but attractive. I sit down a lot in front of clerics, so no front slits."

He clapped his hands together joyfully. "I know *exactly* what you want."

He stood up and began circling the couch, eyeing my shoes and my bag. "I'm thinking feminine but minimalist. I am thinking Armani. I am *not* thinking St. John."

He unraveled a roll of grayish, sea-foam green chiffon, and draped it over a square of the same fabric, in a pearly, light beige. "We'll do this cut like a toga, in two tones, so that when you walk the beige will peek out underneath. It'll be so elegant. So subtle. So modest." He shrugged his shoulders lightly, shivering with delight. He then dropped a stack of Italian fashion magazines in my hands, and said his tailors could reproduce anything I wanted down to the stitch. I was bewitched. It might be worth it to stay in Iran after all, I thought, if I could acquire a custom-made, designer-inspired wardrobe at J. Crew prices.

Fashion as resistance. What an intriguing concept, and how heartening to find style in the land of everything-must-be-as-ugly-as-possible-at-all-times. Immersed in her magazine, Khaleh Farzi looked up to weigh in on color choices, but she couldn't be bothered to have a *manteau* made for herself. For her part, she had worn the same shapeless, navy-blue *roopoosh* every day for the last four years. It looked atrocious the day she bought it, and four years later, it resembled a worn grocery sack. Am I *khar* (an ass), she said each time I nagged at her to buy something new, that I should spend money on this regime's uniform?

The wardrobe she had accumulated throughout her life, the piles and piles of silk scarves acquired during two decades in America, reposed in her vault-like closet, wrapped in tissue. Many of her friends were similarly disinclined to prettify their *roopoosh* wardrobes, as this meant engaging with the Islamic Republic, something they avoided at all costs. They preferred to cloister in the company of old friends, in worlds carefully constructed to turn inward, and deflect the reality of the present as much as possible. That could mean wearing just one *manteau* for years, staying inside all day endlessly redecorating apartments, or supervising the denuding of a leathery old duck. But young women my age weren't prepared to do that—there were parties to go to, hobbies to explore, men to flirt with, personalities to refine. In all likelihood, there would be no other world in which to do all this, and it made no sense waiting the system out, with so much living to do.

"So, are you going to the fashion show tomorrow?" Arash asked me.

"The what?"

"The fashion show. You know, catwalk, models, couture."

"Yeah, I know what a fashion show is, thank you." Arash was charming, but also a bit precious. "But are you sure? Here?" Maybe he meant on the television fashion network.

"It's women only. Maybe I could sneak in under a *chador?* Too bad for me, but you should definitely go."

⚓

The next morning, as I sat in traffic, I called up everyone in my mobile phone's memory and told them I was on my way to a *fashion show!* Just saying those two words was exhilarating, but mostly no one believed me. There had been no fashion shows in Iran since 1979, when the revolution ordered women to cover themselves, and it was easier for my friends to believe that I was wrong (perhaps I had misread some notice in the paper?) than to imagine such a looming wall could crumble. A security guard stood outside the giant auditorium where the show was to be held, making sure only women entered. A few young men loitered outside, trying to peek inside the door when it swung open.

One part of me shivered with delight at the thought of a fashion show in the Islamic Republic. A public event dedicated to the expression and aesthetic of femininity, in a place so hostile to all things feminine and physical. Another part of me registered disappointment, because a regime-sanctioned catwalk signaled a societal entrenchment of the veil. I'd much rather be driving to a demonstration where women burned head scarves, rather than modeled them. But I reminded myself that women's absorption in their physical appearance, in itself, communicated a powerful message. It meant they were not forfeiting their bodies, their right to express themselves, enshrined in the seemingly superficial but deeply symbolic matter of outer garb.

Excited young women filled the auditorium. I couldn't understand why they didn't remove their veils, since men were not permitted, but the veil had been internalized enough that in many such situations, women needlessly kept them on. The murmur of voices subsided, as the lights dimmed and a remix of Sting's "Desert Rose" came on. The first collection consisted of clothes you could actually wear in public, an impressive array of short coats, tunics, and dresses, cut so they could be worn outdoors as *roopoosh,* but fine enough to be worn indoors as a top. This cleverly solved the prob-lem of having to choose two outfits each day: the *manteau*/outer layer, and the under-layer that you would wear upon arrival at your destination. In-spired, I scribbled in my notebook: Have Arash make knee-length tunic with matching pants, and reversible silk coat.

Next came evening wear. Banal prom gowns, mostly, but a ripple of pleasure passed through the crowd, and they cheered energetically, as though they were imagining themselves making grand appearances at par-ties in those very outfits. There were only two looks on display, in keeping with the dated ways of being Iranian culture offered women: tart or lady. The lady aesthetic was demure, with lots of tulle and pastel sheaths. The vampy look involved slinky black dresses with lots of sequins. Both were covered in fur coats the models shimmied out of halfway down the runway.

As the models sauntered up and down the catwalk to the deep bass of jungle music, baring nose-rings, navels, and shoulders, something seemed off. Oh, I realized, it was the absence of clicking cameras and flashes going off. There would be no news reports or reviews of this fashion show in the local press. Like it never happened.

Afterward, I found the designer backstage, and asked her how she had managed to pull off a fashion show. The official sponsor, she said, was a cul-tural preservation organization that had registered the show as an exhibi-tion of clothes embroidered by traditional handiwork. Then she launched into a lecture on how Iranians needed to create indigenous fashions and that we should "cross out the model of the West as inappropriate." An ema-ciated model in designer underwear tapped her on the shoulder and asked if she could wear the finale white wedding dress at the afternoon show.

Between the navel rings and the Kate Moss models, I wasn't sure exactly how the West was being rejected. Don't you think young women favor Western fashion because they associate that style with a freer, more open lifestyle? I asked the designer. She blinked disingenuously, as though she could not fathom what I meant.

Iranian women, like women everywhere, expressed themselves in part through their physical appearance. Because the regime tried to take away this right by giving them uniforms, that task became a time-consuming, of-ten obsessive challenge. This was not an overly intellectual or even original point. And it was breathtaking, how people who accommodated, and were accommodated by, the regime (often out of simple opportunism, like this fledgling designer), refused to admit it.

Oh well. Even if she was deluded or a hypocrite, at least she was creating clothes that Iranian women from all walks of life—not just the privileged women of northern Tehran—could feel good about wearing. She showed me the line she had designed for public-sector workers—well-cut tunic-pants combinations, in violets, and olives, with delicate embroidery, as an alternative to the drab smocks they presently wore. Her best uniforms, though, were designed for Iran Air flight attendants, who for twenty years had flown looking like veiled crows. They were a rip-off of the uniforms the stewardesses on Emirates, a Gulf airline wore, but again, I forgave her. There was only so much you could do to jazz up a navy-blue *hijab*.

☩

Since the revolution, Iranians who had left the country to live in the di-aspora had not, for the most part, commuted back and forth. They came every few years, often much less frequently, some not at all. In the Khatami era, far-flung Iranians began traveling home more regularly. The general at-mosphere had lightened, and there were new incentives on offer. My fa-ther's cousin Mitra, for example, who had left Iran in 1999, came from Vancouver for a very specific reason. Liposuction. We all told her not to do it. I mean, who has liposuction done in a country where doctors are mer-cenaries, out to maximize profit? Yes, in the West medicine is also a busi-ness, but in Iran, it was literally all about money.

For some reason, doctors were exempt from paying taxes. This made medicine the most lucrative career around, save the guiding of the faithful. Say you accidentally chopped off a finger in the kitchen, while mincing heaps of *sabzi,* and called an ambulance. Unbeknownst to you, while you sat in the back nursing your bleeding stump of a finger, the ambulance drivers would be calling various hospitals on their cell phones, to see which doctors bid higher for your admittance. Once they had checked around, they would drive you to the hospital of the highest bidder, even if it hap-pened to be miles farther than the one nearest your house. They *auctioned* you off, like a sheep or an ancient manuscript.

Cosmetic surgery was huge in Iran. Demand for procedures, particularly of the face, surged after 1979, when the Ayatollah Khomeini banned women from revealing the shape of their bodies. It was an investment in feeling modern, in the midst of the seventh-century atmosphere the mullahs were trying to create. It assuaged so many urges at once—to look better, to self-express, to show off that you could afford it, to appear Westernized. The compulsion to work these interior issues out through one's appearance was a curious phenomenon unique to revolutionary Iran. In a way, it was dysfunctional—picking the scab of the right you didn't have.

The voracious demand and the greed of doctors willing to get a quick specialization turned plastic surgery into a thriving industry. Procedures were not cheap (a quality facelift was almost $5,000), but half or less of the equivalent in the West. This obsession with achieving the ideal face, or the effect of trying, had long been restricted to the women of Tehran, who relished adorning what the regime told them to neglect.

But since my arrival, getting a nose job was the hip thing to do—for *men.* It was an unlikely phenomenon in the land of the bearded revolution. Some guys parted with their traditional Iranian nose in favor of a sleeker profile that better matched their Euro-trash pretensions—a nose that said I am vain, modern, and well-off enough to cultivate my image. Some older men chiseled away their noses for a youthful appearance, so they would look less incongruous dating women the age of their daughters. Some men didn't submit their noses to the knife at all, but wore the post-surgical bandages anyway, because they looked cool. In the course of an average Thursday evening out, you could easily count a handful of guys sporting medical tape.

When I went plastic surgery shopping with Mitra, the waiting rooms were full of Iranian expatriate women, from places like Maryland and London, getting bargain treatments on their trips home to visit family. It all seemed so affordable and safe that I felt obligated to get something done. To live in Tehran and not surgically enhance something would be like going to a designer sample sale and walking out empty-handed.

But what? Maybe a nose job. These days you could get a very natural-looking nose in Tehran, unlike in the days of my mother, whose whole generation ended up with the very same profile. Apparently, there was only one man to trust with one's nose in Tehran: Dr. Navab, otherwise known as "Dr. Goldfinger." He used to practice in Paris but had relocated to Tehran after realizing that French women were more into toning their bodies, and Iranian women more into refining their faces. His facelifts were famous. Even the wives of European ambassadors went to him. At parties, if a woman walked in looking magically refreshed, guests would lift their eyebrows and maliciously whisper, "Dr. Navab?!"

The day Mitra and I went to visit him, a small group of *chadori* women stood outside his building, deliberating whether or not to enter. As we rang the bell, one of them broke away, and asked Mitra, in a shrill voice, "Excuse me, *khanoum*, did you get your nose done here?" She, of the perfect nose, shook her head, ignoring the rude question. Ah, I see, so you're here to get your daughter's nose done, the woman persisted, turning to me. My hand flew up to cover the maligned feature, defensively. Is it that bad? I whispered, as we were buzzed inside.

Dr. Navab himself was charming and full of flattery, as all plastic surgeons dealing with insecure, vain women should be. He spoke the esperanto of flattery in multiple dialects *(joonam! chérie!* honey!), and his office looked like an English library, all polished wood and brass. He wore a tie with daisies, and a matching silk handkerchief. There was an ode to his talent, composed by an adoring patient, on the wall: "Slowly, slowly, his artistic hand evokes the work of Michelangelo." Next to it hung a before-Dr.-Navab/after-Dr.-Navab painting, by yet another patient-fan, of a haggard old woman transformed into a svelte model swinging a status handbag.

Mitra queried him about facelifts, and I explored the nose options. In the end, I decided getting a nose job was in poor taste. One day my daughter would go through my old photos, and divide the epochs of my life into pre– and post–nose job days, as I did with certain female relatives.

Preventive Botox would be less invasive, and more subtle. The queen of Tehran Botox, Dr. Fariba, had the same first name as my mother, which I interpreted as an auspicious sign. Her office was done in the same medical spa atmosphere as my Manhattan dermatologist—an airy space both posh and clinical, with Japanese prints on the walls, bamboo flowers in eclectic vases, and cappuccino at the ready. Dr. Fariba was a skilled therapist, beautician, and medical doctor rolled into one and spent as much time ministering to delicate egos as explaining the possible side effects of microdermabrasion. But she had her limits. She would not do Botox parties, though patients requested them. "I run a medical office, not a beauty salon," she said.

In the end, I wimped out on Botox, too, but Mitra finally settled on liposuction, aiming to lose an inch off the circumference of her hips and thighs. I argued this was unnecessary. She was already beautiful, and I didn't see why she should put herself through general anesthesia to go down a dress size. She shook her head dejectedly. At the end of the day, *khanoum,* there isn't much else you can do about this flesh, she said, patting her Iranian saddlebags, our genetic predestiny.

After the surgery Mitra went to her mother's apartment in Niyavaran to convalesce, and that is where I went to visit her, with my twin offerings of tuberoses and *Vogue.* She lay in the day bed of the sunny guest room, propped up against pillows. Outside, the birds chirped at unnaturally loud volume. There were pills and tea on the table. Here, pick out all the skinny pants you can wear now, I said, carefully placing the magazine on her lap. I lay down next to her, and turned the glossy pages, trying not to think about the seeping gauze bandages under the covers.

I reached for the bowl of apricots on the table, picked out a plump one, and passed it to Mitra. She took a nibble with a sip of tea. Our time together was usually spent with her two daughters, dancing in the living room or eating pizza on the balcony. This was our first private conversation.

I had always wanted to ask her about why she had decided to leave Iran, even after Khatami. Was it hard deciding to go, I asked. You stuck it out for so many years, what made it finally unbearable? She thought about it for several seconds, passing her finger back and forth over the apricot. When she finally did speak, it was not about the veil, or the violations of private life, or any of the daily degradations I had lived and expected to hear about. I couldn't stand arguing with them anymore, she said, the Sister Fatimehs and Sister Zeinabs at the girls' schools.

Mitra had two daughters, both teenagers. They would come home from school, having learned nothing useful, but with an earful of reprimands. "I would go down there every day, and ask them why my daughters were being treated like this. And *they,* these uneducated, unforgiving women, would stare down their noses at me, like, who was I to be asking questions about my daughters' education."

Every life in Iran came with its unique set of battles, most of which, like Mitra's, were unknown to me. I had never tried to raise children under the Islamic Republic, so that particular challenge did not even occur to me. I couldn't imagine what it would be like sending my daughters off to school each day, to be indoctrinated against me, their heads filled with an ideology that I would then need to unteach them at home. To be told that I, their mother, was anti-revolutionary, Westernized, immoral. Had I a choice, I realized, I might not have stayed to fight. Not if it meant sacrificing my daughters. The way I had learned to conceive of the Iranian nation, of devotion to homeland, was, after many months, still abstract. If I had children here, being pried from me and claimed for the revolution, if I had to go through a divorce under a system that stripped me of all my rights, then perhaps these notions of patriotism and loyalty would sound hollow.

Mitra's cheek gently fell against a cushion, and her exhalations became regular. In the quietness of the moment, as twilight settled on the willow trees outside the window, I felt some of the guilt of belonging to the diaspora, to the tribe who left, recede. Through living here, through seeing all the complexity that went into people's decisions to stay or leave, I was learning not to judge so harshly myself or others over such an intensely personal choice.

I respected Mitra for boxing up a privileged life, saying goodbye to all of her extended family, and starting from scratch in another hemisphere. Leaving was not an act of treason or disloyalty but of self-preservation. I had always believed that we outside were compromised for leaving Iran behind. That belief had colored my life, filled it with remorse for a decision that had not been mine. But for Mitra, and thousands of mothers like her, it would have been more compromising *not* to leave. Sacrificing a middle-aged life was one thing. Sacrificing two fresh daughters entirely another.

⁂

On the plane, a British businessman sat down next to me, and began chatting as the other passengers found their seats. We both watched women sit down, and, with the exception of pulling their head scarves off, looking pretty much as they had when they got on board. This was wholly unlike the boarding of outbound planes in years past, when women did an elaborate changing routine out of their black *roopooshes,* emerging in full makeup and Western clothes, as though the airplane bathroom was a backstage dressing room. Well, it's much better now, isn't it? he asked, trying to engage me in conversation. Yes, of course, I said quietly. And I didn't elaborate because I didn't have it in me at that moment to extol all the ways Iranians now had it better. I wanted to say: Yes, it's better, but not for me, because I'm a female journalist, and life is still really crap. But of course I didn't say that, because it was so easy to make Westerners think the worst things about Iran, and my private misery was highly specialized and therefore irrelevant.

At that moment, I remember thinking really how stupid the mullahs were. If they didn't intimidate us with their goony Mr. Xs, people like me could be really useful. I'd have sat here chirping away about how much relative freedom women had, and blah blah. I would have been a perfect little commercial for the democratizing Islamic Republic. But instead, they played stupid games and harassed you and pretended to threaten your family and tried to make you rat on your friends and made your friends rat on you. And then they acted incredibly affronted when you wrote that not everything was sublime in the Islamic Republic.

I was on my way to New York. As assignments went, it was relatively painless. It was not a squalid refugee camp, full of ragged children whose torn overalls and forlorn eyes made your heart splinter, or a trip to a desolate border region where you ate nothing but canned tuna for a week. But for me, following President Khatami to New York, for the United Nations General Assembly, held all the appeal of a winter jaunt to Taliban-controlled Kabul.

Under the Clinton administration, the possibility of a stealthy Iran-U.S. détente always lurked around the corner. It seems quaint from the vantage point of today, with the region on the verge of falling apart and Iran branded as one-third of the "axis of evil," to consider such micro-diplomacy a big news story. But at the time, every journalist who covered Iran scrutinized Tehran's relationship with Washington for signs of thaw. Since ties were formally severed, the two countries communicated through what was called "track two diplomacy," where former officials and diplomats acted as intermediaries through private relationships and quiet international conferences that pretended to be about other subjects. The U.N. General Assembly was one of the few occasions when the president of Iran and the president of the United States would be in the same room, so journalists showed up in case the backroom diplomacy went public through some last-minute haggling.

When asked to go, I said yes. Then I went to pack a suitcase and immediately regretted it. I was getting better at existing between Iran and America. Most days one helped me understand the other better, rather than the two squishing me like elephants. But geographically at least, I still preferred them apart. The certainty of vast ocean and great land mass as separator was reassuring. There was always some European airport duty free to loiter through in between, where you could try on ten different perfumes and buy chocolate and prepare yourself for the transition. I did not want the mullahs to come to Manhattan. New York was my American stomping ground. I went there to lounge half-naked in dimly lit bars, sip cocktails with friends, and forget about those same mullahs. Their arrival in New York would taint my sanctuary. Turbans and the Manhattan skyline would mingle in my mind. And the question of "What do I wear?" would take on whole new dimensions.

The morning of President Khatami's press conference, I walked east down 42nd Street toward the U.N., wearing a gray, Donna Karan pantsuit, gripping a soy-milk cappuccino, invisible in the crowded commuter lane of the sidewalk. I was very pleased with this suit because it was my first adult woman suit that actually looked natural on me, instead of boxy and self-consciously suit-like. But inside my bag, glowing like pink kryptonite, was the accessory that would damn it to hell. A carefully folded, rose-colored head scarf.

For months, I had worked around the president and his entourage in Iran, veiled properly, like a professional Iranian woman. Technically, since I carried an Iranian passport and had Iranian nationality, I was legally required to wear the veil everywhere, at all times.

Even secular women activists wore the veil when outside the country, so the system's eyes abroad did not document their violation and use it as pretext to harass them upon return. This probably wouldn't happen to me, but at the same time, I knew the president and his aides were more comfortable dealing with Iranian women who were veiled. Something about speaking Farsi in public with a bare-headed woman distracted them, even though they pretended everything was perfectly normal.

If I appeared before them with my hair exposed, the image would be etched onto their minds forever. Every time thereafter, they would recall me as Ms. Moaveni-whom-I-once-saw-without-*hijab*, rather than simply

Ms. Moaveni. I had gone unveiled before at regional conferences, and half the Iranian delegation ignored me, looking away when we passed in the hallways as though passing a strip club.

The president's men were not so lumpen, and would of course still speak to me. But they would feel mortally disrespected. My youth would render it a precocious offense, rather than a political statement. Who does this girl think she is, they would say to themselves, to be asserting herself so impertinently before her elders? If there was one over-arching value to Iranian culture (at least until the revolution created its own culture of anarchy), it was respect for one's elders. That's why it actually mattered, when you were passing out tea in a crowded room, which elderly woman with purple hair you served first.

Maybe it seems excessive, elevating the question of putting on that scarf to high drama, a Hamletesque teetering back and forth over a square of cloth. But every now and then, I would find myself in these situations, which demanded an understanding of who I was and what mattered to me, and truly felt paralyzed. Putting on that dumb scrap of pink meant betraying my personal beliefs.

First there was my opposition to the veil, inherited from both sides of my family, an heirloom value that every single one of us—monarchists, secularists, socialists, capitalists, dilettantes—held dear. We did not negotiate with the veil. It was the symbol of how everything had gone horribly wrong. How in the early days of the revolution, secular women wore the veil as a protest symbol against the West and its client state policies, and then had it imposed on them by the fundamentalist mullahs who hijacked the revolution and instituted religious law. My generation, Iranians who learned about 1979 at kitchen tables in the United States, absorbed this version of history as truth. Though most women in modern-day Iran might not consider the veil their highest grievance, they knew it symbolized the system's disregard for women's legal status in general. Mandatory veiling crushed women's ability to express themselves, therefore denying them a basic human right.

As a child of this diaspora, how could I wear the mullahs' veil on the streets of New York? As a student of a liberal American education, taught to apply my political beliefs to my everyday life—to recycle and vote, to respect picket lines and observe boycotts—how could I not take a personal stand against the repressive veil? Did I not owe it to the thousands of

Afghani women, veiled by force under the Taliban, the millions of Iranian women who had no choice, to take a stand, when I did?

Of course, even if I'd had days to come up with a position, I wouldn't have known what to do. American individualism and Iranian deference to tradition were irreconcilable. That was the catch that no one ever told you about—that traveling down one of those paths meant turning your back on the other. No commuting back and forth, no shared custody. End of story.

As the flags of the U.N. appeared in the distance, I realized there was no graceful way out. My feet sailed over the pavement, closer and closer to the unmakeable decision. Suddenly, Siamak's voice entered the din in my head. I had spent a lot of time calling him up and presenting him with impossible situations, and by now I could pretty much play his role in my head and talk myself down from the ledge. Okay, Azi jan, stop for a second, he would say. Stop, and imagine the two possible outcomes. Once you can imagine both, decide which one is worse. Decide which one you can live with. If you can figure that out, you know what you need to do.

And so I thought out the worst. Veiled, I would dislike myself. I would brush my teeth in the dark, embarrassed to look at myself in the mirror. But going bareheaded, I would display disrespect for the faith of men I esteemed. Men who had, on their territory, encouraged me, treated me with respect, and always helped me, even when it didn't serve their purposes. On what they perceived as my territory, I would be flinging it all in their faces. This I would carry around like a brick of guilt in my stomach. This I could not live with.

With just a block to go, I unfolded the veil and draped it over my hair, tossing the ends over my shoulders. For a second I felt transported back to Villa Street, that day when Khaleh Zahra dropped her veil and attracted eyes like a lighthouse. On this Manhattan street, wearing a veil was the equivalent of going bare-headed in Tehran. Suddenly, I wasn't invisible anymore. People's eyes actually skimmed over me, instead of sliding past blindly, as they're supposed to do on a crowded urban sidewalk. I had been so busy contemplating "to veil or not to veil" that it hadn't occurred to me anyone else would notice. It was like wearing a neon sign, blinking "Muslim! Muslim!"

I reached the U.N. Plaza Hotel and joined the other journalists, television anchors with brand-name voices, in the lobby. As though the self-im-

molation I had subjected myself to en route was not enough, a prominent
television reporter took one look at my covered head and informed me im-
periously that I was not required to veil (as though I had forgotten that the
laws of the Islamic Republic did not apply in New York City) and that in
fact, I was doing the other women there a disservice by doing so. So now,
not only was I wearing the veil, but I was forced to defend the decision publicly with all these people listening. I live and work in Iran, I explained. My
situation is different. I deal with these officials all the time, not once a year
at election time.

★

After the day's round of meetings, I slunk back to my hotel room, peeled
off the outfit of shame, and poured myself a glass of wine from the mini-
bar. Lying naked on the fluffy white comforter, I contemplated, in between
sips, where my cousins and I should go for dinner that evening. Somewhere
very unIslamic Republic. Tapas? Nobu? Just as the hundreds of small kinks
in my shoulders had begun to ease, the phone rang.

"*Salaam Azadeh Khanoum.*" It was Parsa, the president's translator, and
apparently, he was downstairs in the lobby. *My* lobby. No, no, no, I groaned
face down into the pillow. He had asked me that afternoon where I was
staying, and since *international law* prohibited the delegation from leaving
U.N. grounds, it hadn't occurred to me not to tell him. "For just one second, come down. I have to speak to you about something," he said.

Parsa was arrogant, boyish, and spoke four languages fluently. He had
sneaked me into a bunch of bilateral talks that day, and had given me play-
by-play updates of the president's movements by cell phone, since their arrival. *Now we're on the Brooklyn Bridge, getting pelted by eggs* [anti-regime
activists]. *Now we're at the hotel, and he's taking a nap. Now we're skipping the
photo session, because Madeleine Albright is supposed to be there.*

"*Basheh,*" I sighed, all right. "Give me a minute." I pulled on a pair of jeans,
but refused to brush my teeth. He and his friends were probably drinking
back at their hotel, and I didn't care if he smelled wine on my breath. There
was nothing sadder than official Iranian delegations—journalists, officials,
their assistants—abroad. Half of any group usually couldn't wait to crack
open a beer, but there were always one or two devout spoilers. They argued

among themselves, like those sour couples who are always bickering in the breakfast rooms of hotels. I wouldn't wear the veil, either. He'd showed up on my turf and he'd just have to deal.

When the elevator doors opened, I saw Parsa perched awkwardly on a red velvet chaise longue shaped like a kidney. The Royalton is one of these overly clever hotels that is deliberately invisible from the street. Its lobby is a stark, white, sunken lounge filled with lithe, beautiful people holding flashy conversations over drinks. Parsa had likely never seen so much exposed skin all at once, but he held his head high, trying to appear unfazed. He undid the top button of his collarless shirt as the waitress, an angular blond giraffe in all black, handed us the cocktail menu. Parsa ignored her, for which I gave him credit. It was a rare servant indeed of the Islamic Republic who could avoid checking out a half-naked blonde. Instead, his eyes scanned the rest of the room like strobe lights. I ordered mineral water, and prayed that he would leave quickly.

In a small, nervous voice, he asked me if anyone at *Time* needed a Farsi-speaking assistant in New York, and seeing the incredulous look on my face, revised his request slightly. Or in Tehran. Or Dubai. Or anywhere really, as long he was working for an American company.

"Are you kidding?" I asked him gently. "You have an amazing job. You speak all these languages and get to travel the world. You translated for our *president* in front of the entire General Assembly. Why would you want to give that up to be someone's assistant?"

His face sank in disappointment. In the end, he said, each glamorous assignment landed him back in Tehran, on an Iranian passport. He didn't care about the status; he wanted a life with a future. Besides, there were handfuls of qualified translators who deserved his job, and he owed his to some combination of chance and connections to insiders within the system. If those connections dried up or he fell out of favor, well, he would be just another talented, Iranian twenty-something working long hours for a paltry salary and little chance of upward mobility.

This type of conversation, of which I'd had too many, was akin to treating a splinter. Any tug or pull, whether getting the splinter out or pushing it in further, hurt. And in the end, no one would listen to what I said, because I was not considered an impartial judge. If I argued that life in Iran, for all its oppressiveness, had a sweet, singular appeal, I would be scoffed at. *Nafasat az jayeh garm darmiyad,* as the Persian expression went, loosely meaning: You're judging the coldness of a place from a warm spot. As long as I bore an American passport, any Iranian who didn't would reject my opinions on the livability of Iran. They would interpret my reaction to mean that I didn't think Iranians deserve better, that they shouldn't strive for what I had. But if I agreed, commiserating about how life in Iran could grind you down to a fine powder, like a few strands of saffron crushed under the weight of a pestle, I would be confirming the future's bleakness. And then my judgment would be fresh cause for despair.

Parsa fidgeted, trailing his finger through the condensation on the green glass of the water bottle. I asked if he could find his way back to the hotel. He said he could. Phew. Operation Abort Translator Defection appeared to be a success.

⚘

Presidents Khatami and Bill Clinton had come within yards of a handshake. For weeks before the Assembly, an informal group of senior semiofficial intermediaries had convinced both Iranian and U.S. officials to proceed with the gesture, on the sidelines of the summit, in the first public display of rapprochement between the two countries in decades. The Americans had said yes, provided the Iranians promised not to make any stentorian rhetorical accusations. The Iranians had the same requirement. Both were reassured the other would behave discreetly. Everything was set. It was meant to happen as the world leaders gathered for the annual picture.

But at the eleventh hour, the Iranian side backed out. For reasons I didn't quite understand, I took this failure of diplomatic vision personally. I felt like the Islamic Republic had let me down. Or maybe it was the first time I had front row seats to the Islamic Republic messing up a good opportunity, the first time I had seen its foreign policy so starkly reactive, so absent of long-range strategy or ambition. The leaders weren't taking Iran forward, they were doing damage control and trying to keeping a failed revolution afloat.

At such times, when the puppet-show character of Iranian leadership was put in stark relief against the panorama of the possible that was both the U.N. and New York, I felt crushed by the magnitude of Iran's national decline. How had we been reduced to this? We who had once brimmed with potential, we who had an embarrassing wealth of riches—oil, an ancient civilization, gorgeous cities that would forever draw tourists, mountains and sea, an educated and talented population.

It was impossible for me to form any thoughts beyond what my role was, or what it should be, in relation to this national disaster. One part of me felt involved. I felt like I should make a firm decision, as Siamak had done—roll up my sleeves and take up permanent residence in Iran and in some small, modest way, chip away at the edifice of this rotten regime. At this tendency, my father would have rolled his eyes and said (pointedly and in English), "We raised you in California. We sent you to an American university. Get over it."

Another part of me wanted to listen to my dad and pretend it was okay to do that. I could leave Tehran to study Persian literature at Stanford and buy French cheese at the gourmet groceries in Palo Alto and serve wine to my well-groomed Iranian yuppie friends. I could be Iranian without the Islamic Republic, without the Mr. X interrogations, the nightmares, the veil, and the lascivious mullahs with their temporary marriage proposals.

Being in these political situations, when Iran and the U.S. encountered one another, made me nervous. No one came right out and said anything, but everyone acted uncomfortable if you didn't make your loyalties and politics clear from the outset. If you weren't obvious about this kind of question and suggested things were complicated (that Iran was a rogue state with democratic tendencies; that the United States made lots of mistakes in the Middle East), the possibility lingered that you were some sort of apologist for authoritarian regimes.

I didn't know what I thought. About politics. About patriotic duty. About what or whom I should even have patriotic duty toward. Thinking of myself as a hyphenated entity, an Iranian-American, didn't help in the slightest. It was a sense of self that helped in the banal, day-to-day course of things, but it didn't erase the question of loyalty at all. It didn't help you when two things you loved, countries or people, existed at odds with one another.

When I was a girl, when I tugged on my mother's skirt and made her repeat my favorite story—of her *maman bozorg* (grandmother), the one who chopped down the mulberry orchard in revenge for being demoted to second wife—I remember feeling outrage at the injustice. In the only picture of my great-grandmother we have, she sits on a terrace, next to a line of hanging laundry, hands folded across her lap, a squinting, uncomfortable expression on her face, as though the chair she sat on was missing a leg. How could this great-grandfather be so horrible, I asked my mother, as to cruelly *make maman bozorg* a co-wife? Why was it allowed at all?

Maman explained that in the Koran, it says that a man can take more than one wife *on the condition* that he treats all of them exactly equally. Their quarters must be furnished with equal elegance or simplicity; he must spend an equal number of nights with each. But what about love? I asked. How can he love them equally in his heart? He can't, she said. The heart doesn't work that way. And that's why men should never, ever, have more than one wife. Because the heart is not docile, can't follow literal instructions, can't be cordoned off like a garden—this grove for the first wife, this for the second. Sooner or later, emotions blossom or wither in places they shouldn't, and the pretense of heart boundaries collapses.

CHAPTER SEVEN

Love in a Time of Struggle

In your presence I see the green of my wings,
like the image of grass the feathers of a parrot paint in the mirror,
In the lines that define your being I seek a hedge
to protect the green clove from being trampled.
I grow in your consciousness like a vine,
with my hair covering rooftops, doorstops, and fences.

—Simin Behbehani

To be a young woman in the Iran of the Islamic Republic involved a certain degree of uncertainty over one's identity, or at the very least, over one's romantic priorities. Most of my girlfriends had no idea whether they had a "type." In contrast to California, no one fretted much about being unready for commitment, or the passage from dating to dating exclusively. Perhaps in time, quality of life would improve in Tehran, and along with it, quality of dating. But in the meantime, rather than worrying over arcane distinctions in relationship terminology, or the riddle wrapped in an enigma of "Why didn't he call back?" relationships served a far more vital purpose: taking a fragile identity and anchoring it in a situation or person.

You may think, not incorrectly, that for women relationships the world over involve defining yourself through men. But modern Iran went so out of its way to confuse and complicate the identities of women that this natural tendency became an overwhelming one. The regime fed young people such contradictory messages—women were liberated but legally inferior; women should be educated but subservient; women should have careers but stick to traditional gender roles; women should play sports but ignore their dirty physical needs—that it elevated even basic questions of self (What are my priorities, expectations, needs?) to higher physics.

It was a tough climate in which to be a young woman. It made it hard to know what was truly important to you, what defined you deep down, if all those layers of family/peers/neighborhood/social background/trickle-down-dogma were stripped away. In Iran, a society in flux, every single one of those layers was also undergoing transformation. Constructing a coherent personality out of all the chaos was a formidable task. That's why my generation of Iranians was called the lost generation. And that's why for women, searching for relationships was, if not a search for self, a search to anchor a self adrift.

The intensity of life in modern-day Iran added another complication to finding love. You had to find not only chemistry but a partner who wanted the same sort of Islamic Republic experience, both emotionally and logistically, as you. A dating service would have needed to create questionnaires with such questions—Do you want a partner who (check one): is furious and bitter / resigned and placid; externalizes rage / internalizes sorrow; is itching to emigrate / determined to stay; flouts laws regularly / is cautious and obedient; reads five newspapers a day / does not know what year it is; is addicted to opium/heroin / addicted to food, Prozac.

For Tehrani women who dated within their own milieu, such considerations were psychologically complex enough. For those who strayed across borders of social class, the result was something between agonizing and mortifying.

This proved especially true with a distant friend of mine, Fatimeh. She was the very last person you'd suspect would embroil herself in an inauspicious relationship. When she finally did, she had it the hardest of all, because her relationship, or her would-be relationship, really, had to be conducted in secret, away from the watchful eyes of her traditional family.

The first time I met her, we were waiting for a presidential reception outside one of the palaces at Saad Abad—the royal complex built by Reza Shah in northern Tehran. The press pool stood in the shade chatting, and apart from me, there was only one other woman, Fatimeh. It was only the second or third time I had encountered the Tehran press corps, which was full of journalists who had known each other forever, and I didn't feel comfortable smoking in front of them and the ceremonial guard. I moved to the side of the giant fountain outside the palace, only to find that I had made myself more conspicuous. Noticing the tense way I had my arms folded, Fatimeh walked over to keep me company.

I smiled my thanks to the fascinating, black-clad creature that had appeared next to me. She wore the full-length *chador,* with an elastic strap over the top of her head, to keep the fabric in place. Underneath each arm, swinging back and forth amidst the folds, hung a camera. She chirped hello, in her cheery, brusque tone, and inspected me with equal curiosity. When the officials finally arrived, I ignored them. Fatimeh was a far more absorbing sight, as she maneuvered her way to the front of the photographers, juggling cameras, clicking with one then the other, somehow managing it all gracefully—under a hot sun—while swathed in yards of black nylon.

She came from a traditional, pious family that was exhibiting exceptional openness by allowing her this independence, letting her out of the house at all hours alone, to pursue her work. They did not feel entirely comfortable with this, but that they agreed at all was one of the not-so-small successes of the Islamic Republic. You have to forgive me this brief historical point, and an unfashionable one, at that, but it's important to understanding how Iranians were still struggling with the events of 1979. The revolution rolled back the legal rights of Iranian women, but it transformed the lives and horizons of women like Fatimeh.

Under the Shah's regime, traditional parents like hers would never have let their daughters stray out into society. They preferred to keep them uneducated and housebound rather than exposing them to corrupt, Westernized Iranians who drank, smoke, wore miniskirts, and slept around. The revolution erased all those sins from the surface of society (tucking them under wraps, along with women). In the process, it made it possible for young women like Fatimeh to venture out of the home sphere. They were given the opportunity to do something with their lives besides washing dishes and birthing.

A generation of such middle-class, traditional women were educated under the revolutionary republic. But inevitably, their new freedom stalled the day they graduated from university—when they walked out into an ailing economy that offered no jobs commensurate with their qualifications, back to families who expected them to hang their degree on the mantle and stay home. Fatimeh found a job and started working, so she managed to evade the revolving door that had flung so many of her peers straight back inside the house. She was the first woman in generations of her family to have a career, and her work made her feel capable of more. It raised her expectations of what life should offer her. Captivated by possibility, she was trying to negotiate her future within the conventional role her parents still expected her to play.

Fatimeh worked for a new, conservative-owned newspaper, but talked about its stolid headlines and poor design with disapproval. She brimmed with talent. That was obvious from the first time she dropped by to show me her portfolio. She wanted us to work together on feature stories and asked for help getting her photos published in U.S. magazines. In the end, we never collaborated on anything, because *Time* either used wire service images or dispatched its legendary photographers for special projects.

We saw each other constantly, though, because the months I lived in Iran were dense with news, and the press corps spent endless hours together, waiting for events to start, getting bused around with the president. Fatimeh was totally in love with President Khatami, who in turn had a special affection for her. Once or twice at events, he walked over to say hello and praise her, and her smooth, olive features gleamed afterward for days. "You're so lucky," I told her dolefully. The president had never singled me out, except once on his plane, to tell me he had heard I was a very nice girl.

She called me a lot, and it was clear she wanted to be friends. We met for tea during the workday, but beyond that I didn't know how to include her in my life. It might upset my relatives to bring her over in the evenings, because there would be alcohol around and a stranger in full *chador* would make everyone edgy, like having a nun in a habit at a cocktail party. Dariush refused to socialize with her, and his father had banned her from the house, on the grounds of her *chador* alone.

As much as Fatimeh wanted to hang out, she never discussed her personal life with me. She complained about her parents, of course, but about romance she remained silent. I only learned about this side of her when my friend Davar, also a journalist, informed me she had a crush on him. At first I was skeptical. I couldn't imagine Fatimeh, that intense, purposeful whirl of black *chador* and camera lenses, having a crush on anyone. Maybe you're misreading her signals, I suggested to Davar.

But eventually, her ambiguous overtures turned unmistakably forward. Instead of dropping by his office and lingering for hours, she dropped by his office, lingered for hours, and brought teddy bears holding hearts. Flirting with a guy such as Davar was not in her repertoire, and she probably had no idea where it would lead. So she punched him in the arm a lot, and professed to admire his work. She began phoning him on Fridays, suggesting they go hiking in the Alborz Mountains. I hate hiking, complained Davar. And besides, how can I be seen in public with her, wearing that damn *chador?* Turning her into a proper girlfriend would be nearly impossible.

She had suggested hiking because it was one of the very few activities in modern-day Tehran where people of all different classes and backgrounds came together, trooping up and down the mountains, reclining by riverside cafés. A girl in black *chador* and a young guy in a bright fleece could walk side by side, attracting little attention. But apart from the mountains, where could they go? A relationship could only get so far, when the venues of its evolution were limited to photo exhibitions and newspaper offices. Even cafés would have been tough. It wasn't so common to see a *chadori* woman sipping Turkish coffee with a clean-shaven male in the sorts of cafés middle-class Iranian kids frequented.

The logistics were thorny, but far more complicated was a possible relationship between Fatimeh and Davar. The ocean of difference between them made Davar himself an unlikely choice. He was Christian, secular, middle class, and Westernized, liberal in manner and thought, and an irrepressible partyer. Though on paper, and in person, he could not be more inappropriate for her, I understood the attraction.

Tehran was awash with the male equivalent of Fatimeh. They were journalists and painters, writers and photographers, who had fought in the war with Iraq or were married at eighteen, and were now breaking away from their traditional social backgrounds to enter an intellectual, urban milieu filled with people very different from themselves. The men had an astonishing ability to move in and out of these disparate worlds, hanging onto their evolving personas and sexuality all the while. They easily left their wives and families at home, while finding themselves in the new Tehran.

As a woman, Fatimeh had no such mobility. Her identity as an independent woman, a photojournalist, and a professional in her own right was still wholly vulnerable to the undermining traditions of her family. If she agreed to consider the men picked by her parents—conservatives who would require their wives to stay at home—that fragile new self she had worked so hard to create would be trampled. All this exposure to colleagues like us, people who spoke and socialized freely, who related to one another across the gender divide with an easy openness, had changed her. Davar, she knew, would regard her work as an organic part of her identity, not as phase to be indulged with the expectation that it would end.

How could she not be alienated by that old, familiar world of marriage, babies, and cooking? Yet this other world, to which we belonged, was disturbingly foreign. And Davar was not interested. He wanted straightforward relationships that included sex from the beginning and had no inclination to court a woman like Fatimeh who might never sleep with him at all.

Davar began pursuing a journalist in our circle who was perfectly comfortable going over to his apartment for drinks, and whatever came later. They weren't dating publicly, so it was not immediately apparent to Fatimeh that the object of her affection was embroiled in a side affair. She did, however, sense that something was amiss.

"So you're friends with Davar, right?" she would ask me, tentatively and repeatedly, on the phone. Too timid and embarrassed to go further, she let the question hang, hoping I would pick up the subject, and somehow shed light on the behavior of this young man she was so drawn to but did not understand. I could sense she was already feeling pangs of betrayal, even without knowing the full story. He had spent time with her, and to her, those hours meant something, even if no words had been exchanged.

"Davar has been extremely close to his mother since he was young," I offered lamely. "He has lots of female friends." My answer sounded vague and useless to my own ears. But I didn't know, given the lack of emotional intimacy between us, how to broach such intensely personal matters. In retrospect, I wish I had been less elliptical in warning her about their colliding worlds. I wish I had said, Fatimeh, your conception of a relationship radically differs—in assumptions, substance, and practice—from Davar's. If you judge what exists between you through your attitude, you're going to get disappointed, if not hurt.

I'm certain part of her suspected there was something between Davar and me. In her world, a man and a woman simply did not call each other by nicknames, hang out in each other's houses, go out for dinners and to cafés, unless they were engaged. If they did, their parents would have already met and negotiated their children's potential future. The time alone would simply be a short trial period before marriage, to ensure they did not despise each other.

To disabuse her of this idea, I began complaining about the lack of proper guys in Tehran, making joking laments of my spinsterhood, a refrain in our conversations. Once she realized Davar and I were just friends—that it was possible, indeed natural and common in our milieu, to be platonic in this way—she relaxed. It made her feel less vulnerable to know this was normal, and she sought him out more boldly.

Davar, in his thoughtless but still harmful way, must have mentioned to his new lover that Fatimeh had a crush on him. Though the last person to pose a threat to their new liaison was Fatimeh, uncertain and awkward in her *chador,* the new lover became defensive. I will never forget the afternoon at Davar's office when we all converged. He and I often met there at the tail end of the workday, to walk to our favorite park to smoke *ghalyoon.* Fatimeh called to say she would also drop by, with some photos as a pretext. The new lover phoned his mobile, as she had begun to regularly, and when she heard we were all there, having tea together, informed him she would be stopping by as well. Probably resentful of having her status confined to his bedroom, she showed up to mark her territory.

Painfully unsubtle, she arrived decked out in a glittery, evening veil, with lots of eye makeup and a cloud of perfume. She promptly took a seat near Davar's desk closest to him and made a point of touching him with a casual but proprietary air. Fatimeh looked on, stunned and quiet. The moment groaned under the strain of its awkwardness. It couldn't have lasted more than fifteen minutes, but our collective self-consciousness seemed to slow time.

Davar blinked at me helplessly. "Well," I said brightly, rapping my knuckles against his desk, "who's up for *ghalyoon?*"

Fatimeh stopped calling Davar, stopped littering his office with little fuzzy ducks and bears. Eventually, she stopped passing by all of our offices, stopped calling with pretexts of photos she wanted to drop off or stories to discuss. She blipped off our screens, and when I asked Davar a few months later if he had heard from her, he told me she had gotten married to "some conservative guy." But how? I asked. When did she meet him? When did they date? Why had she stopped working? She kept in touch with no one, and we never saw her again.

⚓

As an equal-opportunity catastrophe, the revolution had generously confused the sexuality of secular middle- to upper-middle-class Iranian women as well. These girls married for love and professed to oppose the rigid morals propagated by the regime, but found themselves as conflicted as their highly traditional peers in the realm where sexuality, self, and future intersected. Should they try to carve away the influence of tradition and family on their life choices, as Fatimeh was gingerly attempting?

Should they look for relationships with men who thought every part of them, including the unconventional, tentative parts, was fantastic? Could they afford to be honest about their sexuality (like the fact that they had some), or should they be guarded, and play to the still-traditional expectations of Iranian men (who liked the farce of believing they were the first—to make you breathless, to make out, to go to bed).

Relationships that were considered successful, that led to weddings and emigration and babies, so often required a total shrouding of a woman's real life and desires. Everyone knew this, because they had watched girlfriends go through lovers, get bored of not being taken seriously, hit upon a suitable prospect, and fake their pasts and camouflage their needs and tastes in order to get married.

Becoming this mercenary—prepared to meet, marry, and live under pretense of being someone you were not—took a while. It took the failure of the relationships where you tried to be yourself, tried to communicate your expectations and passions (hoping they would be adored and encouraged), and watched it all fall apart.

A young distant relative of mine, Mira, grappled with these considerations at the tender age of twenty-two. We weren't very close, but every couple of months I would drop by for dinner, sometimes staying the night so Mira and I could watch videos and raid her mother's stash of French chocolates. "So what'd we get this week?" I asked her. In Tehran, where Western movies were officially banned, everyone had a *filmi,* a video guy, who schlepped a trunkload of new films around to his clients' homes as a sort of mobile video store.

Mira didn't answer, but she slipped a tape into the VCR, and dimmed the lights. She looked at me with an expectant, abashed smile. I need your help with something, she said, winding her thick, ash-streaked hair into a loose knot. Her skin was like porcelain, and glowed without all the layers of foundation and blush she coated it with during the day. If I had skin like hers, I would wear nothing but lip gloss, ever. But her morning ritual before the mirror took an hour and a half.

When summer rolled around, Iranian girls groomed themselves with a seriousness of purpose I had never before witnessed, even in California, a place dedicated to the worship and pursuit of external beauty. Often, a particular feature was singled out for obsessive attention. Tattooed eyebrows, collagen-plumped lips. For the daughter of my waxing woman, it was the fingernails. She grew them out an inch long and painted them a different technicolor every single day. Sometimes she affixed nail jems, sometimes alternating colors on the tips, for particular effect. When finished, she would blast Mary J. Blige and "Nastaran," that year's Persian pop hit, on the stereo in the living room, and dance around alone, waving her hands in the air to the beat, to dry the lacquer. Exhausted, she would splay her fingers for me to inspect that day's creation—the fruits of an hour's labor—which she would wipe off the next day with acetone, priming her canvas anew. I suppose teenagers the world over were preoccupied with beauty—the aesthetics of being not quite a girl, not quite a woman—but in Tehran the attention seemed extreme.

Mira liked to remind me that because of the country's demographics, each year *one million Iranian women were unable to find a husband*. She repeated this figure, or possibly urban legend, with a grave solemnity and tragic expression.

Mira was distressed over my beauty regimen. Since I was neither looking for a husband nor habituated to overcompensating for the veil with too much makeup, I usually went about with what I called a natural look and Mira called self-neglect. Mira's adolescence had corresponded with the years just before the election of Khatami. This had given her a politically weighted relationship to the products of Revlon that continued to this day, when it really wasn't that big a deal anymore.

"You really need to do something with yourself," she told me with a disapproving glance, as though I had a mustache and I walked about in a mumu. "Men are turned on by makeup."

Applied properly, she informed me, makeup is meant to mimic how women look when they are aroused—smoldering eyes, flushed cheeks, swollen lips. I was older and supposed to know these things. They were included in the skills of husband acquisition, which also included: knowing how to make a proper béchamel sauce, being coiffed to gleaming perfection at all times, even when stepping outside in the morning for milk, and smiling pleasantly and disguising any hint of a personality.

The objective of this skill-set was to nab an Iranian software designer from Palo Alto who had flown to Tehran for wife shopping. If I had packaged myself properly, maybe he would pick me. Perfect hair! Perfect sauce!

And I would be rescued and taken back to America, to shop at Pottery Barn and get depressed with all the other imported wives (or at least the ones who didn't ask for their divorces on the tarmac).

Deep down, many friends and relatives suspected something was wrong with me. Clearly I had been unable to find either a job or a husband in the West, and that's why I had come to Iran, to toil day and night before a lap-top hanging out with clerics. They offered sympathy and helpful advice, like how to pour tea more gracefully and rim my eyes with kohl.

Usually, because she loved me and thought it her duty, Mira was the one giving me lessons, in cosmetics and cuisine, but that night, I was supposed to have the answers, to whatever it was in the VCR.

She hit the play button, and a fuzzy image of two very white, very naked people appeared on the screen. I'm not prudish, but neither have I seen much porn in my life. I *definitely* haven't seen German porn from the sev-enties, which is what this appeared to be. I rose and shut the door to the kitchen nervously. If someone were to walk in, there was little doubt who would be held responsible for such a session. Certainly not innocent, sup-posedly virginal Mira.

She expertly fast-forwarded to the next scene. Clearly, this was not her first screening. A towering man, Viking-like, was busily plying his fingers between the parted legs of a frizzy-haired woman.

"Why does he keep doing that?"

I cracked open a pistachio, from the bowl on the table, and studied the shell, encrusted with salt and lemon juice. "He's, uh, pleasuring her."

"But why there? Like that?"

"That's where her, uh . . . that's a very sensitive spot." What was it with young Iranians? How could they be so obsessed with sex, yet know so little about it? Or maybe she was being disingenuous, pretending not to know because she was too shy to straight out say she wanted to talk about sex.

I switched off the video and asked for the real story. I refused to believe she didn't know about her own sex organs, though I suppose it was a slim possibility. As it turned out, her boyfriend had given her a "sex kit" to edu-cate herself with, which included the video and a few lewd magazines. Be-cause their sexual encounters were limited, she explained, he didn't want to waste their time in erotic tutorial. Since Mira was a virgin, and I knew they both lived with family, I asked when and where this knowledge was being put to use. Sometimes we go to the park behind the house at night, or if his parents are out, we'll go to his place, she said. He sounds seedy, I said disapprovingly. I want to please him, she sniffed. Seedy boyfriend preferred the sort of sex that allowed her to remain, technically, a virgin. "Is that a problem?" she asked.

Where to begin? Should I pull up a gynecological site on the Internet, and explain vaginal mechanics? Should I bother asking whether they use condoms, although I was certain they didn't? Do I point out that she is supposed to enjoy sex, too? If Mira started telling her seedy boyfriend what she wanted in bed, he might well consider her loose, acting like a *jendeh,* a whore. Progress in gender relations circa Tehran 2001 meant that men were now willing to marry women who slept with them during the dating phase. But that didn't mean they would marry the ones who had acted like they liked it.

I didn't know what Mira should do. As a starry-eyed romantic, full of passion and dreams of walking into the sunset with her lover, she had to balance her fantasies against her matrimonial prospects. She had to find someone who could accept the many sides of her—the red wine–drinking devotee of flamenco, the bourgeois housewife-to-be with a talent for sauces. On the other hand, as she well knew, Tehran was not exactly littered with suitable guys. Mira had not attended college, had a declining opium addict for a father, and could not afford to let her twenties march by as she worked out what sort of mate would complete her personality and make her an adult and not just a wife.

"Why don't you just go out to dinner more? Are you even friends?"

She rolled her eyes, shooting me one of those exasperated, like, when are you going to get how it is here looks. Curled up in her lilac flannel pajamas, her long lashes sweeping up and down, liberated from all those too-heavy coats of mascara, she looked so innocent.

We sat there silent for a while, occasionally reaching for a square of chocolate. I needed to say something. So I tried to explain that like many men, her boyfriend was intimidated by how much he wanted sex and that it was easier for him to vulgarize intimacy than admit that she (a mere girl/woman) controlled the supply of the most powerful physical experience of his existence. It was kind of an academic point, the stuff you absorb during women's studies classes, and I lost her halfway through.

What an accelerated, demeaning, furtive initiation into sexuality. Their evenings should be spent at clubs, dancing; their afternoons in cafés, ankles lazily interlaced. Of course now they could hold hands in public if they really wanted to. Lots of middle-class couples, who had nowhere else to go, did this freely. But it wasn't nice, being affectionate like that with an eye to your back.

Of all the Islamic Republic's casualties, among the most lethal for young people was the deterioration of platonic friendship between young men and women. As far back as I could remember, the lives of my parents, my aunts, and my uncles, had been full of friends of the opposite sex, who were simply friends, nothing more, often not even recycled former flames. Though highly traditional spheres of Iranian society had socialized along gender lines—with men and women in separate rooms, or separate sides of the room, at parties—platonic interaction and friendship had been ordinary among secular middle-class and upper-class Iranians. The revolution reversed this. It threw up obstacles everywhere to casual coexistence between the sexes: segregated elementary schools and university classes, segregated buses, segregated restaurant lines, segregated passport offices.

Separated most of the hours of the day, young people became mysteries to each other, familiar but alien. It became easier for girls to spend time with their girlfriends, guys with their guy friends. Being together involved sneaking away, into the dark corners of public parks, into the woods in the Alborz Mountains, into each other's empty houses.

I wanted better for Mira. I wanted to see her pretty face radiant with the silly crushes of early womanhood, her weeks filled with candlelit dinners, unmolested strolls through the park behind her house. My adolescence in the decadent, satanic West seemed bubble-gum innocent in comparison to hers—footsy under a blanket at a winter football game, slow dancing at the prom, sleepovers where we drank beer, giggled over Monty Python, and fell asleep in a pile, like puppies, in someone's living room.

The next day the seedy boyfriend would collect Mira, covered in a dark veil and *roopoosh* (still mandated by lots of offices) from work. Maybe they would go out to dinner, but maybe they wouldn't because you can only get in the mood to do this about half the time, when you know there are eyes always watching you. Probably they would go to the home of friends, and then wait for an evening his parents would be out.

It wasn't always, or at least exclusively, as bad as that. An imaginative couple, with some creativity and luck, could create a sparkly courtship out of these circumstances. Sometimes, all the challenges infused drama and romance into a new relationship. Existing as a couple in the Islamic Republic meant facing the petty, the bizarre, and the sorrowful on a regular basis. You had to trust faster than usual, and situations, rather than your own readiness, determined when you would be vulnerable. Islamic Republic coupledom was almost like being in the military together—you got worn down, built yourself back up, and found yourself bonded to the person who had been right next to you the whole time.

In the West, with online matchmaking services, twenty-four-hour restaurants, and the birth-control patch, dating was fast and easy. There was no struggle (worse than not being able to get a dinner reservation) that might elevate a third date from boring to extraordinary. Since romance thrives on mystery and delayed gratification, I had imagined the Islamic Republic would be conducive to excellent love affairs. I thought nothing could be more romantic than love in a time of struggle.

But like most of the conceptions I bore with me to Iran, it ended up being totally wrong. Confronting hardship together didn't magically turn your relationship, or your life for that matter, into Casablanca. Struggle, it turned out, is about as romantic as leprosy. It makes you emotionally absent. It gives you the most compelling, lofty reasons ever to avoid dealing with your emotional problems (you're too busy with The Struggle, of course). It makes you live exclusively in the present. It makes emotions besides hate a luxury. Because in the end, life in the shadow of struggle is really just life in the shadows.

⁎

The next day Reza, my security-obsessed, mobile-dissecting friend, was coming over for tea. The hour before he was meant to arrive, I reviewed the newspapers and munched on a handful of chocolate-covered espresso beans, because you could rely on Reza to have you embroiled in intricate discussion within five minutes of entry. Just once I wished we could have a frivolous discussion.

That day, I of course had to tell him about Mira, and we ended up debating whether the Islamic Republic had made it difficult for young people to fall in love. He said yes, because the mercenary survival skills young people had been forced to develop prevented them from making lasting attachments; because love involved the suspension of selfishness, and the anarchic culture of the regime had made selfishness paramount. I argued that the net effect was neutral, because the mercenary effect was balanced by the incubator effect the Islamic Republic had on relationships. After the twentieth night with nothing to do outside (you can't go to house parties every single night), fiddling with a broken cable box and sipping nasty homemade vodka, you find out quickly whether you actually like each other. The vast stretches of empty time accelerate a realization that might take three months to reach in a Western city, if you were constantly distracted by gallery openings and movies, new restaurants and weekend getaways.

That's how it was with me and Dariush, I told him. Our relationship played itself out in warp speed. We went from attraction to inseparability to power struggle to all-out warfare in something like four months. Do you think that's efficient or awful? I asked.

"I have no comment," he sniffed. "How many times did I tell you not to consort with a child?" Reza had not approved. He had considered it unbefitting for me to have been involved with Dariush, the spoiled, cloistered son of fallen aristocrats. He didn't understand how I could have wasted my time with someone so trifling.

Rather than rehashing the extended cat fight that had been my relationship with Dariush, I wanted Reza to explain to me what the deal was with Mira's orgasm business. So tell me, I said, tell me why Iranian men are such conflicted sexists. They want a sexually assertive woman in bed, but since they don't respect women like that, and women *know* that, they can't get women to behave that way with them. And so everyone acts out a farce. The woman pretends it's her first time, that she doesn't usually do this, that she was too drunk or high to know what she was doing. She quells her instincts and suppresses her sensuality, so she doesn't lose her dignity—her only status currency in this kind of society.

He interrupted. You blame this on Iranian men being Eastern. But this attitude toward sex is actually more Western than anything else, he said, nodding at an old copy of *Vogue,* featuring a bikini-clad model, on the table. The West treats women as objects, but through the filter of consumerism. The underlying attitude is still materialist.

"Yeah, but at least in the West women get to have orgasms." He couldn't top that.

⁂

Iran was not high on any list of top international vacation spots. You would not open up *Condé Nast Traveler* and find breathless recommendations to sip tea at Isfahan's fabled Shah Abbas Hotel or watch the dusk linger over a beach on the Caspian. Shunned by tourists who still imagined it a dark, dangerous place overrun by terrorists, most of the country's scenic attractions—including its magnificent ski slopes—were usually empty. This was bad for the economy, but great for Iranians who skied. During the winter, it made Iranian ski resorts one of the few places in the world with excellent runs and short lift lines. The slopes at Shemshak were only an hour and a half away from Tehran, and up at the top of the mountain, if you managed to ignore the fact that you had arrived via the "women's lift," you could forget you were in Iran altogether.

The figure-obscuring bulk of a ski suit satisfied the dress code requirement, and a wool cap, with hair tucked beneath, stood in for the veil. So on any given winter day, men and women skied down the slopes looking and acting as though they were in Colorado or Switzerland. Altitude and social freedom were proportionally related in Iran. The higher you climbed up a mountain, the safer it was to let your scarf fall around your shoulders, to lean over and kiss your boyfriend, to turn up the Western music in your boombox. The freedom that reigned at these heights made outdoor activities immensely popular with otherwise urban types. It was what made hiking in the Alborz Mountains, just outside Tehran, the thing to do on any given weekend. It was why I, who usually went skiing for what came after (cute après-ski clothes, Irish coffee), was always eager to ski in Iran, for its own sake.

That year, in the late winter of 2001, all the decadent, corrupt, coed swooshing about irked the regime. Some office of doomed ideas, doubtless based in Qom, tried to organize an alpine morality police force to ensure everyone behaved Islamically on the slopes. But the sort of people recruited to such a force were not the sort who had been on skies since infancy. Several broken legs later, it became clear they wouldn't reach ski police levels of proficiency anytime soon. So instead, on weekends when the slopes were crowded, a mullah showed up at the bottom of the lifts to lead noon prayer. He stood there with his turban and robes against the gleaming snow, a Grinch-like figure with no purpose but to inject a little Islam into the atmosphere, in case anyone was starting to feel too glamorous.

During the cold months, the Tehran party scene shifted to Shemshak, and a smaller resort closer to the city called Dizine. Young people preferred gathering in these places to Tehran, because the snow and long driveways between the road and houses muffled the noise and discouraged the police from raiding their parties. Initially I found the parties out in the wilderness refreshing. You could actually see the stars in the sky. You could breathe in crisp, forest air instead of smog. And you could stroll for a good half an hour without seeing a billboard of a mullah or a war martyr.

⁂

I wobbled at the top of the perilously steep ski slope wondering whether one of those helicopter-ambulances could be summoned to take me down. Heights scared me, in the same way as yoga headstands. I needed to feel as though I was in control. At that moment, the panic started in my stomach, and spread until I felt there was no longer blood in my veins but liquid terror.

Siamak was already swooshing down, but when he realized I wasn't behind him, he arced into a stop. You said this was an *intermediate* slope, not a ninety-degree angle, I yelled, waving a pole at him. Come on *aziz,* dear, just make wider turns, he urged. You'll be fine. That one word, *aziz,* caught my fear off guard, conjuring so many primordial sensations of comfort that I felt a warmth spread through my limbs, felt myself lean forward effortlessly and push off.

Until then, I had believed smells were the keys that unlocked memory, uniquely able to transport you back to some distant point in the past, in a heady flash. Words, I thought, exerted their powers more subtly, working through the layers of consciousness over time. But when I heard the word *aziz,* that endearment woven into the fabric of my childhood, which I had heard thousands of times, in the voices of those who loved me first and best, I melted like a cat picked up by the scruff of its neck.

During all of my life in California, I had refused to date Iranian-Americans, because that's what my mother would have preferred, an entrée into a one-size-fits-all sort of existence. My experiences bringing non-Iranian guys home to meet Maman had never been encouraging. The entrance of these English-speaking young men into the home seemed to magnify our distance from Iran, and its imperfect re-creation in our American lives. This re-creation was something of an optical illusion, which we all had to perpetually squint to maintain. It depended on the impossible: my cousins and I forever remaining children, never displaying "American selfishness" (otherwise known as the desire to lead one's own life).

The intrusion of a non-Iranian, in the role of the boyfriend, shattered the illusion that we, the second generation, would grow up in our parents' image. It cemented our displacement, shook the exile stupor and brought us face to face with our California lives. Both my parents, even my grandfather, attempted to understand and adjust, but this resigned graciousness was worse than a tirade. Watching them silently surrender yet another layer of a dream opened up a wound inside me. I almost wished they were more small-minded, more inflexible. Other Iranian-American parents forbade their daughters to date (knowing they did so secretly), preferring the comfort of feigned ignorance; the sanctity of their own fantasy—that they could transplant themselves thousands of miles without exposing themselves to change—was more important to them than participating in their daughters' reality. But my family wasn't so keen on charades. We would scream awful names at each other, throw things, and hold decade-long grudges, but we didn't hide behind lies and fake smiles.

And so they agreed to meet American boyfriends over strained dinners that bored everyone. On these occasions, I would preside tensely as simultaneous translator, making sure observations made it across the cultural divide, hovering with an invisible butterfly net, poised to catch potential gaffes. I kneaded the conversation, tried to make it more interesting, more light. It sunk anyway. I was scared to go to the bathroom, afraid they might offend each other in my absence.

My mother would labor in the kitchen, mincing, like, ten different kinds of herbs into discrete piles, to make some complicated Persian stew, whose name she would enunciate slowly to the warmly welcomed, unwanted guest. My grandfather would beam beatifically, repeat the English phrases he knew: "Hello! . . . Thank you my friend"—over and over again, and then retreat into the living room so we could speak English comfortably, without having to pause to include him with Farsi asides.

Small slights, like forgetting to take off your shoes, or not greeting my grandfather within ten seconds of entering the house, would afterward cause my mother to despair. In her mind, each one corresponded to a more deep-seated disregard or contempt for our traditions. "Don't these people teach their children any manners? What can you can expect from a culture that abandons its old people to die in nursing homes?" she'd say with a sigh. Her eyes would go hard and distant, as she imagined grandchildren with non-Persian names like Jed and Stacy, and then *their* children, who wouldn't even have her around, to sing them to sleep with Farsi lullabies.

Although I knew I was disappointing my mother, dating an Iranian, at the time, would have meant signing up for even greater doses of the overwhelming presence of Iranianness in my life. Being Iranian myself was emotionally draining enough. I didn't want to have to be Iranian for two. I wanted a personal life of order and straight lines.

In Tehran, the equation changed. Siamak and I faithfully and serially dated other Iranians, convinced they would understand us better, fit more effortlessly into our lives. Not out of guilt, or to appease our parents' hopes and expectations, but because we had both been raised outside, and carried a cavernous longing for Iran deep inside us that refused to be filled. We heaped in devotions of all sorts, professional and political, and it still yawned hungrily.

Like Fatimeh, who sought Davar to secure her identity as a photographer, and like Mira, who wanted a boyfriend to mirror her passion, Siamak and I looked for Iranians who would complete the missing Iranian parts of ourselves. Finding and marrying the right Iranian, we thought, would bring us closer to this country we were right up against, but still yearned for.

But I met and rejected the candidates who passed through his life, and he met and mocked mine. One day, I wondered, would we regret the evenings and weekends and social currency squandered on these unsuitables? Would we regret the wasted hours spent trying to will ourselves into happiness with relationships we knew, deep down, would lead nowhere? Neither of us had anything to show for our misguided convictions. Maybe the problem was that we were dating pure Iranians, who had spent their whole lives inside. We found them missing a quality fundamental to our natures, and one they could not be faulted for lacking—the ability to slip easily in and out of more than one culture.

It occurred to me that a fellow hyphen—not an American, and not an Iranian, but an Iranian-American, just like me—was the solution, the missing ingredient required to complete me. Someone who had lived this cleft between two worlds, who understood what divided me, because the same forces tugged and pulled on him, too. Maybe he had made my journey to Iran inside his own head. Together, we would bend our lives to fit the Persian cat's curves. I was so certain of this, that I didn't need to talk it over with ten girlfriends, in two languages, and I congratulated myself on finally getting it together, figuring out how I wanted my life to be.

I spun the fantasy energetically, already imagining my mother and his having coffee together, glowing with satisfaction and planning our *sofreh-e aghd,* the Iranian wedding ceremony. It was almost incidental, the perfect Iranian-American man who would play the role. But because he was the first man I saw at that moment of epiphany, like a duckling whose eyes fall on a galosh and imprint that as its mother, I chose Siamak, my best friend in Tehran. Siamak could be Mr. Perfect Hyphen!

Ideally, he would lack a patriarchal Iranian man's alarming hangups and Taliban-like expectations of women. Mr. Perfect Hyphen and I would grow old together, enmeshed (but not *too* enmeshed) in each other's families, fluent in the old, emotion-laced language of our culture. We would cherish our friends and relatives with intimacy and devotion, but pull back when those ties began to smother our privacy, dictate how we should behave and what we should believe.

When my mother screamed horrible, hurtful things down the phone line ("You are *immoral* and God will punish you!"), he wouldn't be appalled and send me to therapy to recover from being unloved. Instead, he would be familiar enough with my culture to help me put her reactions in perspective, to remind me that old attitudes survived immigration, and that she didn't intend to hurt me. This would be true, and it would heal the ache. These were delicate distinctions that I assumed only two hyphens can make. He would call me *aziz,* and I would call him *honey jaan.* But the chores, those we would divide. Such a brilliant idea. Why hadn't it occurred to me before?

The only problem was, I didn't love Siamak. From the very first moment Siamak and I met, we related as siblings—constantly fighting, teasing, but deeply protective of one another. We joked, expressed affection, sketched ideas across two cultures, in two languages, and the quick, seamless interplay of our halves generated energy that crackled. It was not romantic energy but the intersection of spirits, the synapses of brains meeting and recognizing the familiar. It took just moments, the briefest sentences, to explain anything to him, because he understood so effortlessly, anticipating my arguments, fluent in my various voices. Whether we were fighting or playing, in Tehran or London, it felt like the entire breadth of me was tapped, no crevice left dark.

My uncle played bridge with his mother. Mutual family friends whispered in my ear that it was so *heif*, such a waste, that we were, "how do you call it? . . . 'just friends.'" We did everything together. We watched the president speak at campaign rallies. We sat on the couch in the evenings, working on our laptops. I wrote stories; he drafted Power Point lectures. We took breaks to order take-out Indian, watched *Sex in the City*, and argued whether it was in Iran's strategic interest to build a nuclear bomb. We careened around Tehran listening to Run-DMC. We got drunk, debated whose romantic life was more pathetic, and cooked pancakes at two A.M. Siamak was closer to me than any male friend—or boyfriend—had ever been, but there was no flicker, ever, of anything besides friendship between us. When I looked at him, I saw not a guy, but my brother. This was a problem, since I had decided his was the jigsaw puzzle piece that fit mine.

One freezing, cloudy winter afternoon, we drove up to the northernmost tip of Tehran together, to interview a prominent conservative who had set up his office at the home of Iran's former ambassador to Washington. The sprawling mansion looked out over all of Tehran, once the scene of famous pool parties where American celebrities cavorted with Henry Kissinger. Now a green mosque glowed next to the covered-up pool. We conducted our interview, and on our way out, climbed through the great bales of snow coating the steep, stone stairs.

Look out, I heard from somewhere above me, and suddenly something incredibly cold smashed into my ear, dripping bits of ice down my neck. *Aaaack! No fair, hijab disadvantage!* I yelled, cupping a handful of snow in my hands, and molding it into a ball, to retaliate. We pelted each other all the way to his Nissan Patrol, laughing and falling over in the snow. Tehran looked glorious sprinkled with snow, the white dust coating the homely cityscape of four-story buildings, and Siamak made it feel like home. I stopped for a moment, wiping the slush from my cheek, and tried to memorize the moment. High up in the city, with Tehran seemingly frozen before us, we seemed to float above history. The revolution shrank to a speck the size of the snowflakes. Events, dates, passports, borders—always at the forefront of our consciousness—receded. We were two friends, in the city where we both belonged, engaged in a snowball fight. For just a few seconds, life was as gloriously simple as that. Except that we were not falling in love. Not even a little.

⚓

Each morning, I sat with a cup of coffee at the table in my kitchen, watching the snow fall over Tehran through the tall, steamy windows, and reading the newspapers. Khanoum Shabazy, my housekeeper, attempted to distract me with her latest tale of woe, which inevitably ended in a request for a loan. She also cleaned Siamak's apartment, but to her maternal Iranian personality, he was a prince to dote upon, not solicit for cash.

"Why always me? Why don't you ever ask Siamak to help you?" I asked her one frozen morning in frustration.

She folded her hands together, smiled in her sheepish, actressy way, and pretended to look shocked. "Agha Siamak is a single man preparing for a wife and family. Soon he'll have to furnish his household completely, getting ready for the day when it becomes a *home*. But you, you're alone. You don't have dinner parties. You just sit around. You have no plan to get married, so you don't need to save like he does."

Aha! I had finally forced her to confess what she thought of me—an alien, quickly becoming *torshideh* (literally, *soured*, the Persian term for spinster). She could unlock the door to Siamak's apartment and find a different woman there three mornings of the week. A kitchen strewn with tequila bottles and cigarette butts. But this would not dislodge his halo, dim its glow.

His behavior was judged differently than mine—the return of the collective prodigal son, whose American lifestyle was viewed as the bachelor.

But for me, the tiniest misstep to the left or right of propriety was swiftly catalogued as "Westernized" misbehavior. Even Khanoum Shabazy, whom he either ignored, laughed at, or bullied, adored him, yet considered me—the one who actually listened to her woes—a misfit, uninterested in anything that mattered (cooking, china, dinner parties). I realized that in Iran, just as in California with my mother, "Westernized" was a convenient label for any female behavior that defied oppressive tradition. It could and was attached as easily to an Iranian woman who had never left Iran, as it was to me, raised outside. But men were like Teflon; the Westernized label did not stick. The other names for their conduct—hypocritical, womanizing, temperamental, fickle, bossy, headstrong—were still organically Iranian. The culture made room for *their* transgressions.

That winter morning, I could muster no response to a plea that came wrapped in insult. Instead, I leaned over her shoulder as she prepared lunch, rice with lentils and raisins. She poured, I could have sworn, a full cup of oil onto the soaking rice. She hated me. She knew I wouldn't eat it that way, and she did it anyway, because she knew then I would tell her to take it home. "Remember how we compared our definition of a *drop* of oil?" She smiled sweetly, and said it would burn otherwise, as I would know, if I knew how to cook. It was unfortunate we have no word for passive-aggressive in Farsi, since it is half our culture.

I kept flipping absent-mindedly through the inky pages of newsprint. But wait! Buried on the back page, there was a headline that read "*Ghalyoon* Smoking Now Illegal for Women." Oh God. My one, favorite publicly acceptable pastime, unceremoniously banned. I dialed Siamak's mobile phone.

"Hi. It's me. Do you find it arousing, watching women smoke *ghalyoon?*"

"Not particularly. Especially knowing that a thousand ugly men have smoked from the same pipe before them."

"Well, I have news. One half of the population can no longer smoke *ghalyoon* in public, on the off chance that a pious passer-by notices, and becomes titillated."

That night Siamak invited me over for a homemade *ghalyoon*, in consolation. I sat cross-legged on a chair in the kitchen, as he heated the coals on the oven, and contemplated his back. As we relaxed on his balcony, high above the western suburb of Tehran, passing the pipe between us and inhaling its humid, fruity smoke, I thought about how perfect we were for each other. Well, maybe we weren't perfect. We couldn't even agree on vacations, as friends. He always wanted to four-wheel-drive through the desert, and camp under the stars, and I wanted to lie on a beach, preferably attached to a plush resort, where a waiter would bring me fresh juice and we would sleep on fresh linens at night. Deep down, I thought he was an unrepentant sexist; deep down he thought I was radioactively high-maintenance.

But in Tehran, Siamak was the one I wanted to be with. His manner of speaking and thinking were so familiar to me, as evocative of home as the tart sweetness of sour cherry jam, and the smokiness of *esfand,* the pungent herb we ritually burned to ward off the evil eye. I clung to the belief that in time we could develop feelings for one another. The thought was vaguely gross to both of us, but all those happy, old couples whose marriages had been arranged probably felt that way at the beginning.

I leaned across his boat-like sofa, poked him with a toe and demanded to know why he had never asked me out on a proper date.

"We know all the same people. We would throw the best dinner parties. Can you imagine?"

"Babe, I know you too well now," he replied. "You have no idea what you want. You don't want a relationship. You want a story to tell over cocktails."

"That's so unfair. You don't want a person either. You want an ornament/chef who happens to have a brilliant intellect. Who happens to want to live in Tehran. That doesn't exist."

"I know I'll have to compromise. Eventually. And I know it'll be a big-deal compromise. I'm just not there yet."

I understood precisely what Siamak meant. He didn't need to say anything more, but he did.

"You're not really into *me* in that way. And I'm not really into *you* in that way. And we both know it. If you don't want to hear that reason, I can come up with different ones. But that's really it."

He was right. The whole point of us being romantically involved was flawed, because I had conceived the idea not out of attraction or spark, but out of a frustration with the confusion in my own life. Rather than admit that Iran was disappointing me and wearing me down, it was easier to concentrate on Siamak, a reassuring dinghy in the chaos. Rather than work through my lingering uncertainties about the place of Iran and America inside me, it was easier to pretend assurance by affixing myself to someone who already had it figured out. In the same way Fatimeh sought the company of Davar, instead of challenging the constricting tradition of her parents. As Mira confused dating a consummate jerk with exploring her sexuality. It would take me a bit longer to see it, but I used Siamak as a refuge from realities I could still not bear to admit: that I would probably feel out of place everywhere, always; that my family would be divided forever, between America and Iran; that I would always feel alone.

CHAPTER EIGHT

Summer of the Cockroach

Get used to opening windows wide
to see what the past has done to the present,
and weep quietly, quietly,
lest our enemies hear
broken shards clattering within us.

—Mahmoud Darwish

My face pressed into the plastic strips of the beach lounger, and I wiggled my nose into a crack, so I could breathe and maintain this position of optimal sun exposure. My friend Kim unlaced the strings of my bikini top, so my back would tan evenly. No, we were not in Iran. That would have involved what political scientists like to call step-change, a major and significant transformation in a country's development. I had come to Lebanon to do a story on Hezbollah and had extended my stay for a few weeks, so I could go to the beach with Kim, a journalist friend. We lounged by the freshwater pool, discussing whether she should buy an apartment in Beirut and whether I should buy one in Tehran. She reminded me the Iranian regime was unstable, and I reminded her Israel could reoccupy southern Lebanon.

Real estate did not appear the safest investment for either of us. Our lives, in this region, of this region, always returned to this question: how to put down roots in ground that was so unstable, in ground that was either meant to be temporary, or susceptible to shifts, in response to decisions made by politicians or generals or clerics. Ground that was either being occupied, invaded, liberated, or beginning to tremor, under regimes that seemed destined to collapse.

At the Caspian Sea, where I had chosen not to spend any time that summer, my uncle and his partners had built a gated compound of villas on the waterfront. In our little patch of beach there, I could even swim in a bikini, as long as I waited till I was fully submerged before taking my tee-shirt off. When I told my family I was going to spend the summer in Beirut, they urged me to stay. I thought about all the blissful weekends we'd spent there. We would splash around in the pool, then dry off to play basketball, and grill fresh sturgeon for lunch. When the sun set, we walked laps around the compound and dropped into everyone's open living rooms for tea, and then played games of pool before gathering for heaps of fresh caviar and ice-cold vodka.

It was idyllic, really, if you could get yourself to stop thinking about what was going on outside, or back in Tehran. That summer in Iran, there was yet another anti-immodesty drive underway. The system issued hysterical public warnings against "decadent Western behavior" and sent police to raid the café scene. For Elvis's café, that singular place where Celine and I and countless others took special delight in drinking coffee, it was the beginning of the end. Elvis became tense and moody, reluctant to police the behavior of customers who had become friends. Only twice did he ever tell me to fix my veil, each time with his eyes, his whole posture, radiating apology. He hated having to say such things. Yet if he refused, he could be fined if police showed up and found us as we were, too busy talking to notice our head scarves had slipped back a few inches. He began closing earlier and earlier, and eventually shut down.

Rumors raged that bands of *Basiji* were roving the streets, in search of women wearing sandals and Capri pants. As punishment, they forced them to dip their bare legs in a bucket of cockroaches. Either that, or they sprayed their feet with a paint that took weeks to wear off, so the ankle-flaunting harlots would be forced to wear shoes and socks all summer. When Khaleh Farzi recounted this to me in warning, I laughed it off. Come on, that's urban legend, I said. For one, *Basijis* are too lazy to go around collecting buckets full of cockroaches. But the bucket became fixed in my mind. I've been petrified of cockroaches since that childhood summer in Iran, when they would come hurtling through the air, miniature avian-reptiles, and corner me in a bathroom leagues away from adult rescue. No, I decided, I would not do a cockroach summer. So I went to Beirut.

Splat. A wet volleyball soared out of the pool and hit Kim in the knee. A little boy in orange swimtrunks trotted over to collect it. I *got* it, he screeched, in perfect American English. I pressed my eyes into the softness of the towel, and tried to isolate voices in the conversations around me. A pack of young girls walked by, chattering about the boys around them, and where they should go clubbing in Beirut that night. A serious young voice from inside the pool complained about a detested biology teacher. Further back, from the shady grove of trees, middle-aged Lebanese women deliberated whether an absent friend should have her drooping butt surgically lifted.

Their conversations swung between Arabic, French, and English, but it was the variety of English that intrigued me. I heard British accents, and American ones, and among the American accents, I detected distinct strains—native, ten years post immigration, California, New Jersey.

Lebanese expatriates rivaled the Iranian diaspora in size, but unlike Iranians, many visited their home country en masse every summer. They returned with their children in tow, and all those Lebanese kids growing up in France and Africa, Canada and America, ended up with a tangible sense of origin. They wouldn't have to subsist abroad on stale memories and myths. Memories carried you only so far. They faded steadily over time, and were overlaid by fresh recollections and new longings, until one's consciousness eventually recomposed itself without them. The accents mingled together. Cousins from far away splashed about with relatives who had never left. Their merriment was spontaneous. Young and easy. Borderless.

I wondered, for the thousandth futile time, what would have happened if we had spent every summer in Iran, what would have happened if there had been no revolution. Would my laughter have been this easy, at a crowded pool where my cousins, both the boys and the girls, would have swum together? Would we have felt Iran was ours, felt ties pulling us back, rather than dark fears pushing us away? I thought about my cousins in the U.S. How many of them would bring their no-Farsi-speaking, half-third-generation children to Iran?

That week in Beirut, an editor I knew asked me why Iranians, unlike Lebanese, deserted their country when the going got tough. "We had a war too," he said, puffing self-importantly on a cigar, "but we didn't pick up and leave. Why did you?" Intellectually, I could argue with him. You had a war, but no one ever stole your personal freedom. Your city became a war zone, but you still lived your lives. No one crept into your bedroom, into your mind, and tried to insert their hateful morality into every crevice of your existence. These were rational arguments, but they did not wash away the guilt. Of leaving Iran to *them*, throwing up our hands and collectively moving on. Go ahead, ruin the country. We'll be in exile, if you need us.

I turned over, and studied the sky. My mobile phone rang, and Kim and I exchanged glances. It was Friday, the day Hezbollah usually staged attacks along the southern border. Hopefully it would not be an editor, watching the wires in London, sending us off to work.

"Khosh migzareh, Khanoum?" drawled a haughty voice. It was Dariush, asking me if I was having fun. I shook my head to Kim. He and I were just friends now, but helped each other out when we could, out of an only-child-with-distracted-parents solidarity.

"Listen, something happened a couple of nights ago. I don't want you to get worked up over it. But I think you should know." His voice was calm. "Last night my friend Amin and I were taking a box of stuff you'd left in my garage to your apartment, and we got stopped at a checkpoint on the way. They searched the car, and found a bottle of wine in one of the boxes." He paused.

"Go on."

"He had dropped me off to get cantaloupe juice, and was making a U-turn, so he was alone in the car. Amin told them it was his. I caught up to the car, and told him to keep quiet, that I'd say it was mine. But he said it would be less trouble for him than me. The next day he went to the court, on Vozara Street. They fined him thirty lashes. But he was lucky, they let him keep his T-shirt on, and it was thick. He's fine. We went to a party straight from there."

My lips parted, but no sound came out, as though I had swallowed a shard of glass. What could I possibly say? Tell your friend I owe him dinner, when I get back to Tehran?

"Azadeh? Are you there? Listen, we're used to this kind of thing. As a teenager, I don't think I made it home a single night without getting stopped and smacked upside the head on the way. Stop being so squeamish and American about it." His voice was even, but tinged with impatience.

"Please tell him, from me, that I'm really, really sorry," I said hoarsely.

I hung up the phone, pressed my face back into the beach towel, and wept. Someone had been whipped, like a dog, because of my carelessness. For a stupid bottle of wine that I should have remembered to throw away. I lay there for half an hour immobile. Then I uncurled myself, put on sunglasses, and wound my way through the laughing throng to the rocks along the beach. My little fantasy, of one day being in Iran surrounded by this sort of crowd—Iranians from the West, summering at the Caspian with their children—was shattered. It finally hit me: It would never come to pass. There was no sequel to IRANIANS FLEE TEHRAN ON EVE OF REVOLUTION, and I would never write my dream headline (VILE CLERICAL REGIME FALLS, MULLAHS CHARTER FLIGHT TO NAJAF AS EXILES RUSH BACK). Not even if Iran changed tomorrow. Not even if Siamak and I became the most international, perfect Iranian-American couple ever.

Kim and I drove back to Beirut that night to meet friends for drinks.

From the second floor of the bar, the breeze floated in from the Mediterranean, the lights of the corniche twinkled, and I gazed down into my Bellini feeling utterly alone. I couldn't concentrate on a word being said around me, so I left early to walk my regret home.

Along the way, on a decaying building still riddled with bullet holes from the war, I noticed a giant portrait of Ayatollah Khomeini. I stood beneath it, and matched his glare with my own. A group of men at a nearby ATM glanced over at me, curious. I shrugged my shoulders, basking in their bareness before the ayatollah's sullen grimace. Why are you frowning? I asked him in my head. Everything went your way. You got the country. People saw your face in the moon. I considered sitting down on the pavement to smoke a cigarette in defiance, an anti-pilgrimage. But that was taking things too far. One did not sit on dark street corners, arguing inside one's head with a dead ayatollah.

✦

I returned to a Tehran that was still under cockroach alert. My mother was in town, having come for a month of summer vacation, and during this time she sniffed around suspiciously, detecting a pro-American tilt to my work. She concluded I was "a tool in the pro-Israel, anti–Middle East mainstream media machine," and had taken, in between cooing reunions with relatives, to being cool and dismissive of my ideas, my stories, and ultimately, me. Although she had not visited Iran in a decade, she already knew the country she wanted to find—materially deprived by the revolution, but blissfully unsoiled by the West—and she edited reality to fit this conception.

As luck would have it, the month my loudly anti-American mother came to Tehran, I was doing a string of stories on the popularity of American culture. She refused to believe that young people were transfixed with the United States, that American products were growing more popular each day, that young people, tired of the constrained social life prescribed by the regime, associated brand-name icons of American culture, Coke and Barbie, with the freedoms they were denied. When I told her that young people from all walks of life loved American-style burger outlets, and would choose a Coke over an Iranian cola any day, she chose not to believe me.

I tried to persuade her with fact. I explained that fake American fast food was taking over Tehran. That fake Hardees, KFCs, and McDonaldses were swarming with teenagers thrilled to be tasting and participating in a ritual they associated with openness—eating a burger and fries. Burger places exploited this impulse, I told her, modeling themselves, down to the last detail, after American franchises.

At Tehran's Super Star, which imitated Carl's Jr., smiling employees wore polo shirts monogrammed with the Carl's Jr. star, THANK YOU was printed on the swinging door of the trash can, and a comments box solicited complaints. The only design element that would have been out of place in an authentic branch was the discreet plaque reminding customers to PLEASE RESPECT ISLAMIC MORALS. When rumor spread that Super Star procured its buns from an American burger franchise in the Persian Gulf, the crowds only grew.

Just last week, I said, I stood in an hour-long *line* outside the newest burger place, Apache, while a *bouncer* regulated the flow of traffic in and out. If you don't believe me, come next Friday and see for yourself. She snorted.

One of the hottest new shops in Tehran those days was near Khaleh Farzi's house, in Elahieh. My mother and Khaleh Farzi had not been on speaking terms since 1997, so she had not seen this neighborhood marvel. The store's name was too risqué, by local standards, to be displayed out front, and was painted instead, in gilt letters, on a dusky rose wall inside: Victoria's Secret. It wasn't a real part of the chain, of course (U.S. sanctions forbade American companies from doing business in Iran). Some savvy merchant in West L.A. probably bought out his local VS, threw copyright to the winds, and set up shop in Tehran. Iranian women flocked there to rapturously fawn over delicate silk negligees, lace underwear, and other fripperies. All over the capital, it seemed Iranians were craving consumer symbols of American culture. The scarcity of supply only drove more demand, even for faux versions of everything you could imagine.

I tried to refine the point. Perhaps Maman might understand that young people embraced the "Great Satan's" products not out approval for U.S. foreign policy in the region but as a way to register their discontent with the religious conservatives who controlled their country. But none of this heartfelt explaining did any good at all, and she just gave me that narrowed, skeptical look that said I feel that you are lying, but because you are my daughter, and we are polite people, I will not point this out to you. "I understand that you and your five yuppie friends feel that way," she said.

The stories about pro-U.S. sentiment in Iran, she insisted, were concocted by the American media (and its journalist-propagandists, like me) to pave the way for American cultural/political/military/culinary domination of the region. The U.S. wanted to keep Iran either weak and isolated, or weak and dependent. That's why the CIA overthrew the country's democratically elected government in 1953. The United States cared only about securing its own interests, along with Israel's, in the region. Given this, Iranians had a duty to be anti-American. I had a duty to be quiet, and not criticize the Islamic Republic, because in the short term I would be making things easier for a neo-imperial America bent on undermining the country.

If I have to function that way, I told her, I'd rather not be a journalist. The whole reason I do this is to document reality, not cover it up. Besides, why isn't it possible to criticize both? Do America's abhorrent Middle East policies somehow oblige us to defend the Islamic Republic?

Our arguments were never-ending. Frequently, they sunk to absurd depths. One afternoon, irritated that my work had me undermining Islamic solidarity, she made a theological critique of my outfit as I prepared to leave the house.

"You're not going out in those sandals, are you?"

"Yes, I am. Is that a problem?"

"You're disrespecting Imam Hossein."

"Mom," I said, "Imam Hossein has been dead for a thousand years. Surely he doesn't care about my footwear."

"Fine. Disrespect your culture. People won't say it to your face, but *know*, Azadeh, *know*, that in their hearts, they are insulted."

I tried to take her censure about my clothes, my understanding of Iran, my work, lightly. Rationally, I knew I was in charge of my reactions. In the split second after a standard maternal provocation ("I regret how bourgeois you have become"), I could choose patience over fury. But most of the time, I regressed in nanoseconds to my disconsolate fifteen-year-old self, mute and wounded at being told she had betrayed her real culture.

The only difference was that now, I was armed with my own arsenal of

Iran savvy. This insane traffic that made her shudder? I could navigate it from the top of Tehran to the bottom. With short cuts. The politics she made pronouncements about? I actually understood the fine points and could recite the history of its evolution by rote. When our arguments in Farsi became heated, I no longer had to switch to English, in liquid wrath, to make a point. After months of dislocation, my mother's arrival demystified what I had been seeking all along—a shared history with Iranians living inside, a history in modern Iran. And now, finally, I was more at home than she was in Tehran, street-smart in the city where she grew up and that she now no longer recognized.

Now I could see how much of my journey back had been directed to this very point—the point where my relationship to Iran was bilateral, not negotiated through a third party (my mother) and at the mercy of our turbulent relationship. Before I came to Iran, my mother essentially *was* Iran to me. During her long stretches of estrangement, I felt exiled from Iran as well. No matter how many Iranian restaurants I dragged my friends to or Iranian films I sat through at art-house cinemas, I hadn't been able to fill the cat-shaped hole in my life.

Looking back, I saw that my return to Iran was partly to preempt my fear of a loss I knew was inevitable. One day my mother would die, and with her my Iran would disappear. Once, when we were driving together from Carmel to San Jose, I shuffled through the tapes in the car, and slipped a tape of classical Iranian music into the stereo. The drawn-out twang of the sitar filled the car. She smiled softly. "Do you remember," she asked, "when you were little, and told me, 'Mom, it'll be sad when you die, because no one will listen to this music anymore'? I think *you* will."

✦

That summer of 2001, the summer of the cockroach, was a time-marker for both my life and Iran. It was the last summer Iran would be boring old Iran, and not a member of the "Axis of Evil," the Bush administration's rogue-state triptych. It was the last summer the country would have relative calm on its borders, instead of the wars that were to come, in Afghanistan and Iraq. It was the summer I stopped tormenting myself with such enthusiasm, and began to admit that Iran was disappointing me horribly.

As the mullahs waged a multi-front war on fun, stirring rumors of a cockroach menace and siccing the morality police on cafés, young people's hunt for entertainment found a new outlet: post–soccer match celebrations. The regime considered exercise healthy and virile, and the national soccer team represented Iran in a sport associated with populism, all worthy in the regime's calculations. So celebrating the team's victories became a pretext for kids to pour into the streets, make noise, and be young. Eventually, people even began "celebrating" the team's losses and dismal wins over inferior teams.

It became such a phenomenon that the media started covering soccer nights as news stories. The evening Iran played the United Arab Emirates, I packed a reporting satchel and got ready to go out. The Iranian team performed badly and failed to secure a spot in the playoffs. But teenagers poured out onto the streets as though we had won the World Cup. Hundreds of thousands of people descended into the Tehran night, under a velvety sky occasionally lit up by lightning. Najmeh, my anti-smoking journalist friend, and I drove over to Shahrak-e Gharb to check out the celebrations. The square was thick with teenagers and families, waving Iranian flags, honking their horns, setting off firecrackers, and chanting "Iran!"

Police in riot gear lined the square, eyeing the crowd uneasily. People were so high-strung and excitable that any spontaneous gathering could easily morph into protest against the system. The security apparatus knew this, and often preemptively disbanded crowds, before they could turn.

I have a bad feeling about this, I said to Najmeh. There are too many police. Moments later, a teenage boy on a motorbike shot through the crowd, crying "Death to Khamenei." The police didn't move, but they shifted uneasily in their positions. Emboldened, another teenager ripped a small tree out by the roots, tied an Iranian flag to its branches, and brandished it in the air. A procession of hundreds began following him down to the main square.

Najmeh and I followed, until we saw two young men dousing the lawn of the square with kerosene. Run, I yelled, grabbing her arm. We sprinted back up the boulevard as giant flames engulfed the square behind us. Najmeh glanced over her shoulder to make sure I was close behind her. Azadeh, *roosarit!* she cried, your head scarf! The scarf had slipped back slightly, exposing my hair. Najmeh was always immaculately covered. She could be fleeing a burning building, or a burning square for that matter, and stay modestly put together.

Suddenly, without sounding a single warning, the police stormed the square. They charged in all directions, swinging their batons. They moved into the crowd of middle-aged women and children, beating them on their backs and legs. They beat trees.

Najmeh and I climbed up an embankment and huddled against the wall of a nearby apartment building. We thought we were safe, never thinking the police would spread out so far. But they did. They came storming up the hill, just meters away from us. I stood paralyzed. This cannot actually be happening, I told myself. This is a very bad movie. You will snap out of it in a second, and realize you fell asleep on the couch. But then I felt Najmeh's nails digging into my arm, as she grabbed me and pulled me further up the hill. I tried to run sideways, so I could watch my back while moving. But it slowed me down. They were nearly on top of us now, so I turned to sprint.

Before picking up Najmeh that evening, I had run miles at home on the treadmill, and my legs felt like jelly. They were too tired to carry me. Really, you would be such a fool, I scolded myself, if you couldn't outrun some pudgy Iranian cop. Thud. I heard the sound of a wooden baton slam against my neck, before I felt the pain. Thud. My tailbone. Thud. Thud. Thud.

I doubled over, but I kept running, weaving between shrubs and trees, trying to escape more blows. Naj, I screamed. I couldn't see her anywhere. My veil twisted around my neck, and I pulled it off, so I could see all around me. Everything blurred. I saw men and women fleeing, heard cries and the stamping of feet. Finally, I reached a small park, near the back door of another apartment building. By now I was above the melee. I turned to see Najmeh trudging up behind me, her face splattered with black tears of running eyeliner. Naj, they hit me, I repeated over and over, lightly touching my fingers to the throbbing in the back of my neck. I know, she said. They hit me, too. We held each other for a few seconds.

The scene from the hill was flashing before me. I had seen a girl, about twelve, being beaten and the image filled me with a wrath I had never experienced. I screamed, using the foulest Farsi I could manage, cursing the police, the system, the revolution. Najmeh rocked back and forth on a park bench, clutching her stomach. I thought she was crying again, until I realized the sounds were belly laughs. Oh no, I thought, she's hysterical. Do I have to slap her?

Azadeh, she gasped, you can't say those things, anatomically, those are *male* curses. The woman was amazing. If you woke her up from a nightmare, she would speak in correct, full sentences. Whatever, they deserve it, I said.

Slowly we walked up a creek bank parallel to the road, and peeked through fences to see if we had come far enough. A few teenage boys ran into the creek, scooped up rocks in their T-shirts, and ran back out onto the street, flinging them at the police. But they were no match for batons. Fifteen minutes later, the police had cleared the main avenue. If we walked back to the square, we would probably be detained, but it was the only route home.

A green Paykan slowed near us, and Najmeh begged the family inside to take us as far as the expressway. As we drove toward the square, she told me not to look outside, but I couldn't help it. I saw about ten young men lined up against a fence being savagely beaten, their arms above their heads. In the square, a group of those arrested—at least forty—sat crouched on the ground in a circle, heads down, awaiting the security buses that would take them away.

"*Baba,* are they beating these people because they're not husband and wife?" asked the little boy in the car, as he gazed out the car window, transfixed.

"No, *baba jaan,* it's because the police are afraid of them," replied his father. He did not explain, and the little boy went quiet.

The family dropped us off beyond the square, where we scanned for a taxi at the freeway entrance. Naj, I know that you're going to hate it, I said, but I think at this moment, I really deserve a cigarette. She glared wordlessly. I took the pack from my satchel, lit up, and as if on cue, cars began pulling up alongside us, heckling, offering rides. Islamic dress codes made it difficult for women to dress in a totally distinct fashion, so prostitutes distinguished themselves to potential clients with coded signs. One was to hold a plastic bag in the left hand. Another was to smoke in the street.

Najmeh gritted her teeth. She ignored the cars, but her full, arched eyebrows grew closer and closer together, until I thought she would go crosseyed. Do you want me to put it out? I whimpered. Yes, she exploded, they think we're *jendehs*, whores! I crushed the cigarette under my foot, and looked up at the sky, hoping for some sort of divine intervention. How was it possible to be thrashed with a baton and solicited sexually in the space of thirty minutes? I felt like I was trapped in a Quentin Tarantino movie. What would happen next? Maybe we would get run over by a car, and then auctioned off in the ambulance?

It took two hours to get home. The scene in Shahrak had repeated itself in squares all over the city, and the streets were locked with traffic. After spending half an hour immobile on an overpass above Vali Asr, contorting in various positions that didn't pressure my tailbone, I got out of the car to walk home. All along the overpass, people had turned off their engines, turned up their stereos, and were dancing between lanes. High above the street, protected by a parking lot of cars, they were safe. It was the first time in Iran I had seen that many people dancing anywhere besides a living room. My body ached. I needed to get home.

⋆

For an entire week, I did not leave my couch. I simply could not sit. Outside my apartment, life ground on as usual, with the bizarre sameness that followed severe mass disturbances. Perhaps for a couple of weeks, illegal satellite dishes would not be raided, coffee shops would be left alone. Maybe the price of bread and meat would drop, or state television would show *Harry Potter* in the evening. With these token gestures, the system would twist the valve to let out just enough pressure. This time the regime masterminded a slightly more creative official response to the riot: a mammoth confection. After the next soccer match, the government baked a towering, fifty-layer pink and yellow victory cake, requiring some 12,000 eggs and 1,200 pounds of chocolate. They transported the cake to the lawn on Azadi Square, near the soccer stadium, and distributed it by refrigerated trucks all over Tehran. Reformists said nothing about the cake but instead raised questions about the system's core problems: the multiple power centers within the Islamic regime, the imperviousness of its legal structures to amendment. The discussions went in circles.

Stranded on my couch, I expected a little sympathy from Siamak. He offered none at all. He said I should stop being neurotic, and sent me emails that read: "u LIKE drama too much baby. Must-stop-drama." Lately, he took this patronizing tone with me.

I rose every few hours to pull up my nightgown, and stand before the mirror, monitoring the dramatic evolution of my bruises. The colors shifted as spectacularly as a sky at sunset, from inky purple, to iris blue, to a sickly olive-yellow. The more everyone brushed off the incident ("So, I hear you got a little spanking . . . *teflak,* that's too bad. . . . Can you do lunch Wednesday?"), the more obsessed with them I became. I lay face down on my bed, over a white sheet, and made Khaleh Farzi take pictures of them.

Siamak was not getting the message. What I wanted to explain, were he to give me the chance, was that we had a moral obligation to care when awful things happened to people around us. That by treating beatings, lashings, or checkpoint arrests as commonplace—ordinary, like going to the ATM—we were becoming dehumanized to the sickness around us. A heightened threshold of suffering was necessary for getting through the day, but mentally, we had to retain some sort of perspective. Of how a functional government should behave. Of what was unacceptable. Otherwise, we would become like those blasé reformists, who would look you in the eye, and say: "Look at how much progress we've made . . . See! I'm wearing short-sleeves. . . . Could I have worn short-sleeves ten years ago? . . . No! . . . What are you whining about human rights for? . . . Aren't we better than the Taliban? Than the Saudis?" Yes, there would always be some junked, lost country we would be superior to, but that wasn't a proper ambition, was it?

Siamak and I lamented many things, but most of all how the revolution had lowered Iranians' expectations. How it made them dream more modestly. Iranians considered a soulless shopping mall like Dubai, in the Persian Gulf, the height of modernity. There were few sights more painful than watching Iranians shopping in Dubai, gaping in awe at this trussed-up backwater, wondering whether someday, in the distant future, Tehran would be lucky enough to approach a fifth of its greatness.

Why did Iran's vision have to contract so minutely? When did we start dreaming so small, start considering violence against our bodies normal? For the average citizen of Tehran, years, possibly a lifetime, would probably pass without an arrest, a beating, or some other random, unearned act of brutality. But the *potential* still colored the mental context in which everyone lived.

I could not say these things to Siamak. He was too busy drafting a Pow-
erPoint presentation about the new investment law. So instead I told Reza,
who came to visit me the very next day. He brought strawberries and the
new James Bond movie on DVD. When he called to tell me he was going
to do this, I told him I didn't have a DVD player, and so he brought one of
those, too. All morning, he treaded back and forth between the living room
and the kitchen, bringing me cups of tea and heating towels to put under
my neck. *He,* like any normal human being, considered it a tragedy that police would beat unarmed women and children. At least they should invest
in a giant water hose, he mused, fiddling with the television wires. After all
these years, they still haven't figured out how to control a crowd of people
without bashing their heads in.

Watching him, I was struck by how evolved he was. Though he had always lived in Iran, there was nothing traditional or dogmatic or chauvinis-
tic about him. He was always criticizing something, having absorbed essays
and books that I only managed to skim. We had more in common than I
ever expected, the same taste in ideas, the same conclusions about people.
Once upon a time, at the very beginning, I had assumed he was an arche-
typal Iranian male—raised to believe he was the center of the universe, de-
serving of women's constant, tender ministrations—who concealed his
sexism with jargony intellectual debate. How wrong I had been.

I had been wrong about Siamak, too. When I first met him, I was convinced that Siamak, the U.S.-educated consultant, was necessarily broad-
minded, in every realm of his life. When these judgments collided with
reality—Reza's worldly intellectual openness, Siamak's boring, airhead girlfriends—I was embarrassed to admit how deterministically I had viewed
them both. How quickly I had outlined dictums about the sort of life or
person I wanted, so naively convinced I would think that way forever. As I
came to understand all of this, I slowly let go of the belief that Siamak was
my perfect Iranian-American alter ego, without whom I could never be
whole and at home.

Siamak was precious to me, touched my life in a special way, because no
one else's history had paralleled mine so closely—American cities, Cairo,
then Tehran. We shared that kindred bond I had with my cousins, woven
from the intimacy of shared experience. As with them, I didn't need to continually recompose myself before him, because he had grown up in the

same sort of living room. But this kind of bond is what made people family. It was wholly separate from the question of who could make the grown-up you happy, with whom you could fall in love. Just because on paper, and in the eyes of others, we were a suitable match did not mean his soul would sing to mine, or mine to his. I had to let him go.

⋆

I was too proud to discuss how excruciating it had become, just getting through the day; how the beating had grafted itself on my consciousness, putting my senses on an exhausting, permanent danger alert. In the full light of day, at the produce market, the rev of a motorcycle engine sent my heart racing so fast I could hardly see.

Covering crowds, the vigils or lectures where confrontations with the *Basij* or the police were inevitable, was like rubbing gravel into an open wound. If a group of people began moving quickly, if a line of police shifted positions, if a *Basiji* raised his voice, I started to run away, my feet driven by raw, lizard-brain reflex. On multiple occasions, covering demonstrations, I sat trembling three blocks away, pestering my friend from the BBC on the mobile phone to tell me what was transpiring. "Don't be silly, Azadeh. Get back here," he would say. "There's absolutely nothing happening." But I couldn't. I had seen how you could go from absolutely nothing to having your neck smashed in bare seconds. There was no way to predict when things would spiral out of control. No way to know if that night the *Basij* had been instructed to intimidate or attack. I wasn't sure how to deal with this skittishness. How to forget the cockroaches.

CHAPTER NINE

Not Without My Mimosa

When we saw the wounds of our country
appear on our skins,
we believed each word of the healers.
Our ailments were so many, so deep within us,
that all diagnoses proved false, each remedy useless.
Now do whatever, follow each clue,
accuse whomever, as much as you will,
our bodies are still the same,
our wounds still open.
Now tell us that we should.
you *tell us how to heal these wounds.*

—Faiz Ahmed Faiz

It was September 14, 2001. For three days, I had not budged from a twenty-yard perimeter of my television. A moat of empty water bottles and apple cores surrounded the couch, the single piece of furniture on which I now ate and slept and lived. It was as though a close friend that no one else here knew had been murdered, and suddenly all the nice people in my midst had been transformed into cold monsters, unmoved by death. The phone rang as it usually did, with invitations to dinners and lunches. Life proceeded as normal, though for me time had slowed, and even the tree outside my living room window somehow looked different.

One evening, a youth group organized a candlelight vigil for the victims of the attack on the Twin Towers at a square in north Tehran. A decent and varied number of people turned out, the *Basij* attacked, and I, of course, hyperventilated. But the vigil, with its undercurrent of sympathy and openness to America, was just one strand of the Iranian reaction. It was only in the astounding indifference around me that the depth of accumulated resentment of American foreign policy in this region became apparent to me. The fraught, emotionally charged conversations I had in the days that followed left me stricken, but in their course I learned many things. The first was that the U.S. government was viewed as a greedy, heartless *uber*-power in pursuit of domination of the Middle East, indifferent to its civilians.

Reza and I fought heartily. Aren't you going to tell me you're sorry? I asked accusingly, overwhelmed and infinitely sad. Don't you want to ask me whether I have friends in New York, and whether they're okay? Did you know that two of my cousins live in lower Manhattan?

He lit a cigarette carefully and looked away, a flicker of anger passing over his freshly shaven face.

"Don't you care that thousands of people died?" I pressed on. I needed desperately for someone to register that this was tragic. My voice pitched high, and I hated its strident, hysterical tone. "Are you so dehumanized that you can't even feel sympathy for dead office workers?"

"Don't preach to me about dehumanization," he said.

"Reza, *they jumped out of burning buildings,*" I said.

"Why did no one talk about dehumanization when America armed both Saddam Hussein and the mullahs, and allowed us to bloody each other during eight years of war," he replied, his arms tightly folded across his chest.

"But these were civilians—" I interjected.

"Civilians!" he snorted. "What about our civilians? Do our lives count for less? There's no outrage in the West when we die, no one talks about civilian deaths, because by now our loss of life is ordinary. What about the Iraqi civilians dying because of sanctions? What about Palestinian kids who get shot in the street running out for candy?"

In all the instances he named, the injury inflicted on civilians was considered to be encouraged or abetted by America, the instigator of sanctions, the ally of Israel. Surely those deaths, the thinking went, could not have been silently facilitated by the United States unless it considered us, people of this region, animals, whose slaughter was less regrettable than that of Americans. It was from this sense of having already been dehumanized, counted for less, that the attitudes around me seemed to come. Understanding the origin of these views depressed me profoundly, because I saw they did not arise from cultural rage, jealousy, powerlessness, or religious hate, all the explanations that emerged to explain why anyone should feel anything other than absolute horror at what happened that day. The heartlessness was political, linked to specific events and places and ways in which America was seen as having behaved cruelly against the civilians of other nations. I saw only a reluctant satisfaction, as though a mirror was finally being held up—now *you* see what it feels like to die, you who have for years reserved death only for us.

⚓

Though Iran played no role in Sept. 11, it was, like Iraq and Palestine, contaminated by the fallout. President Bush declared Iran part of an "axis of evil," which did not bode well at the time, since it was becoming clear that Iraq, our neighbor and fellow axis member, was going to be invaded. The term "axis of evil" sounded funny in English, but in Farsi it struck a bizarrely familiar note: It was ideological and inflammatory, the sort of phrase a mullah would think up and bellow out during Friday prayer. For years the clerics behaved like madmen, screeching at the Great Satan from their pulpits, and suddenly there was an echo from the other side, someone screeching back in the same tone.

Do you want to throw an "axis of evil"–themed cocktail party in honor of our fresh national relevance? I asked Siamak. I pictured appetizers on skewers, and drinks with red and green food coloring, but he vetoed the idea. The Islamic Republic, of course, could not strike back against George W. Bush's Washington, and instead released its anger at home.

The newspaper headlines, their criticism tempered out of fear of the press court, became inane. Important acts of legislation, like a bill that would have allowed single women to study abroad, landed in the trash bin of a clerical adjudicating body. Being in the axis made reporting thorny, too. Sources were afraid to say anything at all, lest they be dragged before a court for endangering national security. It was as though an unspoken emergency law had gone into effect, terrifying the skittish and silencing the outspoken. It was a divine gift to the hard-liners, who were running out of excuses for their ongoing repressiveness.

The label seemed to signal no policy shift by the Bush administration, which before had refused to deal with Iran and continued to do so. The difference was that now there would be name calling. And so Washington said there should be "regime change" in Iran, but the task would be left to the Iranian people.

In the immediate months that followed, the already painfully slow process toward change ground to a halt. The sorts of organic debate that had been commonplace in 2000—on the role of *sharia* (Islamic law) in society or the degree of social freedom that custom could tolerate—were now muted, or avoided altogether. The country was under attack, said the hardliners, and everyone needed to band together. Internal conflict would no longer be tolerated. If the ostensible goal of the Bush administration was to promote tolerance and democracy in the Middle East, thereby discouraging militancy and religious extremism, then its policies had neatly produced the opposite effect.

When the world's biggest superpower puts you on its top-three hit list and begins talking about regime change and the possibility of military attacks on nuclear power plants, the national attention span can scarcely focus on a bill to adjust women's marriage dowry for inflation. I imagined the clerics sitting in Qom, rubbing their hands together with delight, cackling with glee. For two decades, they justified their neglect of Iran in the name of fighting "enemy plots." Finally, the "enemy" was acting its part.

Many people, including some Iranians, said this was not such a bad thing. That given the failure of the reform movement, American pressure could push Iranian society to look more seriously for another option. Were there an alternative, they might have a point. But there was none. The Shah's son, sitting in Maryland, lunching with congressmen, and waiting for conservatives in Washington to install him as the next president of Iran, was out of the question.

Iranians did not take him seriously. He had no popular following, though lots of people enjoyed tossing his name about, as it made them feel like at least they had an option to reject. One day, if the plates underneath Iran shifted, the regime crumbled down, and the choice came down to a U.S. occupation force (à la Iraq) and Reza Pahlavi, then okay, Iranians would choose him. But it would be a choice of that order. An anti-choice. Like President Khatami.

Admitting there was no alternative to the reform movement deeply disappointed me. A devotion to a secular Iran ran through both sides of my family, and everything I had learned about religion and freedom convinced me secularism was the only way to safeguard people's basic rights. The reformists, in their agenda and its pursuit, were highly flawed, but there was no alternative waiting in the wings—no charismatic student leader with an organized following, no ambitious Boris Yeltsin–type figure who saw personal gain in rocking the system.

The first year I lived in Tehran, over family lunches on Fridays, my family asked me, so, this Mr. Khatami, what is he going to do for us? Now they asked, so, this Mr. Bush, what is he going to do for us? They said this in one breath, and in another said they didn't want another revolution. They wanted everything to change, they wanted to hurl the mullahs into the mosques and double-bolt the doors, but they did not want their society to fall to pieces all over again. They did not want to be Iraq.

When I first walked the streets of Tehran, during the war in Afghanistan and, later, during the war in Iraq, people were thrilled. When will it be our turn, they would ask me eagerly, eyes gleaming at the fresh sense that entrenched orders could collapse. And then we would go over to a shop corner and talk quietly, and it would become clear they did not, in point of fact, want the U.S. military to carpet bomb Tehran. "When will our turn come" was a cry of helplessness, an admission that change was out of their hands. The Islamic Republic appeared immune to internal change, and so it could only be fixed by being toppled. It meant: We would *immediately* like something *extremely* different from what exists now. When meaningful change was reduced to a speck of light down a very long, very dark tunnel, there was nothing left to say but "When will our turn come?" The very phrase was an affirmation, in its repetition, people reminding themselves that one day, they would have a turn.

⁂

With the United States at war in Afghanistan, my work in Tehran now centered on Afghan exiles. I found myself interviewing ex-warlords with Taliban sympathies, and their inflammatory quotes about fighting the infidel American invader surfaced in my stories. Mr. X, my interrogator, did not appreciate my associating with such types without his approval.

One day he phoned to complain. "What did you and Mr. Hekmatyar talk about?" he asked, referring to a shady tribal chief I had met with recently.

Whenever I picked up the receiver, and heard his voice, the urge to be flip overtook me. "Spring hemlines!" the urge whispered. "Oh, you know," I said. "The war. The Taliban. That kind of stuff. Listen, I have something on the stove. I have to go." The "axis of evil" had amplified Mr. X's suspicions about everything.

Up until that point, I had been working with a relative freedom that surprised even me. The red-lines had seemed lenient enough that I kept pushing, and finding a give, pushed even more. I wrote about torture, public lashings, show trials, attacks on demonstrations, and attempted assassinations of the regime's opponents. I wrote that young people were fed up, hated the revolution, and considered the reform movement only one degree better than the ruling clergy. I wrote that the regime staged its rallies.

Throughout it all, I listened patiently to complaints from Mr. X that I had got the story wrong, that I wasn't being sensitive enough to the red-lines, that unbeknownst to me, my editors at *Time* were collecting cash gifts from the Iranian opposition and the CIA. The criticism was sometimes overt, often oblique, mostly friendly, occasionally intimidating. But in the course of it all, I was never, not even once, told not to write. Until the day the Bush administration declared war on terror, invaded Afghanistan, told the world it was either "with us or against us," and declared Iran evil.

Mr. X, who had until that point harassed me in ways I could mostly bear, became intolerable. He accused me of having worked on a story that must have been either a CIA or a Mujaheddin-e Khalq (the country's main armed opposition group) plant. When I denied this, several times and at several different octaves of voice, he shrugged his shoulders.

"Fine, maybe you weren't in on it. But that means your editors are on the CIA payroll, and you're their blind servant. Not even getting a cut." It wasn't clear which he considered worse. It was all so bizarre and seedy, I didn't know how to respond.

He insisted we talk on the phone several times a week, and turned our charged, uncomfortable meetings into full-blown interrogations. Who told you to write this? Who are these "opposition sources" you keep quoting? What do you mean you can't tell us? Doesn't national security mean *anything* to you? Khanoum Moaveni, *the country is falling apart.* And you're not doing enough for us. Perhaps it would be useful if we saw your work before publication, just in case we have any helpful ideas.

I had rejected many of Mr. X's suggestions in the past. When he asked me to email him from Damascus or Cairo, to tell him what people were saying there about Iran, I said no. When he asked me to brief him on what foreign diplomats in Tehran had to say, I talked in broad terms about the day's headlines. Most of the time, between flat-out refusals and empty blather, I managed to evade his attempts to make an informant out of me. But this request, to have my articles vetted, was too specific to slip out of.

Over the past year, I had exhausted all the resources at my disposal to extricate Mr. X from my life. The Culture Ministry was no help. I had gone to my one friend in a high place, the vice president, and asked him to help. He had a talk with the minister of intelligence, and promised things would get better. They did not. Now Mr. X was pressuring me even harder. I couldn't take it anymore.

I phoned Siamak and we convened an emergency summit over sushi at an Asian fusion restaurant that was pioneering the trend in mood lighting. We ordered our rolls and bent our heads low over the lacquered table. What should I do, I whispered, I can't say yes, I can't say no. I'm totally screwed.

For once, he wiped the smirk off his face, muted the teasing twinkle in his eyes, and listened to me seriously. You're right, he said, there's only one thing you can do. What? Leave.

The waiter returned with steaming cups of jasmine tea. We pulled back, careful not to appear too tête-à-tête.

They're so stupid, he fumed, jabbing a chopstick into the air for emphasis. They're freaked out—which is understandable, being in the axis and all—but instead of trying to use you to their advantage, they're bullying you.

As usual, Siamak's mind was working like a consultant's, whirring to prescribe the self-interest-maximizing course of action a rational government would take (generally, the opposite of what the Islamic Republic chose to do).

I agree with the stupid part, I said, but I'm not sure about the using part.

Our summit lasted only an hour. Instinctively, we both knew there was not much to discuss. There were certain questions to which there was only one answer. Siamak was right. It was time for me to leave. The ground had become too unstable. Until it settled, working in Iran would be impossible.

The next day I sent an email to my editor in New York with a John le Carré subject line: coming in from the cold. I knew my editors well enough to be certain they would want me on the next flight, if anything jeopardized my ability to report or to work safely. I followed it up with a phone call and bought a one-way ticket to New York.

I did laps around my apartment, gazing at my belongings, at the telephone, in confusion, unsure what to pack, or who to call. I didn't know whether I would be back in three weeks, six months, or never. How many seasons of clothes would I need? Should I arrange someone to water my plants, or store my carpets with mothballs? I didn't know what sort of mood the occasion called for. Should I go out to dinner? Should I stay home, listening to old Iranian music and feeling somber? I felt an unnatural detachment, as though I was watching myself in silent, still-frames. In the end, I took a sleeping pill and went to bed.

At the buzz of the alarm just a few hours later, I got up and made what I sensed would be my very last espresso in my beloved, moonlit Tehran kitchen. I threw some jeans and scarves into my suitcase, sent emails canceling my meetings and dinners for the week, and then set about combing through my office. I did this each time I left Tehran for work, but this time I was diligent. I went through piles of old notebooks, blacking out names and phone numbers of student organizers or activists, erasing disks with notes from sources, throwing old tapes of interviews into a bag to take with me. Should Mr. X or his associates end up going through my things, my files would be sanitized, my sources would be protected.

My uncle drove me and my one bag to the airport in the dead of night (the uncivilized hours when flights out of Tehran are routinely scheduled) and waved his medical badge so he could accompany me up to the dreaded passport control. We were both tense, uncertain whether the life we shared together in Tehran was ending or simply being interrupted. A loud, clucking woman, weighed down by several bags, and two boxes of pastry, was making the rounds of the passport lines, begging someone to carry her sweets onto the plane. Please, she said, lumbering from line to line, I have too many bags; I don't want to leave my *shirini* here in the airport.

I bet I'll be stuck sitting next to her, I whispered. Iranian mothers who carried Tupperware full of cooked, smelly food onto planes were our family joke. They were convinced that the Persian stews they cooked in Tehran to bring to their sons were wholly distinct from the exact same thing they would make for them upon arrival. If you had the misfortune of being seated next to one, you were likely to come away either smelling of stew, or getting oil stains on your bag. She waved at me with a questing look.

Don't even think about it, my uncle said, that baklava could be filled with cocaine. Caviar, I replied, is the only acceptable food item to export on one's person. We distracted ourselves with this sort of light conversation, avoiding the question neither of us could answer: When will I see you again? I waved goodbye from the other side of the line, and watched my uncle light a cigarette, take one last look at me, and turn down the stairs.

During the interminable wait for my flight, my mind flitted back to my most vivid memory of Mehrabad Airport, the day my mother and I left Tehran after that summer of 1981. When we stopped at the female security check, a woman in *chador,* with a thick caterpillar of hair above her lips, told my mother to take her pants off. I was only five, but old enough to realize that was an alarming thing to be told at the airport. In those days, many women leaving Mehrabad were emigrating permanently, trying to take their worldly possessions, most importantly their jewelry, with them. Since the revolution had abolished private wealth, suddenly Iranian women's jewels were part of the revolution's assets, and confined to its borders. So women devised elaborate ways to hide them upon exit, a favorite method being to hide them not *on* one's person, but *in* one's person, if you know what I mean.

I stared at Maman, who stared at the mustached woman. Maman pulled her shoulders up and gazed at her with blazing eyes. Shouldn't you be going after the thieves who're robbing the country blind? Her voice was high and forceful. Caterpillar woman flinched. Okay, she said, just sit down, open your legs, and wiggle. For years, that encounter fascinated me. I devoted free minutes, in the backseat of the car being shuttled to Farsi lessons, waiting to be picked up after school, trying to invent ways to smuggle jewelry out of Mehrabad. Then I would run them past my parents. What about a secret compartment inside the heel of a shoe? Tucked inside a Cabbage Patch kid's diaper? Stop thinking about stuff like that, sweetheart, my dad would say.

I wondered if he and I would ever travel through Mehrabad together.

Finally, the loudspeaker called my flight to board. As soon as I stepped onto the plane, I tore the scarf off my head, a motion that felt no less wonderful with months of repetition. The lights of Tehran disappeared into distant flecks as the plane ascended, and I pressed my forehead against the vibrating window, until they were fully out of sight. I had called no one to say I was leaving, because in my mind, I was not prepared to leave. Uprooting with the conscious intent of transplanting myself to New York would have taken me weeks. Had I known the move would be permanent, I would have roamed the streets disconsolately, trying to memorize the bends in my neighborhood, the clean, frigid smell in the air after a night of snow. Worst of all, I would have had to call each friend, each relative and source and acquaintance, and say goodbye. I am leaving, as you always knew I would, leaving you behind.

☙

Tormented by jet lag, I rose every morning well before dawn, and sat by the window of my Upper West Side sublet, waiting for the first rays of sun to shine on the Hudson, trembling with loneliness. I was no stranger to this city, whose streets I knew well from years of visits and extended stays, where I had cousins, close friends, and even a chelo-kabob crew that met once a month for dinner at Persian restaurants around the city. But after two years in Tehran, where the combat zone of everyday life made people dependent on one another for constant spiritual fortification, I was used to my days being suffused with intimacy. In Tehran, at any given hour in the day, at least four different people could have told you where I was, what sort of mood I was in, and what my plans were for the evening. Here, I could die of food poisoning from takeout, and no one would find me for days.

Living in Tehran was like being stuck in an elevator all the time, the snug common rut almost eroding stranger as a social category. In comparison with the fullness of those hours, my days in New York were a disconcerting, cold void. No one called to complain that the garbage man was now asking for a bribe, a conversation that would begin as a gripe and dissolve into jest.

While the intimacy of daily life retreated, work inflated in proportion. Soon after I came to New York, the magazine hired me as a writer on the world desk. After two years in the field, working at the Time Life Building in midtown lent a welcome but unsettling composure to my days. I wrote and reported on the same stories—militant groups, U.N. sanctions, al-Qaeda, weapons of mass destruction, Afghanistan—but I couldn't smell or feel them. Interviews were easy. Sources called back. The phone wasn't tapped (I think). No one proposed temporary marriage. But my life felt empty.

One weekend, in an effort to cheer me up, my cousin set me up with a colleague, an investment banker named Matt. We met for drinks. Like so many Americans, Matt's perception of Iran was skewed. You can drive there? he asked. Wait, hold up, that means you can go outside? I didn't blame him for not knowing, but I also didn't have the patience for these conversations anymore. I was too angry to slow down and explain—angry that to be a Middle Eastern person in this era meant you were maligned and condemned, occupied and threatened, all ambiguity discarded.

We were having dinner at a steakhouse with vaulted ceilings, and the enormity of the meat that arrived on our plates distracted me. Matt's cuff links shone. I was wearing a thin blouse, and felt myself shrink with cold. The stories that plopped out of my mouth sounded self-consciously exotic, in this robustly corporate atmosphere. Matt didn't really know how to respond. That doesn't sound like it checks out on the old safety meter, he said gamely. Do you just have a Hemingway-ish thirst for adventure?

No, I said, it's not just me. That's ordinary life. I could have taken the time to explain, to illustrate this strange-sounding world and fill in the lines of the axis-of-evil caricature. But I couldn't work up the energy. I was being sullen, and I knew it, but I couldn't be anything else. The starched table felt like a witness stand, and my role was defendant, to argue why my story contradicted the one on Fox News. Matt sat back, swirling the red wine around in his glass, waiting expectantly. He did not feel obligated to speak for the Bush administration, for the pro-Israel lobbies. Why then, was I expected to speak as an envoy for the Middle East? I had no desire to be an envoy.

Before I moved away from California, my energy for explanation was boundless. At the slightest sign of well-intentioned curiosity, I was eager to share that Iranian women could drive and have bank accounts and work, that the population was modern and sophisticated, that we spoke Farsi and did not by and large consider life cheap and support suicide bombings. But before, the curiosity wasn't tinged with such confident suspicion, this mix of pity and mistrust.

By the time dessert arrived, we had retreated from these uncomfortable subjects, toward the common ground of things—Italian weavers of cashmere, Florentine paper.

I stared at Matt's hand against the white tablecloth, searching for character clues. It struck me that it would take months to know one another properly, without having our deepest selves tested and displayed on the way home by a terrorizing run-in with the *komiteh*. When we walked out of the restaurant, I did not immediately reach for a pack of gum, to cover the martinis on my breath. It hit me with novel certainty that no one would stop us outside and ask how we were related. We could plan to meet again any evening of any week, without shifting plans to avoid the death anniversaries of imams, or other inauspicious nights.

How unaccustomed I had grown to American life, where my Iranian instincts served no purpose. When a bank clerk told me to come back in three days, my instincts buzzed "Obstacle!" and I tried to figure out how to bypass him, used to a system where you were constantly navigating blocks, until I realized he actually meant it. Not having to react this way, not having to think and maneuver as much, did not feel great, as it should have. Mostly it all felt too free, too oppressively light.

I noted the unhealthiness of this thought, and chalked it up to withdrawal pangs from a life overabundant in adrenaline. After a few weeks, the nightmares stopped. In Iran they had become so regular I no longer thought of them as nightmares. They were simply my dreams, always bad—of standing next to President Khatami being shot, getting his blood splattered all over me; of being strangled by my own head scarf, running out the door and having it catch on the knob.

                      ⚕

I moved downtown to be closer to my two cousins, Pouria and Alidad, and our proximity to each other made Tribeca feel comfortably village-like. We could stay up late drinking wine and watching Fardin movies, old Iranian black-and-whites, and arrive home on foot in minutes. During the week we were all busy frantically succeeding at our jobs—apparently the only mode of being for serious people in New York City—but we blurred through weekends, inseparable, in a continuous whirl of brunches, movies, drinks, and dinners.

My best friend from junior high school, an American, asked me if living in the U.S. felt different after September 11. Not really, I said, except that my cousins and I are turning into our parents. But the truth was that we co-cooned in the shelter of each other's company, as an ever-yawning gap developed between our inner sense of reality and the world around us. Now we felt—again—as though our lives were touched by a historical event we had no part in, but were somehow tainted by. Like the hostage crisis, which forced every Iranian in the United States to walk around with a scarlet letter of association, September 11 and the "axis of evil" revitalized suspicion and hatred for the religion, however secularly, we belonged to, and the part of the world we did not live in, but were shaped by and whose citizens we looked like.

Pouria might be a banker, hailing a cab down to the financial district each morning, or Alidad a corporate lawyer, merging and acquiring, but they were rather obviously young Middle Eastern men—the villains in the post–September 11 history of the world. We grew resentful enough, and paranoid enough, that we stopped mentioning September 11 in public.

People, our own friends, confessed the strangest, most insulting things, without any intention of offending ("I was sitting next to this guy on the subway, saw him reading the Koran, and wondered whether I should call the police, since the terror alert was on yellow"). You had to wonder what they were thinking, and why it was suddenly okay to think and act like this. What other people, what other religion, could you so openly slander?

After a two-hour brunch one Sunday morning in the Village, our waiter told us the owner of the restaurant was Moroccan. As he stacked our plates on his arm, he gave us a look, like surely you agree, and said, "He's cool, but Muslims these days, who knows what they're *really* thinking. I had an Iranian girlfriend, and I just had to get rid of her." He actually said that.

Often it was like that—stupid little stings—but sometimes it was cruder and more disturbing, like when I called my aunt in California and was told that some redneck had punched my uncle (the gentlest soul you could imagine, an avid baker) in a mall parking lot over a parking space, bloodying his nose and calling him a dirty Arab. What if suddenly the country turned on us, we wondered, like it did on Japanese-Americans during World War II? We mused about this half-jokingly, as we did about our mothers, who were all deciding where to move when they finally came for us. Mine said Vancouver. Alidad's said London.

We spent the week around colleagues and work friends, for the most part, concealing what we really thought, remaining silent when outrageous things about Islam and fundamentalism (aren't they the same thing?) and the Middle East were said in our presence, and we were expected to agree, or not notice. And like our parents, who drifted through the 1980s, Iranian in America, with polite masks, and then rushed home to the kitchen table, to vent, and argue, and exercise their real selves, we did the same. Except at restaurants and bars, rather than the kitchen table. Raw with a week of pent-up frustration, on Friday evenings we drank far too much, and yelled at one another, upset enough that the waiter would hover nearby, waiting for one of us to pause mid-screed, so he could deposit a plate and mutter "Yellow tail sashimi with jalapeño" before scampering away.

Even our conversations took on familiar dynamics—the ebb and flow of frustration and resignation—though we often pretended detachment, and were careful to interrupt ourselves to gossip and decide on skiing versus island vacations. It did not really work, this attempt to mix serious and uncomfortable subjects with the effervescent, urbane tones we usually spoke in. This was supposed to be the inheritance of our generation, the privilege of shedding history. We were supposed to be citizens of the world, comfortable everywhere, released from the concerns of political conflict. Our lives were supposed to make up for our parents' lives.

We became predictable, in our now distinct modes. Alidad was the deliberate and aggressive one, maneuvering the discussion around with disdainful purpose. Pouria got steely and quiet, and asked lots of questions, because he didn't have the time to read enough, to arm himself with facts, and the bareness of his intellectual defense incensed him. Generally, I was defensive and jumpy, because Alidad would at some point have slammed his glass down on the table, and attacked me as propagandist for the U.S. government ("Can you stop talking in *Time*-ese?"). Like our parents, who saw a conspiracy in every corner, we too developed the unattractive tendency of paranoia, though we despised ourselves for it all the while. If an airline lost Alidad's plane reservation, he became convinced he was being monitored by the FBI, his travels disrupted by some software at CIA headquarters that automatically canceled last-minute plane travel by people with Ali in their name.

When the conversation relaxed, we lingered over port, smoked, and discussed exit strategies. Alidad plotted a move to London, where he insisted the base level of ignorance would be elevated a few notches, and where you could criticize Israel without being called an anti-Semite, damaging your career and becoming a social leper. Pouria speculated about oil and power, as he had decided to retire at forty and devote the rest of his life to writing a book about neo-imperial energy politics. I dreamed about buying an old house in Beirut, and renovating it with friends, making a home in the only city I knew where the duty to fight occupation and the passion to live richly were sustained with equal energy. Around the edges of these evenings, I felt it creeping up again, the shadow of history, dogging the next year, the next decade, each decision. At the end of these nights, we filed out into the street, throats sore from talking, and headed toward an intersection to hail a taxi. I walked in the middle, linking us together with my arms, trying to extend the intimacy that had risen up between us, like an invisible shield, another hour, another block.

⊥

As the weeks passed, it became clear that I would not be going back to Tehran. I called finally to announce this to my relatives. Khaleh Farzi had a spare set of keys to my apartment, and she went over and packed my life up into boxes. The apartment went to Siamak, as we had originally agreed, upon discovering it together, falling in love with its view of Tehran, and co-signing the lease.

Still, five months later, on an exploratory mission to see if the ground had firmed up, whether it might be possible for me to return permanently, I boarded a plane to Tehran. I expected it would still be difficult to work, and that I would have to go through the ceremony of leaving that I had avoided the first time around, with my unannounced, middle-of-the-night departure. So I arrived in Tehran, bracing myself for the emotional drain of multiple good-byes, desolate at the prospect of becoming one of the ones who left for good. But one of my first mornings back, as Khaleh Farzi and I were drinking coffee, the phone rang.

"Your grandfather passed away last night": it was my father's voice over a crackly line. He spoke in that clinical, over-enunciated tone he reserved for anything Iranian and emotive, as though he was explaining the pathology of a complicated cancer. "The service is in four days. In my opinion, there is no need to interrupt your work to return. You know how I feel about this mourning business. But your mother might feel differently."

Because my mother was a professional weeper (she had wept her way through the last decade, for Iraq, for Bosnia, for Afghanistan, and, eternally, for Palestine), because she wore all-black for 365 days when her mother had died a decade earlier, I didn't bother to check.

And so I returned to the airport. This time, as I gazed at the city disappearing below, and ticked off another deferred farewell to Iran, it occurred to me that perhaps there would *never* be a proper good-bye. I thought of my Agha Joon, my grandfather, and how strange it was to be leaving Tehran, the city where he spent his career and raised his children, to bury him in California, a land he passed through like a ghost.

He should be buried in Tehran, or in his home province of Azarbaijan, where everyone spoke Farsi with the same gentle, Turkish lilt, or in Shiraz, near the tomb of his beloved Hafez. Certainly not in Los Gatos, at an interfaith cemetery surrounded by tract homes and a strip mall anchored by a Borders. But perhaps he wouldn't mind, I told myself; maybe he would just blink widely and repeat a few lines of verse about untethered spirits.

I had visited him in the nursing home the last time I was back in California. Oh, how my cousins and I tortured our parents over that nursing home. You said they were only for Americans, for savages who didn't care about their old people, we accused them. Their faces pinched, pale with pain, they blamed each other, and everything else they could think of, for why it had come to pass. The truth was that like most Americans, they had jobs and could not suspend their lives to care for their sick. They were living their American nightmare, at one of those exile crossroads where bitter reality stares you in the face—when you are forced to confront the fact that the temporary stay has become permanent, that you will never smell the old smells again, that there is no other life to regain.

The nursing home's peach, textured walls, its room filled with the shells of men and women, sapped the remains of Agha Joon's spirit. Tacked on the wall behind his bed were instructions, written out by my mother: *Please include yogurt with Mr. Katouzi's meals.* I saw that note, and felt my stomach cramp with pain, because I knew then that he would die. He would rather die than keep breathing with the knowledge that he was a burden.

My mother referred to him pointedly in these notes as Mr. Katouzi, lest some young nurse accustomed to the easy familiarity of such places venture to call him by his first name, Gholam-Hossein. Should this happen, I warned my mother, he might have a stroke on the spot, murdered by indignity.

Frail, surrounded by strangers, unable to communicate in their tongue, Agha Joon was stranded at an antiseptic, alien rest stop on the way to death. And he knew it. When I went to visit him, he played the usual game, decades old, of not recognizing me, until I stepped right in front of him and bounced up and down, *Manam, manam!* It's me, it's me. A real fog seemed to have replaced the make-believe one.

I perched on the side of the hospital bed, and pressed his smooth, brown-speckled hand between my own, to draw him closer. Is it you, *dokthar,* daughter, he asked, finally focusing on me. Where have you been? I was in Iran, Agha Joon. This reply intensified the fog. He never really understood that I had gone to live in Tehran; it was a twist too strange for him to absorb, at the end of his years. The family emigrated en masse to America, adjusted slowly, and watched the second generation put down roots— it was all for them, in the end, so they could bloom and learn in a civilized, modern place. I told you last time, Agha Joon, that I moved to Iran. He just looked at me, tempted into prose by the oddity of my words. His prose was rusty, and came out lyrical anyway: "What were you seeking, in that distant place?"

I took small pride in how his face lit up, when we spoke. I had scarcely seen him since early college, when my Farsi groaned under an American accent, like all of the diaspora's children. This handful of years later, when we sat together, and I recounted where I had been, I could speak naturally, not hesitating each minute for the right word. His eyes glittered, registering that something unexpected and interesting had occurred. Listen, Agha Joon, listen to all the poetry I've learned. And as I recited everything I could remember, his face finally became animated. *Bareekalah dokhtar,* he praised me, beaming. *Ustadat ki bood?* Who taught you?

He delighted in everything we learned. Perhaps it was because he himself refused to learn English, used the same five phrases for thirty years, and in comparison, our easy acquisition of local skills seemed impressive and dexterous. More likely, because he had learned to savor the smallest things—an old tape of Banaan; the postcard of the Blue Mosque I sent him one summer from Istanbul, which he carried in his pocket for weeks; an unlikely new bud on what seemed a doomed plant. When I first learned to drive, and stopped at yellow lights, he said precisely the same thing from the passenger seat, with the same smile. Who taught you?

We took a slow stroll down the hall of the nursing home, an alley of parked wheelchairs, and he guided me to the front lobby with his walker, toward a waist-high cage of canaries. He sat down in the padded, green armchair next to them, gesturing proudly. "Look! . . . What birds! . . . See how they sing!" One of the poems he recited often opened with a couplet about nightingales; "a bulbol bore, in its beak, a petal. . . . "

As far back as I could remember, Agha Joon had a talent for filtering out the ugliness around him—the suburban sprawl, the gas stations like warts on every corner—and spotting only what he wanted to see. We would be sitting at a traffic light, at the most soulless intersection conceivable, and he would point to a tree in the distance, at a far-reaching branch. See *dokhtar,* this thing of such beauty, that God has created? And I would strain my eyes, and finally spot a nearly invisible bird's nest perched at the end of a distant branch. Even here, at the very, very end, his vision blurred out the foreign trappings of senility and death and strained to admit only the birds.

I arrived to a quiet house, not bustling in preparation. In the two decades since the revolution, enough Iranians had died in America that there were now people to call to handle the elaborate rituals and commemorations. A caterer would cook the feast for the service, would buy and pit the dates and fold them into pale squares of *lavash,* would cook the four-day-in-the-making sweet halvah, and send waiters to circulate with cups of tea. Scratched down in address books was the number of the local Sunni volunteer committee, who offered to wash the dead, even the dead of the Shia, in the ritual fashion Islam required.

The day before the service, we lingered over breakfast, taking progressively smaller bites of toasted *barbari* bread, smeared with sour cherry jam and fresh cream. We were miserable, and chose to provoke one another as a diversion.

"I think I won't wear nylons tomorrow," I announced, even though it was cold out, and even though I didn't know what I was going to wear.

"I think we should serve wine," said my aunt. At this we all looked up in surprise, but she immediately turned her back to pour tea, to hide her expression.

"Feri, have you gone crazy!" my mother exclaimed.

"Agha Joon loved wine. He didn't believe in all this pious ritual, and I think if we're going to be true to him, we should have wine," my aunt argued. This outrageous thought, as it was intended to, short-circuited my mother, who excused herself to make phone calls to Tehran (where people were sane and did not suggest serving wine at *khatms*), punching in the numbers of the international calling card as she cried.

There was nothing for me to do but buy some extra candles and a black dress. Oh welcome task! I could not wait to escape the cloying atmosphere with an afternoon of religiously sanctioned shopping. Everyone was lost in private regrets, angry self-condemnation. As I was about to leave, my mother came back into the kitchen and reminded me, as though this was her first not fifth mention, that I needed to write an elegy for Agha Joon in English, "so the American guests don't get bored sitting through an hour of Farsi."

"I don't know why we have American guests in the first place. Agha Joon didn't even speak English. How could he have had American friends? Who've you invited?" I asked accusingly.

It turned out my mother and her sisters had invited their friends, some colleagues from work, in the Iranian tradition of expecting even the outer rings of one's social galaxy to make an appearance at a funeral. I was furious. The language in which I loved Agha Joon was Farsi. To speak about my adored grandfather to an audience of American strangers in English was an obscene idea to me.

"It's out of the question. How do you expect me to write a tribute of grief to Agha Joon in an alien tongue?"

"Azadeh, jaan. You're a writer, aren't you? Just write." Hah! When there were elegies to compose or long complaint letters to airlines or insurance companies, I was elevated to the status of writer. Otherwise, I was a collection of other things: a non-attendee of law school, a gypsy doing "God knows what" in the Middle East, a rejecter of suitable Iranian-American doctors, an exceeder of bank accounts, who liked to write as a "hobby."

"Can't we just pass out a flier with explanations?" I asked, as we had done for the Iranian wedding ceremony of my cousin to an American.

That night I sat for hours, poring over reams of Persian poetry, trying to find a few stanzas of verse that might be appropriate, that might translate. In Farsi I found the perfect lines—playful, elegant, profound—but they stubbornly refused to be led into English. I traced the Farsi words under my finger, in frustration, wanting to tear them off the page, command them to cross the border and not cling so willfully to just one world. The pile of rejected possibilities grew. Their translation was stale and constricted. So wearily, I sat before the screen, and just let my fingers type. And eventually something came out, mostly on its own, that I did not love, but I felt spoke the truth about my grandfather. And that is what I read.

My cousin Daria stood next to me. After I finished, he talked for a few minutes about our grandfather in broken Farsi, charming the audience with all the love that shone through his jagged words. He didn't think, of course, about what a conventional Iranian gathering expected to hear at a *khatm*. He simply spoke of Agha Joon, as he knew him.

My grandfather, he began blithely, never prayed once, not a single *rakat* of *namaz*, his entire life. The crowd, a hundred Shiites, dressed in head-to-

toe black, prepared to weep in our thousand-year-old tradition of mourning, broke out into laughter instead.

Our mothers, standing next to each other along the wall, eyed each other in alarm. Everyone quickly covered their mouths, peering around, discomfited to have stepped so dramatically out of character. But once they saw that the spirit of Karbala would not strike the room with a bolt of lightning, they relaxed.

Daria continued. He didn't pray, my grandfather, but he was more ethical, more kind, than any other man I have ever known. I smiled, and rested my fingers on Daria's arm, proud of his Iranian heart, and his simple, American naturalness.

That moment resides, a precious still-frame, in my consciousness. Exiles spent so much of their lives adrift through time; grieving for the past, pruning regrets, bracing for a future that was anticipated rather than lived. But in those seconds of surprised laughter we lived, collectively and wholly, in the present, an unfamiliar place we seldom met alone, even more rarely together. Afterward, a stooped-over old woman, wearing a head scarf of black lace, tottered over to us. Good for you, *pesaram*, my son, for not forgetting your culture, she said, patting Daria on the back and swinging the braided chain of a worn Chanel handbag in my direction. Tell that cousin of yours she should learn Farsi.

That night we assembled at my aunt's house in Los Gatos, heaving the towering trays of leftover fruit, herbs, *lavash*-wrapped dates, into the garage. If you had swapped a few of the stews, the menu would have resembled a wedding. I bit into a Persian rice cookie, the kind that immediately crumbles upon contact with your lips. We didn't like to admit it, but these cookies, like many Persian sweets, tasted better here in America. The quality of the butter and flour were finer than what bakeries used in Tehran. The taste buds, at least, can't be tricked by nostalgia.

Maman was on the phone with relatives in Tehran, speaking three decibels louder than necessary, as though to compensate for the fiber-optic distance. Daria was locked up in his room, inconsolable. He and Agha Joon were closer than any of us were to either of them. The bass of his angry hip-hop reverberated throughout the house. It made me feel better, too.

The house was full of people, yet it also felt empty, composed of negative space. It was vibrantly the house that it was, yet at the same time, it was not the houses in Tehran, where on the other side of the world, our estranged relatives were registering that Mr. Katouzi, nearly the last of his generation, had died.

Ever since I had put down my pen the night before, and surrendered the obsession to translate poetry, a possibility had slowly crept over me. Maybe the fixed lines I had drawn around worlds, around countries, around languages, were distorted, like a flat map of the earth.

The urge to translate, this preoccupation with language I had dragged around with me, had been a resistance to the sense of foreignness I felt everywhere—a distraction from the restlessness that followed me into each hemisphere. If I could only have conquered words, purged from my Farsi any trace of accent, imported the imagery of Persian verse into English prose, I had thought, then the feeling of displacement would go away. Just as I didn't like to admit, even to myself, that the *shirini* here tasted better than in Tehran, I didn't want to accept that displacement was an inescapable reality of a life between two worlds.

I felt the weight of my mother's arm around my shoulders, as she introduced me to a distant cousin, who smiled kindly. Iran existed here, in the interior intimacy and rhythm of our lives. This enclave in California felt as much home as did the strange world of Tehran, the homeland itself, where our Iranian relatives lived as strangers. I resigned myself to never saying goodbye, because I now realized that I would perpetually exist in each world feeling the tug of the other. The yearning, which I must embrace and stop assaulting, was a perpetual reminder of the truth, that I was whole, but composed of both.

⋆

On a summer night in Manhattan, my Iranian crew of friends assembled at Lincoln Center, for one of those avant-garde performance art productions put together by Iranian artists who had been away from Iran for years. I expected in advance that it would be disappointing, as art produced in exile often was (or at least our art)—either flat, from want of creative synergy with the changing homeland, or predictable, for the reuse of dated themes, the visuals of Iranian suffering going back to the revolution. We settled into our seats, and the lights dimmed. In the background, shapeless figures trekked through woods. A single woman emerged, and sank into a pool of water. Black and white landscapes flashed on the screen, the woman keened, and the trekkers trekked. The story was inspired by *The Conference of the Birds,* a twelfth-century Persian epic poem by Farid Ud-Din Attar.

These static, arid images evoked nothing of the Iran that I knew. My Iran was alive with ideas, a place of clumsy fashion shows and sophisticated bloggers. They were like artifacts, these visuals, remains of an era when my parents' generation used words like Mao and SAVAK instead of tech bust and stock split. Bored by the incoherence of the performance, and only partly entertained by the singer's divine voice, I peeked over to my right, to see if I was alone in my thoughts.

Hafez Nazeri, whose father is one of Iran's preeminent classical musicians, was sitting next to me, and could compare as well as I the caliber of art being created in Tehran, and the vacant, atmospheric spectacle before us. He raised an eyebrow, and leaned back with a skeptical expression.

I closed my eyes, and thought instead of the poem, *The Conference of the Birds.* It was a story I remembered well, the story of the mythic bird the Simorgh. When I was young, my mother and Khaleh Farzi and her husband drove down to Big Sur nearly every other weekend, to perch on the terrace of a magical place called Nepenthe, a restaurant you reached by climbing up through a small forest of redwoods, to a terrace that wound around the side of a cliff, high above the south coast of the Pacific. The terrace, the horizon, and the proud trees blended into one enchanting space, and we would sit for hours near the outdoor fireplace, listening to the logs crackle, gazing at the white foam of the crashing waves, the stars on the velvet sky. Khaleh Farzi and my mother sipped cognac, and talked about Iran. I drank creamy hot chocolate, and ran around asking pesky questions. Nepenthe, I found out, meant a place you go to forget your sorrows. I was young, and glad the sorrows drew us to a place with such crispy French fries.

There was a carved wooden statue of a phoenix at the tip of the cliff. What's that? I asked my mother. It's a phoenix, which is really like our bird, the Simorgh. The Simorgh, she explained, was a mystical bird, the leader king of all birds thousands of years ago. One day, the birds were summoned and asked to undertake a journey to reach their king. They accepted, though it was a hazardous journey, fraught with obstacles and valleys. Some of the birds—the nightingale, the sparrow—dropped out along the way.

With closed eyes, still tuning out the ululations around me, I tried to remember the story, as it had been told to me on that terrace so many years ago. Yes, in the end, the birds that made it through to the final valley gathered and waited expectantly to meet their leader. Their guide turned to them, and announced that there was no leader, no Simorgh—that if they looked around them, they would realize that they *themselves* were the Simorgh. The tale relied on a play of words; in Farsi, *si-* means thirty, and *morgh-* means bird. The birds looked around, and realized there were thirty of them. The goal of their journey, which they had imagined as a quest for their king, was actually their quest for self.

I edged out of the aisle, into the lobby, and finally outside, to sit on the cool cement steps, and breathed in the night sky. The notion of the Simorgh sifted through my mind, its end—the shock of the coveted mystery unveiled as the familiar—uncannily resonating with the recent twists of my life. My journey to Iran was meant to be a search for homeland, the prize for which I had trudged through the long days, the frightful, sleepless nights.

I had taken the first steps assured in myself, intent on discovering Iran, and I had eventually found that Iran, like the Simorgh, was elusive, that it defied being known. Its moods changed mercurially by the day, the scope of its horizon seemed to expand and shrink by the season, and even its past was a contested battle. Though with each day there I accumulated as many questions as answers, like those steadfast birds, something kept me honed on course, a belief in the obscured value of the destination. The knowledge had been unfurling in me slowly since the day of Agha Joon's funeral—that the search for home, for Iran, had taken me not to a place but back to myself.

Inside, the lights went on, and my friends filed out. We gathered at a Moroccan lounge in the East Village, and raised pitchers of mojitos into the air. Pouria and Hafez were engrossed in a discussion of Iranian classical music. Maryam talked about her upcoming wedding on a Greek island, how she had carefully chosen the destination because both Iranians from Iran and Iranians from America could get visas to attend. The axis of evil had made the choice of neutral-visa territory a foremost consideration in wedding planning. These were our preoccupations.

We spoke Farsi in different accents, or not at all. Some of us had extensive memories of Iran, others fewer. Our individual blends sparkled distinctively. In Hafez's voice, I heard the steely assurance of the fearless new generation; in Pouria's, the melancholy nostalgia of our family; in Maryam's laughter, the fusion of Iranian femininity and sharp New York attitude.

All our lives were formed against the backdrop of this history, fated to be at home nowhere—not completely in America, not completely in Iran. For us, home was not determined by latitudes and longitudes. It was spatial. This, this was the modern Iranian experience, that bound the diaspora to Iran. We were all displaced, whether internally, on the streets of Tehran, captives in living rooms, strangers in our own country, or externally, in exile, sitting in this New York bar, foreigners in a foreign country, at home together. At least for now, there would be no revolution that returned Iran to us, and we would remain adrift. But the bridge between Iran and the past, Iran and the future, between exile and homeland, existed at these tables— in kitchens, in bars, in Tehran or Manhattan—where we forgot about the world outside. Iran had been disfigured, and we carried its scraps in our pockets, and when we assembled, we laid them out, and were home.

Acknowledgments

This book wasn't meant to be a memoir, but since it turned out that way, I need to thank the many people whose presence in my life made the stories possible.

The spirit of Kaveh Golestan, the bravest, most talented photojournalist I have ever known, runs through these pages. With his unrivaled zest for poking into Iran's darkest corners, he taught me, and the Iranian journalists and photographers of my generation, that resistance could be an art and that art could be resistance. His place is permanently empty.

My aunt and uncle, Farzaneh Katoozi and Hamid Rasti, made Tehran home with their humor and love. The rest of my family—Sharokh and Mimi Moaveni, Shahla and Mahine Jamali, Pirouz Azar, Ferial Katoozi, Mohsen Mahdavi, Pouria Deghanpour, Nadia Babella, and Ardavan, Khosrow, and Forouzan Moaveni—spoiled me with graciousness on multiple continents. The companionship of two beloved friends, Carmen Nersessian and Siamak Namazi, sustained me throughout. My colleagues in the Tehran press corps practiced a solidarity I have never before or since encountered. My comrades, in the truest sense of the world, included Najmeh Bozorghmehr, Hossein Rassam, Suraj Sharma, Nazila Fathi, Negar Roshanzamir, Guy Dinmore, Jim Muir, Lily Sadeghi, Mohsen Asgar, and Ali Raiis-Tousi. Many others shared their Tehran world with me: Ali, Mitria, Nikki, Goudarz, Babak, Aresu, Roxanna, Kiarash, Maryam, Cyrus, Amirhossein, Kamran, Ardeshir, Hadi, Kavous, Nooshin, Yazdan, Ano, Kami, Koroush, and Armen. To protect their identities, certain friends appear in this book camouflaged.

Two friends in Tehran made special contributions to this book. Goli Emami, whose conscience and literary sensibilities I value immeasurably, read an early draft of the manuscript and in the course of our discussions, helped me hone my ideas. Ali-Reza Haghighi's sophisticated insight into the Revolution, reform, and the sociology of the Islamic Republic illuminated my own understanding every step of the way.

I owe an intellectual debt to Farhad Behbahani for explaining the intricate meeting of theology and politics in Iran and to Massoud Filsouf for sharing his accumulated knowledge of the post-revolutionary system. Many thanks to those who kept their doors and phones open during the tensest of times, particularly the student organizers and activists who are probably better left unnamed. My discussions with Ahmed Bourghani, Hadi Semati, Abbas Maleki, Taha Hashemi, Neil Crompton, Simon Shercliff, Saeed Laylaz, and Mohammed Sadeq Al-Husseini always demystified the rapidly changing political moment. Perhaps no one in Tehran helped as much as Mohammed Ali Abtahi, a uniquely devoted friend and a uniquely truthful vice-president. At the Ministry of Culture and Islamic Guidance, Mohammed Hossein Khoshvaght and Ali-Reza Shiravi struggled valiantly against the bureaucracy of seemingly ten different systems to help us do our work. My driver Ali Khatami, unflappable and fiercely loyal, treated my deadlines and dangers as his own.

I am forever indebted to my editors and colleagues at *Time Magazine*— Howard Chua-Eoan, Joshua Cooper Ramo, James Geary, Michael Elliott, Tony Karon, and Jim Kelly—for trusting my instincts, encouraging my ideas, and for a never-ending string of extraordinary reporting opportunities. My deepest thanks to Lisa Beyer, confidante and mentor, for standing behind me from the first moment. At the *Los Angeles Times*, my home during the writing of this book, I thank Marjorie Miller, and especially Dean Baquet, for his support and inspiring example. Both Terry McDermott and Michael Muskal shared their superb expertise with the written word.

My agent, Diana Finch, nurtured my embryonic ideas with great patience and steered me as expertly through the creative process as she did the world of publishing.

At PublicAffairs, Peter Osnos and Kate Darnton came up with the idea of memoir and then gave me the chance to write one. Kate edited the manuscript with a friend's insight and a diplomat's tact. Her ideas were routinely brilliant and she deserves credit for everything that works. Lindsay Jones and Lindsey Smith pointed out the rough spots and Nina D'Amario's cover ideas were truly inspired.

Many thanks to Conn (Ringo) Hallinan, Laurel Elmsey, Elahé Sharif-pour-Hicks, Gary Sick, and Michael Slackman for lending me counsel along the way. My friends in the Middle East and in America were the anchors that helped me live in between. They include Sarah Weigel, Geoffrey Smick, Matthew Gould, Shweta Govindarajan, Jeffrey Gettleman, Rana Boustany, and Kim Ghattas. Joe Logan endured me with special forbearance and kept me sane. Ranwa Yehia and Ali Shaath gave me second homes in Beirut and Cairo. Ramy Shaath taught me to be honest about the place of country in my psyche. Without Scheherezade Faramarzi, I might never have moved to Tehran at all. And without Anthony Shadid, I might never have finished.

Finally, I must thank my parents for the fascinating clash of their politics and personalities—growing up with two radically different versions of the same tale left me, among other things, curious about the truth. My mother, Fariba Katouzi, passed on a bottomless, passionate affection for our culture that has made my life incomparably rich. Her example is a source of great strength and her acute sense of justice is more a part of me than she knows. From my father, Sassan Moaveni, I inherited the Iranian hobby of politics, a healthy suspicion of ideology, and an allegiance to secularism. I am enormously grateful to him for being the most un-Iranian father in the best way possible and for not giving me too much hassle when my elephant remembered India.

Permissions

PublicAffairs is a publishing house founded in 1997. It is a tribute to the standards, values, and flair of three persons who have served as mentors to countless reporters, writers, editors, and book people of all kinds, including me.

I. F. Stone, proprietor of *I. F. Stone's Weekly,* combined a commitment to the First Amendment with entrepreneurial zeal and reporting skill and became one of the great independent journalists in American history. At the age of eighty, Izzy published *The Trial of Socrates,* which was a national bestseller. He wrote the book after he taught himself ancient Greek.

Benjamin C. Bradlee was for nearly thirty years the charismatic editorial leader of *The Washington Post.* It was Ben who gave the *Post* the range and courage to pursue such historic issues as Watergate. He supported his reporters with a tenacity that made them fearless, and it is no accident that so many became authors of influential, best-selling books.

Robert L. Bernstein, the chief executive of Random House for more than a quarter century, guided one of the nation's premier publishing houses. Bob was personally responsible for many books of political dissent and argument that challenged tyranny around the globe. He is also the founder and was the longtime chair of Human Rights Watch, one of the most respected human rights organizations in the world.

.   .   .

For fifty years, the banner of Public Affairs Press was carried by its owner Morris B. Schnapper, who published Gandhi, Nasser, Toynbee, Truman, and about 1,500 other authors. In 1983 Schnapper was described by *The Washington Post* as "a redoubtable gadfly." His legacy will endure in the books to come.

Peter Osnos, *Publisher*